THIRD EDITION

DECEMBER 2024

FAHIM A.R

USC.FAHIM@GMAIL.COM

To all the young people of the world, please read this book before you start any kind of business.

Introduction

What made me write this book is that I noticed many young people believe that making money is easy. They think that if they were to start a business or open a shop, a restaurant, or any kind of business, they will be rich within a few years. Many times I heard young people mentioning the stories of some people who became very rich in the world of trade and business, without knowing that there are a lot of factors of success which helped those people get rich.

I grew up in a family surrounded by business. Later on, as time goes on, I noticed that a lot of business men and merchants do not have the ability to explain things about the factors of success in the world of trade and business like school teachers and university professors. Because, explaining things is a skill and a talent that not everyone has.

When I was a student at the University of California for 14 years, I impressed many of my professors and peers, during the years. I took many classes and wrote many papers during my time in USC. My peers and university professors would complement my writing style and were extremely impressed with how well I wrote my papers. Several of my peers even told me that I should write a book because I always have many stories to tell and have the skill and talent to write.

After 30 years of my experience in business, I decided to help young people around the world and show them the road that led to success, and make them avoid the pain and suffering of financial problems and bankruptcy. So, I ended up honestly explaining the truth about the world of trade and business in this book.
Since this book is an international book for all young people in the world. I tried to put different stories from different parts of

the world just to make everybody around the world happy.
In December 2017, I started writing this book about the factors of success in the world of trade and business, I completed it on February, 2024. Most rich people and successful people in the world of trade and business have some of the factors of success and not all of them. No one is perfect and no one has all of the factors of success I mentioned in this book, I am not saying that you should have all of the factors, because no one is capable of having all of them. By mentioning the factors of success in this book, I am not trying to discourage young people, I just want to be realistic and tell them the truth and show them the road to success in the world of trade and business; the road to money.

Even though this book is mainly about business but the 25 factors of success in this book can also help an ambitious employee to be promoted in his job in order to be a manager or even CEO of a company.

FAHIM A.R

Chapters of this book:

Chapter 1

Patience

1- You cannot do any kind of business unless you are patient. You must know that the years go by quickly, the time is passing quickly. If you open a shop or a restaurant, you need time until your shop or restaurant would be known to the people and the public. If you have some products, it ould take time until your products grow in fame and popularity. A lot of people make mistakes when they think that their business will be known and famous within a few months. In reality, it may take five years or possibly even ten years. All successful people are patient they are patient with their employees, and they are patient with their clients.

2- Many people in many different countries around the world started to buy real-estate or land for very cheap prices a long time ago. After 20 – 30 years, the same land became very expensive. Those people became very rich and successful today, because they are patient.

3- Today, many large banks, companies, and corporations which started from 50 to 100 years ago, first started very small. Over a pro longed period of time, they started to grow and become bigger and bigger. Today they have grown into entities that are very big and veryfamous.

4- The inventor of the Television is a Scottish man named John Baird. He was not able to convince people to lend him money. Baird's dream was to make the T.V accessible in every house and work exactly like a cinema. The people of the time thought of him as a mad man. The idea was alien and unheard of. Bird was poor. He borrowed money from several of his friends and relatives in an effort to fund his invention the Television. Unfortunately, he died poor and indebted to a lot of people. However, today, after many years, we see televisions in all houses around the world. If one thinks about it, it took a very long time for this to happen.

5- One of the most important stories I read during my childhood and helped me a lot in my life was the story of the rabbit and the turtle. The turtle was awfully slow. Walking steadily but never giving up, it finally reached the finish line and won the race. A saying that I like and am quite fond of is, 'Slowly but Surely'.

6- In Switzerland, they plant pine trees and wait for 50 years to cut the pine trees to sell the wood. People and companies wait a very long time, even for as long as half a century.

7- During the 20th century, there was a famous billionaire from Greece named Onassis. He was primarily invested in the shipping business. He started to work on ships when he was a child. He worked as a person who cleaned the ships. After several years, he gained a lot of experience about the ship industry. The experience that he gained did not come over night. The time he devoted translated into fortunes. He married Jacqueline the widowed wife of the late John F. Kennedy, former president of the United States.

8- You must have patience like the character in the novel of Gabriel García Márquez *Love in the Time of Cholera.* The author is from South America. The story is centered around a teenage boy who was in love with his neighbor. The father of the girl didn't like the boy (their neighbor), and they moved to a different city. He was writing letters to her for many years, and over 50 years later, they got married.

9- When Alexander the great decided to invade a city, he sieged the city for months. If the city he was invading did not surrender, he would leave the city. This was to make the inhabitants of the city feel comfortable. He then sent his people disguised as merchants to buy the food in that city for very high prices. The people in the city thought that Alexander would not come back. Alexander however came back again, and sieged the city. The city no longer had any food, meaning that they could not defend the siege, forcing them to surrender in one to two months. The point to be drawn from here is that Alexander was a great and patient leader, due to the fact that he could wait for 10 or 11 months to take over a city. Patience was never a problem for Alexander the Great.

10- There are some people in the world who are not patient. If you pay someone 100 dollars to wait 7 - 10 minutes, the erson will not wait. Some taxi drivers will not wait even if you pay them. There are also people who are pushy and want things immediately, not able to wait for several minutes or a few hours. People like that cannot succeed in business. Sometimes I meet with businessmen, and wait for 2 – 3 years to finish the deal. Sometimes I give my phone number to people and they call me after 2 – 3 years.

11- When you want to start any business, you must take steps and there are no shortcuts. For example, if you want to open a restaurant, you must know people in order to borrow money or in order to have good credit with the banks or start saving part of your income and this will help you to open a business. Also when you open a restaurant, it will take many years for the restaurant to be known to the public.

12- Every kind of business has a business cycle.
For example,real estate business, stock market and shares

business, shipping business, oil and gas business. So, sometimes the business is booming, sometimes it goes down. So, when the business is down, you must wait a few years for the business to go back up so you must be patient.

13- There are a lot of famous companies in the United States and around the world. When they started, they lost a lot of money for many years and the owners of those companies went through a lot of pain and suffering but they were patient. Then at the end they started to make money.

14- One of my companies in oil and gas started to make money after
10 years so I was patient for 10 years or 11 years.

15- If there are two friends living in the desert, one of them is patient and planting seeds in his land. The person hopes that there would one day be rain, waiting for the rain for two or three years. The other person does not want to wait for a long time. After two years - three years the rain will come, and the man who planted seeds in his land and waited for three years will be rich, and the other person will remain poor.

16- In conclusion, any kind of business needs time and takes time to
succeed, so you have to be patient. No patience no money.

17- Also, in order to be promoted in your job you must be patient. For contacts and connection , you need patience. Patience is important in everything in life.

Chapter 2
Manners

1- When you have good manners, all people will love you and listen to you, and try to help you.

2- Always try to make friends not enemies. If someone is nice to you, be nice to him. Do not criticize or make jokes about people. Everyone is different. Try to not offend people or hurt one's feelings – they are different than you. One day, one of these people may end up helping you.

3- One's first impression is generally your manners. Common people in the street judge you by your manners. They do not know how much money you have, nor what level of education you have achieved. Whether you have attained a PhD or a high school diploma, it does not matter.

4- When people like you they will one day help and bring clients to you. So, keep the door open and have good manners.

5- It happened to me a lot. I met a lot of people, and because I am nice to people, a lot of people bring clients to me.

6- There was a young man from the middle east who went to Europe. He worked in Europe and made money then he came back and wanted to open a bakery in the middle east so he hired some people to work for him and wanted a manager who is an honest person to run it so he deiced to hire his father but the problem with the father is that he does not have manners and he always shouts at people. Everybody in the bakery was annoyed at the father because he was shouting day and night and was not respecting them. The employees at the restaurant decided to leave their jobs t the restaurant then the owner of the bakery

ended up selling the equipment in the bakery for less than half the price and he lost all his money and he was in debt.
This happened because his father has no manners.

7- Sometimes, people will not listen to you nor help you when they
believe you to be a threat, when you compete with them. This happens when you are both selling the same product. To deter this from happening, you must explain that you are not a threat.

8- If you are a manager or owner of a company and have good manners, your employees will love you. This will enable you to make them love your company.

9- One time, I had a new employee in my company. At first, my employees did not like him. They said he was ugly and looked like
Dracula, I told them not to judge people based off how they look, but by their performance in work. After a while, I came to notice he was rude to some of my clients, as well as to some of my employees. There were some women working in my company, he was very rude and very pushy to them. One of the girls told me that he kept telling her that he will be very rich and she will regret not marrying him. After a while, I fired him because of his behavior – I gave him the opportunity and chance, yet he lost it. Today, after twenty years, he is still poor and does not have a good job.

10- I met a poor old man who wanted a job and wanted to make money, he said that he one day wished to have his own business. I gave him a chance to work with me. The first week he was very happy. Because of me I opened the door for him to meet many important and key people. He had no contacts nor connections prior to working with me. His communication skills were very limited. He told me that he is the luckiest person.

After a while, I came to realize that he is a hard, honest, and dedicated worker. However, he lacked manners. He was pushy and annoying. He called me many times a day, even after repeatedly telling him not to call me more than once a day. This is because I am a very busy person. He also made appointments for me with other people on my time, when I am busy and tired, having many appointments and other things to do. He always had an excuse for me to meet with some of his friends, or some of the people he knows. whether it be travel. This added pressure to me. Even though I told him that he is bothering me when making such appointments. He never listened, never giving me a break, or time to take a breath. When I once asked about his parents and his childhood, he said that his father was an officer in the army. His father was a serious person, being both tough and harsh on him. Finally, I fired him, telling him to leave me alone even though he was honest, educated, experienced, dedicated and a hard worker. But, he was pushy, annoying, and had no manners. He had a good chance with me but he lost it. The Chinese proverb, if you cannot smile, do not open a shop.

11- I know another person, who is an ambitious hard worker who thinks he is very smart, yet is poor. His dream in life is to be rich and famous.

I gave him a good salary and a chance to gain experience with him.

He was very happy at first, he thought he was the luckiest person after meeting me.However, he has no manners, always fighting with other people, and not knowing how to deal with others. Not even knowing how to deal with me, angering me very often. I then fired him. He had a golden opportunity and lost it because of his bad manners and personality.

12- You must also appreciate people who have good manners, even if they are not your type. This is due to the reality that there are a lot of bad mannered people in the world. When I was in college, I remember a beautiful girl who had a Japanese roommate. Her roommate was very quiet and had good manners. So, I asked the beautiful girl to invite her roommate to lunch or dinner. The girl replied, saying that her roommate is not her type. I told her that I am impressed by her manners, and that she has very good manners. The following year, the same beautiful girl had a different roommate. That roommate was very rude, very mean, and very bossy.

She argued and shouted a lot to the beautiful girl. Then, her life became so terrible, she was unable to concentrate on her schoolwork. She was calling her parents every day and complained about her rude roommate. Later, she remembered her ex-roommate, the Japanese and had regrets that she did not appreciate her Japanese roommate. The point here is that you must appreciate people with good manners.

13- In India, there is a large company for the car industry named TATA. They manufacture many large cars and automotive. But in 1998, they started to manufacture a new brand of cars named INDICA, which did not do well in the market. The owner, Rattan Tata, later decided to sell the brand to ford. He and his team then traveled to the U.S.A. Bill Ford told Rattan "You do not know anything, why did you manufacture a car for passengers?!" Bill said that "We are doing you a favor by purchasing". Rattan Tata felt he was insulted in front of his team, he then left the meeting. He walked, he went back to India and decided to work hard and to improve his car. Then by the year 2008, this brand of car became the most successful car in Indian market. By coincidence, Ford then began to lose money because of its competitors such as Jaguar and Range Rover. So, Tata decided to buy Jaguar and Range Rover. So, Bill Ford traveled to India to finish this deal. The deal was then settled, and Bill Ford said that "You are doing us a favor by buying Jaguar and Range Rover, thank you".

14- I always consider a businessman who comes to a meeting on time and never late, a person who has good manners. This is because he has respect for other people who he has a meeting with. This person has both discipline and good manners. There are some people who are always late for meetings.

15- There was a good seafood restaurant I used to go to. I used to give a lot of tips to the waiters for their service. One of the waiters, a young man, started to say that he wanted to be rich like me. I laughed, because I knew then that he didn't have the factors of success that are mentioned in this book. To me, he's just a dreamer. After a while, every time I came to the restaurant, he repeatedly said the same thing – this began to bother me. Then, finally, after giving him tips, he told me that he didn't want tips, he wanted to be a partner with me. He was very interested in my business.

I looked at him as an annoying person, I didn't like the way he spoke to me. I did not like his approach. I told his manager to tell this young man not to talk nor serve me any longer. The manager knows that I am a good client to their restaurant. He told the waiter not to talk to me anymore. Maybe, this young man is ambitious and a dreamer, however, he doesn't know how to approach people.

I didn't like his manners, nor his behavior.

16- Since my childhood, I talked a lot. My mother did not want me to talk a lot. My father told me many times that I talked a lot. My aunt also got mad when I talk a lot. I still talk a lot. This however is my personality; I cannot change it. You cannot change one's personality nor behavior. If you see an employee with such a rude and disrespectful character, it is best to ask him to leave. There is no chance of them changing.

17- Also, behavior is important. Sometimes you see a person has better behaviors than other people. Also, people will judge you based on your behavior and reactions to things. There is a story about Ford the billionaire. Ford the billionaire invited two people who were candidates for a job to lunch because those two young people went to the same university, had the same grades at university, were excellent students and studied the same subject who were also friends. Mr. Ford had to decide on who of the two friends to select since he could only choose one of them. After lunch, he chose one of them and did not chose the other person.
After lunch, the other person asked Mr. Ford why he chose the other person over him. Ford replied saying that he noticed that the first one had good manners when dealing with the waiters. He was nice to them and was dealing with them with good manners. As for the second one, he noticed that he was rude to the waiters. The person who is rude to the waiters will one day be rude to the clients and people. Mr. Ford told the other person that he did not know how to respect the waiter.

18- The point here is that a person cannot change his personality so if one of your employees has no manners or has a bad habit lying to clients or stealing, don't give him a second chance because you cannot change his personality.

19- In the year 1919 King Jai Singh Prabhakar he was the king and the Maharaja of Alwar in India. He visited London in England. During his visit to London he went to the Rolls Royce showroom alone without his entourage and body guards and was wearing casual clothes. The Manager of Rolls Royce showroom thought that he was a poor Indian immigrant, so he did not respect him and kicked him out of the showroom. So the King wanted to revenge so he ordered 6 of the best and highest quality of Rolls Royce cars and the most expensive ones from the Rolls Royce showroom in London. Then he made those cars collect the garbage off the streets of India by removing the top of the cars roofs in order for the garbage men to store the garbage easily. The news papers in India took pictures of the cars and started to make jokes about the Rolls Royce cars. Finally all the news papers of the world started to make fun of Royce Rolls cars that are only good for garbage. This problem caused millions of dollars in losses to Rolls Royce company. Then the Rolls Royce company apologized to the King and gifted the King a few rolls Royce cars for free to stop using the Rolls Royce cars to collect garbage.

Chapter 3
Self – Confidence

1- You need self-confidence for everything you do in your daily life. Whether it be for your social life, or your business life. Unfortunately, however, more than 95 percent of the people of the world do not have full self-confidence. It is not an easy thing to attain like going to the pharmacy and purchasing some pills for self-confidence like it is with vitamins, and the next day you will be fine. You have to go through a lot of challenges in your life to accomplish a lot of things in order to attain self confidence. You will find some people who inherited a lot of money who do not have self-confidence. This is because they inherited their money the easy way, without any challenges. You may sometimes see a beautiful actress who is rich and famous, but she does not have self-confidence because she became an actress by knowing producers or directors.

2- You need self-confidence in business to talk to people and to negotiate with people. Also, to sometimes give a speech. It will be embarrassing for someone who has no self-confidence to start blushing. I have seen a lot of people who have been embarrassed, where their faces would blush (turn red), their hands start to shake, and sudden changes in their voice.

3- Self Confidence varies from one person to another. For Example, you may find someone who studies hard and does well in exams has 50 percent of self-confidence while his brother who does not study and cheats on exams has 20 percent of self-confidence. You may find a lazy girl who only has 25 percent self-confidence, while her sister has 45 percent self-confidence because she participates in more sports.

4- Usually, young people have less self-confidence than older people. The older a person gets; the more challenges they go through in their life. This is why that when you get older, you have more self-confidence. But still, some older people do not have self confidence because they did not have enough challenges in their life.

5- Hard working people who start their business and work hard in their life usually go through a lot of challenges and have more self confidence than people who inherited their riches from their wealthy father or family.
A professor who knows a lot because he reads a lot and writes a lot of books and gives a lot of speeches, usually has more self-confidence than a normal professor who does not do much.

6- If there is a student at the university who is working and going to the university at the same time who has two-part time jobs to pay for his tuition at the university. Also at the same time he studies very hard and doesn't waste his time on the weekends. He may even only have one meal a day to simply save his money. So, this student will have very high self confidence, maybe 85 percent because he is getting things the hard way and facing a lot of challenges in his life, and struggling hard. You may find a smart employee who knows everything about his job works very hard, and after he gets promoted, he has more self-confidence than a person who got promoted without working hard and knowing the job. He might have 70 percent more self-confidence while his lazy co-worker only has 40 percent self-confidence because he got promoted in an easy way.

7- Hard working people who start their business and work hard in their life usually go through a lot of challenges and have more self-confidence than people who inherited their riches from their

wealthy father or family.
A professor who knows a lot because he reads a lot and writes a lot of books and gives a lot of speeches, usually has more self-confidence than a normal professor who does not do much.

8- In business, it is very important to have self confidence for the following reasons:
- Negotiating with companies that have more money and power than you.
- Being confident when talking about your product
- Giving a speech to either a small or big group of people in meetings
- In order to convince the contributing parties about the product you are selling.
- You will listen and understand to what other people are saying in
meetings, people with little self-confidence prefer to talk about themselves and brag a lot. They should instead listen to others and concentrate on
others during the meetings.

9- Sometimes, an employee with low self-confidence will try to show the other employees during a meeting that he is smarter than his boss simply to get attention. However, his boss will hate him and hold grudges against him.

10- Sometimes even if the manager has an inferiority complex, he will act like an arrogant person, and may try to show off to the other manager, from another company, in the meeting and insult the person, not respecting him without realizing. This will have negative effects on the meeting and the business.

11- I have very high levels of self-confidence because of the challenges I have gone through in my life. I started my business with little money and very few employees. However, during

meetings with big companies and big corporations who have thousands of employees and billions of dollars, I argue with them and negotiate with them comfortably.
This is why self-confidence is very important.

12- Self Confidence is very important when you start your business.

13- Before you start your business, if you have self-confidence, you will not be affected by friends and other people who may discourage you. Also, in the beginning of your business career, you need self-confidence because no matter what idea you have, some people, especially your friends will discourage you. You should have enough self- confidence to believe in yourself and ignore your friends and other people, and not listen to those who make you change your mind and business ideas. So, do what you think is right because if you listen to people, everybody will say
something, and you will get to nowhere. You must believe in yourself and have self-confidence. So, self-confidence is very important when you start your career.
I remember when I was in high school my friends at school (my relatives at the same time), called me an idiot, stupid, and a moron. This also
happened to me in the university as well, but I did not care. This is
because I knew that some of them are stupid and others are jealous.
14- Self-confidence will also enable you to meet with very high leveled people. Self-confidence will push anyone to approach others whether it be at a party, night-club, restaurant or at the beach. I met a lot of key people and high – leveled people because of my self confidence. A lot of people who were sitting with me were impressed when I approach famous people, as they are lacking in their self-confidence to approach others.

15- Some young people who start their business, and do not have enough self-confidence start having a lot of advertisement on TV, Newspapers, Billboards, Etc. They then start spending a lot of money on big parties, going over their budget simply to show off and impress people. With big houses, very expensive cars and expensive furniture. After a few months, you will find that the same company will not have enough money to continue their business and go bankrupt.

16- Sometimes I feel sorry for when a salesman is selling a product and has no self-confidence. Because I see him trembling, not knowing how to put his words together to explain his product in the right way.

17- I sometimes also see a business development manager who has no self-confidence, when he sees a key person, suddenly he jumps on him to introduce himself and gives him his business card not giving the other
person time to take a deep breath. This approach is wrong.
A person like this does not know how to approach key and important people.

18- The CEO or manager of a big company, or even a big arrogant business man who is rich and famous, when they make an interview with him on T.V he starts trembling and shaking because he does not have enough self-confidence. This person may sometimes even lose control when he talks.

19- The people stated above remind me of university life when I was a student at USC. At the beginning and end of the year, we had an annual ceremony where students would give speeches yet some of them were trembling to talk, and some would not speak at all. I had a specific instance where a student panicked when giving a speech, resulting in his friend escorting him out of the stage. This shows a lack of self confidence. Also, when a young man sees a beautiful girl, he starts trembling and makes mistakes when he speaks to her. Speaking of girls that see a man they like, they start blushing and become very quiet. When the man she likes approaches her table on his way out of the cafeteria, she starts blushing more.

20- There at the university of Southern California (USC), I took several speech communication classes. In these classes, they would train students to give good speeches to people without panicking or getting scared. To give a speech in front of many students in a classroom or lecture hall, requires a lot of self-confidence. Average students, with about 45 – 55 percent self-confidence can manage to give a speech. You can still see that they get tense, and they become flustered. Their eyes and legs tense up, their voices change, their hands start shaking, and their legs begin to quiver. At the same time, there are very few students who have very low self- confidence, about 15 percent. These people are afraid to give a speech in front of other students in a classroom. So, these students would make a deal or agreement with their professor, that they would give the speech to the professor alone, without anyone else being present in the classroom.

Speech classes are very important to give students confidence in case the student one day becomes a big manager, CEO, or any other important job.

This would work as readying the person for any high position.

21- I remember when I was at university, in our geology class, there was a beautiful girl who was our teacher assistant for our geology class helping our professor for the geology lab. There was a stupid student in that class who liked that girl a lot. But because he has no self-confidence, he was mean to her by showing her that he is smarter than her in geology. Also, he always called her "big thigh". He just tried to tell her that she is fat so that one day he can cut her down to make her feel that she

is on the same level as him – giving him a chance to be with her. He knew that she is too good for him and higher than his level. This girl is a nice girl; I always give her compliments because everyone likes compliments. This girl liked my personality a lot, whenever I invited her to dinner, she always came.
The stupid guy in my geology class became very jealous. He does not understand the difference between me and him. I have high self confidence and always give compliments to people, not insulting them and cutting them down. Because I know most of the people in the world do not have self-confidence, so they always need compliments and they don't need people insulting them and cutting them down.

22- Sometimes you might see a person who attracts attention by saying that he is very smart, and that he is even smarter than his boss during a meeting, his behavior would make his boss hate him, and hold grudges against him. Today, in the world of business if you have enough self confidence, you can apologize to your client and make him happy, even if he is wrong and made a mistake. Sometimes I see a client who is wrong and stupid and made a mistake, and I know he has no self confidence.
I simply apologize to him to boost his ego and make him happy. For example, I would say phrases such as "Wow, you are right", and "How did you know this?". If I see someone who is not educated, I would tell him that he knows a lot of things, I would then see a smile on his face and become happy. Sometimes during business meetings, I would see somebody with no self-confidence arguing with his clients, angering them. This was to show others that he knew everything. This reminds me of my life at University, where I used to argue with my roommate or other stupid people on my floor. They would then get mad at me. I would just tell the person that he was right and I was wrong and he won and I lost. The person would become very happy and I would see a smile on his face.

I used to say that to simply maintain our friendship.

23- If you are an owner or manager of a restaurant, and one of your
customers did not like the chicken or the meat, you should try to tell him that your food is very high quality. You must apologize at the same time to make the customer happy. It needs self-confidence to be able to apologize.

24- Also, when I was at university, I saw a stupid guy with no self confidence, joking and teasing two girls, eventually fighting with one of them. One of them was very beautiful. Her friend, who is big and strong was not beautiful. He wanted to impress the beautiful girl by proving he was stronger than her friend. After a while, he took the matter seriously. He started pushing, hitting, and hurting the girl badly. This was all to impress the beautiful girl and prove that he was a strong person. By the end of the fight, the big girl was hurt and hated the guy. Her beautiful friend ended up hating the guy as well.

25- The main point here is that if you are an employee, don't make your boss hold grudges against you. Don't make your boss at work mad at you by showing others during a meeting that you are smarter than your boss. Because your boss will not promote you. Also, if you are a business man, do not make your client mad at you during the meeting. Do not argue with your clients, your clients are the people who give you the money. This is the same idea in business. Try to be calm during the meeting, and nicely argue with the clients. Don't over react and try to control your temper. When they criticize your products or your services, be a gentleman don't fight with them. All of this needs self confidence.

26- Sometimes, if a person has low self confidence he will spend more money to impress people and to show off.

27- A person with no self confidence will say I cannot do this and he will never try but a person with self confidence will say I can do this and he will try.

28- Don't listen to negative people, because negative people will always say that "this is impossible". For example, I heard horses don't look left or right when they walk which means when you have a dream, go for it with confidence and believe in yourself, there is nothing called impossible.

29- When you have high self-confidence, you will think and dream that you can have big businesses and others are not better than you. When you have self-confidence, you will feel you can achieve something and the others who achieved things are not better than you.

30- When you have self-confidence and your friend or people criticize you, you will think positively to fix the problem in your company or your behavior but people with no self-confidence might over react and shout at his friend then his friend will be discouraged to tell him and will not tell him about his problems.

31- Do not impress others by buying a nice car, big house, big farm, you must use your money for investment. Usually, people who don't have enough self confidence they will like to impress other people.

32- There is a story about a small stone which is not shaped very well
located in a dam. That dam was reserving the water coming from the mountains for the entire city. That small stone thought he's not an
important stone, like the others. He's not a diamond rock or a gold nugget. So, he said "why don't I commit suicide and jump off the dam?" When he did so, the entire dam collapsed and all

the people in the city died and the entire city was ruined.

The wisdom and the main point here is that everyone is important in life. Every human being is important and you must have self confidence and not to think that others are better than you.

Chapter 4
Money

Money is very important, you cannot start business without money. You need the capital to start a business. Because, you need money to open an office, to buy products, to do services for people, for daily expenses and operation, and to pay the salaries for your employees. You also need money to pay for your telephone and internet bills etc. The proverb is saying "You cannot buy honey if you don't have money".

So, if you have the ambition to start a business, you should save your money from today. You must save 15 percent of your income from your salary for your future business. This money should be put in an independent savings account. You must also save 5 percent of your income for emergencies, and put the money in a separate savings account preferably another bank. In all, you should be saving 20 percent of your income or salary no matter how low your income or salary is. So, if you start doing that at the age of 25, after 5 years or 10 years, your savings will be a lot of money. You may then start your ownbusiness.

A person may think their salary is not sufficient enough for a savings account. The truth is that if you have a goal and ambition, you have to start from now by putting pressure on yourself. You have to tell yourself that you are not poor and save your money by staying away from purchasing luxurious things. This can be made by:

1. Going on vacation once a year instead of three times a year, because you are an ambitious person and have a big goal in your life, your colleagues and friends are not as ambitious as you.

2. Instead of buying a new car, buy a used car, because you are an ambitious person and have a big goal in your life, and your colleagues are not as ambitious as you.
3. Instead of renting a big house or apartment, rent a small apartment.
4. Instead of going to dinner and movies five times a month, you should only do it once a month, because you are an ambitious person and have a big goal in your life, and your colleagues are not as ambitious as you.
5. You might say that your life will be miserable by buying a used car, or living in a small apartment, or going on vacation just once a year, you might also say that you are used to a certain standard of living. So, don't worry, you will be fine, and you can adapt your life to it. There are a lot of people around the world who are living a life like this, and they are very happy.

6. It is always wise to keep some properties or building you own and not to sell it because once you sell your properties and get alot of cash it will be very easy for you to spend it for example you might spend the money on buying new car or new furniture for the house or you might go on a vacation with your wife etc..
   Then a year later you will have no money left and of course no properties.

7. Maybe now, when you are poor, you will see that 100 dollars is like (10,000). Like how most of the poor people are. But one day, hopefully when you are rich, you will see that 10 thousand dollars (10,000) is like 100 dollars. So, when you start your business, you have to spend your money carefully, thinking that 100 dollars is like ten thousand (10,000) dollars. By doing that, within a few years, you may notice that you have much more money than your friends and your colleagues.

8. There is no need for credit cards because credit cards will encourage you to spend your money plus it will charge you high interest rates. You can live without it.

9. There are a lot of rich people known in the history of business who established their businesses by following similar steps. When they started, they were very poor and sometimes did not even eat three meals a day, just to save money and start their business.

10. When you start your business, try to save money. A lot of people started their business either in their houses, or in their garage or in their garden. A lot of famous people started their business from their houses. When you have cash in your hand you will always be ready for opportunity to buy things. For example:

1- Steve Jobs who established Apple with his friend Steve Wizneiak in 1976. Personalized computers, then made the iPod and iPhone.

2- Jeff Bezos, the man who established Amazon in 1994, who started
selling books on 16th July 1995.

3- The main point here is that the start of a successful business does not rely on the place or office. You can start from your own house.

11. There are a lot of people who make a lot of big mistakes when they open a shop or restaurant and don't have enough money for it. They think that their office or shop will generate money in a few months or a very short period of time. But a lot of times, it doesn't work that way. So, within a few months or a year, they do not have enough money to pay for the rent, salaries, or daily expenses of their business. This is entirely due to a depleted budget. The reason behind all of this is because their savings is not enough, and did not

calculate things in the right way.
Most people think about starting a business, but do not think about maintaining and continuing the business. Because in order to continue your business you still need money.
Money for your employees' salaries, rent, buying products and materials, and paying for your telephone bills, internet bills, etc.
So many people around the world have this problem. They cannot continue their business, because they thought that the minute they start their business, their business will start making money from the first year. You have to have the money to continue your business for three to five years, until your business starts to generate money and stand on your feet. At the same time, you have to shrink your budget in order for your business to survive.

12. Business always has a high season and a low season. For example, you may have seven good years, when the economy is booming and seven bad years when the economy is getting bad and shrinking. So, if you already had seven good years, when business was doing fine, you should get ready for the bad years. In this case, when the economy is bad you should stop wasting your money, and should instead start shrinking your budget. You should also start laying off your employees. It is exactly like how when you have food poisoning and diarrhea, you should suddenly stop eating and only drink water, until you recover, where you will eventually start getting back to your normal life.

13. A research study shows that 90 percent of people who open any kind of business, lose money, while only 10 percent make money. For example, if there are 100 people who open restaurants, 90 of them will lose money sooner or later. And only 10 restaurants will be fine. The same thing would happen with shops selling clothes, or any other shop selling

any other product, where 90 percent would lose money while only 10 percent would make money.

14. There are many reasons why 90 percent of the people are losing money. These reasons include:

1. Wrong place
2. Wrong time
3. Employees stealing money
4. Not enough experience in the business
5. Bad Management
6. And many other reasons that will be mentioned later in this book.

15. Most people lose money when they start their first or their second project. You may lose money, but may also gain experience and other things, so don't panic. When a person starts his first business, it is more likely that he will lose money. Try to not put all of your money in one business – do not put all your eggs in one basket. I know some people who borrow money from banks, their friends, and their family. They put all of their money in one project, because they have dreams.

    Suddenly, they lose everything.

    A person should not give up when he loses in the first project.

16. When I started my first project, which is related to amusement parks, I was in freshmen year at university. At that time, I was a very ambitious person, hard worker, had a lot of dreams. I was very active and had a lot of energy, so I sold my sports a corvette to finance my first project. I worked very hard for it. Unfortunately, however, I lost. The reason why was because I was only thinking of the first, second, and third step. I never thought of the steps after that.

But I do not regret that. This is because my first project allowed me to meet with very key and important people. This opened the door for me for many other things in the future.

17. My second project was related to publishing. It was a successful project that made money, not as much as I expected, and where I made a name for myself as a successful person. This second project made me more respected among my friends and family. It also gave me the hope for the future. I became more optimistic. The real problem of this project was that the money I made was much less than expected.

18. My third project was related to shares and the stock market. This opened my eyes to the world of real money and banking. And dealing with many big people and big banks. The problem with this business however is that it is a high risk, and that there was a high season and low season. This means that there are some good years and some bad years.

19. My fourth project was oil and gas. It is making good money, has less risk, and is a good business that made me more in touch with big companies around the world, meeting key people with different nationalities. The problem of this business is that it has high season and low season.

20. It is always better to start working with a low budget so don't start with a fancy office because most of the big companies started working in garages with a low budget. Try to save money when you get started. For example, google started in a garage. Disney started in a garage and so did apple. Facebook started in university dorms; Samsung started in a small house.

21. When an employee does not have enough money and have financial problems he can not concentrate on his work.

Chapter 5

Experience

1. The key to success is to know your business, you must know your
   business very well. The more knowledge you know from business comes from experience. A lot of people fail in business because they invest money in a business they do not know and do not have any knowledge about it and do not have enough experience in that business.
   Experience and money are important to start a business. But if you ask me, "if there is no choice, what is more important: money or experience?" I would say experience is more important.

2. Experience make you focus on one thing you know then you will be an expert in that type of business in that thing and the other business will grow.

3. As time goes on the merchant and businessman will start to gain skills and talents.

4. A lot of people who inherit the money from their parents or a lot of people who get rich suddenly because of lottery or are football players or from sports, they do not have experience so they invest their money then lose everything. Same thing happens to people who steal money from somewhere, they try to invest money in places where they have no experience.

5. In order to become successful in any kind of business you must know that business very well and to know the little secrets of that job. For this reason you should work there for at least a year. A bank manager knows little secrets about banking, a doctor knows little secrets about hospitals, a

waiter knows little secrets about restaurants so those little secrets are very important.

6. If you want to start in any business you have to work there for at least one year just to get an idea about that kind of business. For example, if you want to make a manufacture for ice cream you have to work there as an employee or a worker just to know the secrets of that manufacturer. The same thing if you want to build a hospital, you have to work as an employee in that hospital. If you are a rich kid, you can work in a different city away from your friends to gain experience then go back and open a hospital.

7. At one time I asked the waiter I know in a restaurant because I always go to the same restaurant to eat and I used to give him good tips about how long or how many years of experience a waiter needs in order to open a restaurant on his own. He replied he needs at least 10 years of experience or 15 years then I asked him what would happen if that person has only one year of experience, he replied that that means he is stupid and he will fail because he must know other things than serving the clients. He must know how to buy the products, meat, fish, bread, salad, vegetables. And it must be at the lowest prices and must know from where to buy and what time to buy it and there are many things he has to buy for the restaurant and there are many things that are more complicated than what you think about restaurant business.

8. Experience is more important than money, you cannot start business without experience, but there are chances that you can start business without money. Nobody was born with knowledge and knowing everything. People learn only through experience. So, experience is more important than money. Experience is extremely important.
   Experience is the most important thing in business, it is more

important than anything else. I always consider a person who has experience as a person who has treasure or gold. It is always good to have both experience and money, in order to start a business. But choose experience over money if you were given the choice. There are a lot of people who inherited a lot of money from their father or their family, or suddenly they won a lottery, and they lose their money in a year or so. This is because they don't have enough experience in business. However, a poor person with a lot of experience has a better chance of getting rich. Today, 86 percent of the rich people were born poor. But, because of their experience and their hard work and the other factors of success written in this book, they became successful.

9. If somebody gave you a chance to work with him at the right place or at the right company, it is like someone giving you gold, not money.

10. If you are a young man, and you do not have enough experience, it is always good to ask people who have the experience. Or to read books, on the people who have the experience.

11. The most successful people in business are those who open a business in something they know. For example, a doctor must open a hospital or clinic, a school teacher must open a private school or a teaching institution, a waiter in a restaurant must open a restaurant, a pilot must open a flying school, and a policeman must open a security company. If you want to start a business, you start a business about something you know.

12. The story of Kentucky Fried Chicken started with Harland Sanders who was born in 1890 and raised on a farm outside Henryville, Indiana near Louisville, Kentucky. When Sanders was five years old, his father died,forcing his mother

to work at canning plant. This left Sanders, as the eldest son, to care for his two younger siblings. After he reached seven years of age, his mother taught him how to cook. After leaving the family home at the age of 13, Sanders passed through several professions with mixed success. In 1930, Sanders took over a Shell filling station on US Route 25 just outside North Corbin, Kentucky, a small town on the edge of the Appalachian Mountains. It was here that he first served to travelers the recipes that he had learned as a child: fried chicken and other dishes such as steaks and country ham. After four years of serving from his own dining room table, Sanders purchased the larger filling station on the other side of the road and expanded to six tables.

13. Every job or every business has little secrets, nobody knows the secrets aside from those who experienced it. This is why it is important to have a business in something you know.

14. Don't make a mistake and start a business with something that you do not know. Most of the people who fail in business, fail because they start a business in something that they do not know. They simply start the business because of greed, and think that there is always money. After a while however, they lose their money. This results in disaster, where they lose everything.

15. Just start any business you know and are good at, and can do it well. Once you start this business, you will get the feeling of business. Later on, all the doors will open for you. Don't worry, things will work for you. This is how life is. Within two years or three years, you might start a different kind of business related to your first business. This is life and this is business. One door will open another door for you, and your business will grow. One business will lead to another business. Later on, after a few years, other businesses will be

easy for you. They will come to you due to your experience, and things will work out for you.

16. I'm sure that when you were in 7th or 8th grade you were worried about how you could survive when going to high school. You may have thought that things were going to get harder for you. High School would have been harder, and you would have questioned having friends in high-school. However, things would hopefully work out well for you in high-school. The same process would repeat itself when going to university. You may have asked if you were going to survive in college or university, as you held more responsibility and had to read more books and do more exams. You may even worry socially, asking yourself if you would have friends in university. Things would hopefully end up working well for you, having friends in university. Once you graduate from university, you may worry about surviving in the real world, questioning if you would get a job or find friends at your place of work. Do not worry, things will work out for you. So now, when you start a business do not worry, but you have to start with a business that you know and things will work out for you.

17. The person who has the experience will know how to choose the right people to work for him.

18. A long time ago, there was an aerospace engineer who was working in Airplane manufacturing. His name is James Smith McDonnell who was born in Denver, Colorado, on April 9, 1899. He graduated from Princeton University in 1921 with a bachelor's in physics. He then earned a Master of Science in Aeronautical Engineering from MIT in 1925.In 1928, McDonnell left Huff Daland and set up J.S McDonnell & Associates, and with the help of two other engineers, McDonnell set out to design his first aircraft with his company name. He was working for many years without

getting promoted. He joined another aircraft company and did not get promoted there either. He then went to a third company for aircraft and didn't get promoted. He felt bad because he has a lot of experience and did not get promoted. Then, in 1938 he decided to open his own company related to aircraft production. He borrowed money from his wife and his friends. He needed even more money from banks; however, they refused to lend him money. In 1939 Adolf Hitler invaded Poland. He founded McDonnell Aircraft Corporation. Then, World War 2 started. The United States started to produce more things for the war. There was a lot of business related to the aircraft industry. James Smith McDonnell found one bank who was willing to lend him money. He then started his business. He started growing and making money. More banks started to lend him money. In 1967, McDonnell Aircraft merged with Douglas Aircraft Company to create McDonnell Douglas. He kept growing. Finally, he made a lot of fighter jets, such as the phantom and the f series (F-15, F-18), dc-9, dc-10. He became a billionaire. The point here, is that James Smith McDonnell started a business related to his job (aerospace engineering). It was something he knew.

19. I always look at one's experience. A person's experience is like gold. Someone can translate his experience into business and money making. I always look at someone's experience as a treasure, but a lot of people do not know that. No matter what experience you have, it is like treasure, you may not know how valuable it is. Invest in your experience in something you know, and you will make money. Do not stem away from what you know. A bird in your hand is better than 10 on the tree.

20. I have a lot of friends who have no experience in restaurants, yet opened restaurants, failed, and lost their money. I once

rented a limousine, and was talking with the limousine driver. He told me that he used to work as a food delivery driver at a restaurant. I asked the driver if the restaurant was making money, he said that it was making a lot of money. He said that the restaurant owner was very successful because he used to work from a very young age at his father's restaurant. The owner of the restaurant learned a lot from his restaurant. His father was also working in the restaurant of his grandfather. The whole family had a lot of experience with restaurants. This is why they are making good money.

21. In every business, and in every job there are a lot of little secrets that not many people know, but they are very important. This is the same with anything else, this is why they know their business and this is why they are making money, for example in cinema. Let me give you an example of a young man from England whose name was Robert Bolt. He was interested in writing scripts for radio stations at that time. In the 1930's he was attempting to sell his scripts to the radio stations, but they didn't buy them. Robert Bolt went to college. He was only able to attend college for one year; he didn't have the money to fund his tuition for the second year. His poor father told him to find a job. The only job available was that of a post man. He didn't like his job, it was very boring for him. That year was a very bad year for him. After he worked in the post office for one year, and collected the money, he went back to college. He then started to think about writing a script about the daily life of a postman, because he experienced it, he knew every little thing about it, all the secrets about it. He did very well in it. This was because he lived that life. He knew how to describe every little thing about a postman's daily life, because he lived it. He was then able to sell his script to the radio station in England. This script made him famous. It opened the door

for him to write other scripts. Over the years, he wrote the script for many famous movies such as, Lawrence of Arabia (which won 7 Oscars), Amazon, etc. The point here is that this man, Robert Bolt did well in his first sold script about the postman because he knew about the job, he knew every little thing about it, he knew what it meant to be to be a postman.

22. One of my ex-roommates in college used to work in construction.
Every summer, since he was in high school he got the same summer job in construction. Finally, after he finished college, he opened an office with the help of his family in construction business and making houses. He is now successful; making money, and going on vacations. The point here is that since this man was a teenager, he kept working in construction – a job he was very familiar with. He started early, learning the little things about construction.

23. There was a story I heard from a good friend of mine from the middle east. The story is that a poor teenager approached and asked a merchant if it was possible to work in his shop. The merchant told him that if he were working at his house, he would get his full salary, however, if he worked in the shop, he would get half his salary. The boy asked the merchant why there was more money working at his house than at the shop. The merchant said that if the boy were to work in his house, he ould not gain any experience nor knowledge, but if he were to work in his shop, he would gain both, and could one day be a competitor. The boy chose to work at the merchant's shop, for half the salary. After fifteen years the boy gained enough experience, and opened many shops, becoming very successful and competed with the older

merchant. Even though the boy has no education, through his experience he knew the most important things in business which are the three P's – Product, Prices, and Place. He knew how to sell the good products with low prices, and open shops in the right places.
This is how he made his fortune and his business flourished. Because, he started to know the quality of products that the customers want. Also, he knows how to buy things and at what price. He started to know where to buy big quantities of products at the lowest prices. So he can make more money. At the same time, he knows how to maintain good quality.

24. I know a person for the last 39 years who is a government official.
I rarely see this person however. Every time I see him, we talk about jokes and funny things. He thought that I am an idiot or a moron. So, one day, when he was about to retire, he asked me about my business. I told him that it is in oil and gas. It is a good business, making good money (millions). He thought that he is smarter than me, forgetting the experience I had. The next day, he opened a company for oil and gas services, and spent all of his money and savings, just to imitate my money and business. After three years, he closed his office without making one dollar in oil and gas.

25. There was a young man who graduated from college who was looking for a job in a bank. He was not able to find a job like all other young people in that year. This man however knew the importance of experience and knowledge, he is a smart and unique person. He told the people in the bank that he is willing to work in the bank for free, just to learn something. They gave him a chance to work for free. He used to come every day very early in the morning, because he liked his job. He learned a lot. The people in the bank noticed that he is very smart and ambitious. The man was

very friendly, had good manners, and was a hard worker. The people started to like him. After six months, they offered him a job with pay. Today, this person became a multi-millionaire, owns a famous bank in the middle east, and many financial firms.

26. I always consider a person's experience like a treasure. Most of the people don't understand that. Most of the people do not know how to transfer their experience into making money. This is like giving a three-year-old child a piece of gold. He will not understand or know what to do with the piece of gold. He doesn't know how to sell it or go to a shop where they purchase gold. He doesn't understand that the piece of gold can get him a lot of money, which can get him a lot of ice cream and chocolate.

27. A lot of times kids from wealthy business families learn things about business and factors of success in business from parents indirectly, more than others kids in their schools for example the child or the young man will hear his father talking about their neighbor who failed in business because he did not have experience or he will hear his father is talking about the importance of contact and connections or his father is complaining about some of his employees who are stealing money from him or he will see his father working very hard even on the weekends or he heard his father talking about patience and how his grandfather lost his money, he waited for many years and until he recovered after few years and then started to make money and became successful again. Many times it happened to me that when I talk to some of my educated friends who came from families who are not from business background I notice they don't know about the basic things about business or the concept of business or the factors of success in business they just talk like they are from a different planet and they think making money is easy.

28. People who do not know how to use their experience to generate money must have the other factors of success which are written in this book. This is because the factors of success are the tools to help people to make money.

A. I know a lady in California who didn't like her son in law that married her daughter. He is a geologist. Because she didn't like him, she didn't like what he was working as. She said that "he studied geology, a rock in the crack". She didn't understand that him being a geologist was something of value. I personally started out as a geologist, and because of the factors of success, I was using my knowledge in geology and my experience in the oil companies to make money. This man can make a lot of money if he had the other factors of success mentioned in this book.

29. Once you start your business in the first year you will be approached by all kinds of people. Some people will try to borrow money from you and not pay you back. Other people will try to buy products or other services from you, and won't pay you back. So, many people will try to take advantage of you, cheat you, or steal money from you even your employees will try to steal money from you. So, as time goes on, you will be aware and careful no longer naïve. A new person in the market will be fooled and cheated easily.

30. There was an engineer who inherited money from his family, who likes farms and nature. When he received his money, he decided to quit his career as an engineer, and instead went into the farming business. He started to buy some farms, and started to sell the fruits. Then, he found a company from Europe that was willing to buy his fruits. He was happy and excited. The first time, he sold them in a small quantity and they paid him. The second time, he sold them three times as much product, and they paid him. The third time, he sold them five times as much. The fourth time,

they bought an enormous amount of product, and didn't pay him. The man paid for the transportation and delivery. He ended up losing all his money and filed for bankruptcy. The man then went to Europe to find their office, however it didn't exist. The office shut down and the thieves ran away with the money.

31. I heard a lot of stories such as this. The buyers who are not honest would pay for the first, second and third shipment, but anything exceeding the fourth would go unpaid. This resulted in many of my friends and people I know losing money, and very large setbacks for their business careers.

32. I always feel sorry for some people who have no experience in business, and no money. They always jump into big businesses,possibly not even having 500 dollars in their pockets. There are a lot of them everywhere. You may see this person on the street with no experience and no money. He may tell you that he wants to import 200 cars and sell them. He has dreams, and ideas, but doesn't know anything about business, or the subject, lacking the experience. They would be lacking the contacts and connections. Or, this man may tell you that he wants to import big quantities of certain foods which costs millions. Perhaps, he will tell you that he wants to build a big oil refinery in south America or Asia, which would cost billions. These kinds of people waste many months or many years of their time, without even making one dollar. A lot of times they approach me and try to work with me, however, I reject them because they have no experience in business or making money. They waste my time.

The problem with these people are:

1. They are not patient and are always in a hurry, they want to make quick money.
2. They have no experience. For any kind of business, you have to start from the beginning. After many years of experience,

a doctor in the hospital can have his own business and open his own hospital. A school teacher, after many years of experience, can open a private school. A waiter after many years of experience can open a restaurant. A pilot, after many years of experience can open a flying school. But, these people want to start from the top because they don't believe in experience, they just think that they are smart.

3. They have no contacts or connections
4. They don't have any factors of success mentioned in the book.
5. They are greedy and have a dream that they will one day be successful by striking out on pure luck. This will never happen to them.
6. They are following fantasies.
7. Those people are ignorant and shallow people, who have no knowledge about the subject – they don't have the experience nor the details or little things about the subject they are trying to do. This is because they never worked in the job they are trying to do. Unfortunately, some may be retried lawyers, or retired teachers, not having any experience in business or to their previous job. They go into big new businesses that is not related with their career. They think they know everything, but in reality, they only know a bit about everything. These people are simply following a trend. If these people were to see success in oil, they would follow that success, or jumping onto selling fish, the second month they would be selling chicken, and meat for third month, and the next month selling big quantities of food, five months later selling cars, seven months later selling medicine and healthcare, ten months later they would be in steel, gold and shares. These people would jump from one business to another, looking for opportunities and thinking they can be as successful as others with experience. The problem with these people is that they have an ego and don't want to start from the beginning. It is exactly like a student who drops out

of seventh grade and started to fool around.After a few years, this person would realize that all his childhood friends are in university. He will then have a dream to go to a big school such as Harvard. So, a person like that will have no chance to be admitted to Harvard. Because of his ego however, a person like that will not want to start from the beginning. If you hypothetically assume that he was admitted into Harvard, he will not be able to survive in Harvard. He will not be able to write papers or take exams in Harvard. He will be lacking all the experience, prior education, and a strong background needed to succeed. Even socially, he cannot get along with students at Harvard University, because the other students will think that he is mentally retarded.

33. The main point here is that you shouldn't venture out of your comfort zone and work in areas that is not related to your expertise, where you have no experience in. You must conduct a business in something you know.

34. They must hire a financial firm to see if the project they are investing is realistic, and can make money or not. They are not successful; they do not have the other factors of success written in this book.

35. Some young people want to invest their business into another country, or invest their money into another country, because they think it's easier, just like the saying the grass is greener on the other side. They don't know the rules and regulations in another country, neither do they know the culture of the other country. They don't have the key people, nor the contacts or connections - the right people. They then fail and lose their money.

36. For every business there are steps that you have to take. The first step is knowing what your customer or client want.

Knowing what kind of services, they want, not what you want or like. You must think of what the client wants. Give the fish what the fish likes to eat, not what you like to eat. For example, you may be a rich young man who only stays at five star hotels, and want to open a five-star hotel. You must however think of the other people and what they can afford. Maybe, building a three-star hotel or a two start hotel would be the better and more successful project, because many people don't have the money to stay in a five-star hotel.

37. In every business there are steps that you have to take. You have to have good planning. Most young people don't have the plans, nor the steps and details. This is why they lose money on their first project. For example, imagine that there's a person who found a map for hidden gold during the 19th century. In this case, he must have a good plan for it and follow the steps. For example, step 1 is to find the gold. Step 2 is to find the horses and mules to carry the gold. At that time, he was counting on finding the mules, so he might stay for a few days for the mules and horses. Step 3 is to find a boat to put the gold in it to cross the river. He may have to wait a few days, possibly assuming that a boat would be there every day. Step 4 is to return to his home or village, and hide the gold in a safe place. A good and safe place for the gold. Step five is to find the right and honest people who will pay him money in exchange for the gold.

38. When I was young, like most young people, I had simple dreams.
My dream was to open my own restaurant. I thought it was an easy and simple business – not complicated. Like many other young people. In 1976, I used to visit my friends in San Diego, California. I used to go with them to Jack in the box late at night. We used to sit and eat delicious cheeseburgers with onion rings. On a cold and rainy night, we would be

listening and watching the rain while I was talking to my friends as I savored the hot and delicious burger and crisp onion rings. I told myself that I must open a restaurant like Jack in the Box. Similar food. In 1977 I used to go to mammoth mountains for snow skiing. We used to stop in McDonalds in the middle of Mojabi desert on a cold night. At that time, the hot hamburger in McDonalds taste so good, on a cold night – it was so delicious. In 1978, I started to go to a restaurant named Tommy's Burger close to downtown Los Angeles. The place was always full and delicious. There were plenty of celebrities and famous people eating at the restaurant, I was impressed. I then had a dream to open a restaurant that could attract many people and celebrities at the same time. In 1980, I went to Hawaii with my friend John. We used to eat healthy food – tuna sandwiches at a tuna restaurant (it was very healthy food). I always loved Hawaii. There are many activities people could enjoy while staying healthy. For example, Jet skiing, Scuba Diving, watersports, or walking at night listening to the waves – it was the right place to have fun and have a healthy life. It was the perfect place to have healthy tuna restaurants on every Hawaiian island. In 1984, I started to go with my friends to Hard Rock café in Los Angeles. I noticed that all the young people liked to gather there. So many young people also bought T-shirts and Hats with the name, Hard Rock Café. I asked myself why I didn't open a restaurant with good food that can sell merchandise, which would give me more money. In 1990, I started to go for a walk along the beach in Newport-beach, California and had hamburgers on the beach. I used to eat the hamburgers while watching the waves, and the clouds overhead. I said that having many hamburger joints along the beaches of California will lead to very good business and profit. In 1993 I flew from California to Louisiana to visit a friend of mine. There we went to a nice and unique place where they have donuts and coffee. The taste of the donuts and coffee there is very unique. I decided to create something unique. There, I heard that everyone who goes to Louisiana has to go to this place. I asked myself why I should bother myself. It is very easy to make donuts and coffee. In 1997, I noticed that some of my friends like the Cheesecake factory. In Los Angeles, I was impressed by the large menus and that it is always crowded. I had an idea to have a restaurant like that with such a large menu, so that it could always be crowded. In the year 2000, and 2001, I used to go to in and out burger in Irvine, California. I used to go there a lot at night. That place is always crowded with students who like the tasty hamburgers. I then thought, why I don't have tasty hamburgers similar to IN and Out burgers, but next to every University in California. By doing that, I can make more money. Today, when I think about those ideas, I just laugh. I tell myself that I am glad I did not follow up. They were not for me. I didn't have the experience of cooking, or the experience of working in restaurants.

39. The point here is that not all the things you like you can do. You may like hamburgers, but you don't know how to cook hamburgers. Maybe you like to drive cars, but you can't be a taxi driver. To be a taxi driver requires a lot of patience and hard work, that not many people have. Maybe you like to watch movies, but you cannot work as an actor lacking the talent. You possibly can't produce a movie lacking the funds and money. Maybe, you like to watch football on T.V but you cannot be a professional football player.

40. Every time you start your business, it is not guaranteed that the first or second project in your life will make money. However, you will gain experience. My first project was related to amusement parks. I worked very hard for it. I sold my sports car to finance the project. But then, my project

failed. I was really depressed that year. But, I gained something. I gained the experience. I came to realize that I needed much stronger planning. I also attained many contacts and connections because of the project. Looking back, I am happy that it failed, I see it as a blessing, I do not regret it because I gained a lot of connections, which helped me for the rest of my life. For example, in my first project, I was planning on making money, but I made contacts and connections. I then remembered what my friend said sometimes in life when you grow apples you get oranges, and when you grow potatoes, you get onions. My second project was about publishing. I made little money, not as much as I dreamed. My second project opened the door for me to meet with other people, and formed connections with other people. I gained a lot of experience. In both publishing and other things. Here, I just wanted to mention that one of my friends told me that in life, you get very unexpected things. It is like planting apples, and getting oranges. When you plant potatoes, you get onions.

41. The key to success is to know your business. You must know your business very well. The more your knowledge you have, the more successful you will be in your business and the knowledge comes from experience over a long period of time. A lot of people fail in business because they invest money in a business they don't know, and they don't have any knowledge about it. They not have experience in that business, they just do it based on dreams and imagination.

42. Experience makes you focus on one thing you know. You will then be an expert in that thing and that type of business. In the long run, your business will grow. When a merchant or a business man starts his business, he starts to gain skills and talent. So as time goes on, he will have in depth knowledge,

large skill set and experience in that business.

43. There is another way to learn how to make money, which is that you start with a small business. For example, selling shampoo on campus at the university, just to learn and get the feeling of how to make money and you will learn the method of making money and the method of losing money in small quantity. By doing that, you will learn the business of making money and also you will gain the self confidence.
44. There was a 12 years old boy who ended up working in a chocolate manufacturer. By working there for many years, he gained the experience. At the beginning, he didn't like his job but after a few years he started making a chocolate manufacturing company. Today, it is a 21 billion Dollars empire called Hershey's. It is the largest chocolate manufacturer in the world. The point here is that the reason behind his success was that he used to work in a chocolate manufacturing business for many years and after that he gained the experience and he knew everything about making chocolate.

45. There are many people who like to eat food at a restaurant but they never worked as waiters or cooks in restaurants so they do not know about the restaurant business. When they started opening a restaurant, they fail because they know nothing about the restaurant business. They do not have the experience, they never worked as waiters or cooks in a restaurant.

46. The best way to know the business and the secret of that job is to work there.

47. So the point here is that skill and knowledge come from

experience and implementing your skills and knowledge making experience so important. No one has skills and talent in business without the experience.

48. Every project or business starts with an idea but the best idea is when you have the experience or based on your work experience.

Chapter 6

Working Hard

1. Working hard and dedication is the key to success, and you must dedicate all your work and your time to your business, and you must focus entirely on your business. Do not think of other things. There are some people who dedicate their time to sports and social life. They rely on their employees and others to help them. If you want to be successful, you must do things by yourself. Don't rely on others. Sometimes,employees steal money from their superiors or business owners because they would not be present. A successful businessman is a person who works seven days a week, 24 hours a day.

2. Most people want things the easy way. People looking for business in the easy way and there is no easy way to make money.

3. You must be unique by working hard even if you are in a bad mood.

4. I know a lot of people who have better chances than me to make
   money. However, they are lazy. These people do not want to work hard. They want things the easy way. I tried to help these people many times and give them chances.people never listen, many times laziness is the cause for poverty. They are simply lazy. Many times, laziness is the reason for poverty.

5. So many people approached me, complaining that their income is very low, and that they need more income and more money. I tried to help them by showing them the way to make money, however, it did not work. They are only

interested in making money, not working hard for it. Without working hard, nothing will happen.

6. A person that I know very well once asked me a long time ago to help him make money. He has no experience, the only thing he has is contacts and connections. I asked what his specialty was and questioned if he could help me. He told me that he knew a very important businessman and that he could set a meeting between the two of us. After I agreed, he told me that we can meet up the next night. When I called this associate, he told me that he was busy. This was his repeated response after I called him. I was never able to meet with the business manager due to the associate sometimes going to the gym and other times going to the movie theater or the barber shop for a haircut. Every time I called him, he had a different excuse to not see me. This person had many opportunities to make money but missed them. His laziness is the reason as to why he is still poor today. There are a lot of people like this person who don't use the chances given to them. These types of people are uncommitted and lazy.

7. My time is precious and I do not have much time to spend on others. When people ask for help however, I try to find the time, telling them that I will contact them in the near future. I meet them to show them how to make money. When I call these people, they always have an excuse not to see me. Whether it be plans to go the movies, exercising at the gym, or going to the barber for a haircut, they are always busy. A person cannot carry two dishes in one hand. You are either busy with business and making money, or busy with other things.

8. A study shows that 86 percent of the wealthy were born poor. Most worked extremely hard to reach the point that they are

at now.
Interviews about the most successful people in business have a similar saying. They say that they worked very hard to reach the position that they are at. A lot of these people focused entirely on their work and profession, sometimes even disregarding their health and well-being.

9. Even in other things, aside from business, a lot of successful people in history were very hard workers, they work all day and all night. For
example, Napoleon, was a very hard worker. A lot of successful directors and producers in Hollywood are hard workers.

10. When you work hard in business, you will learn a lot and gain experience. The longer hours that you work, the more experience you will get. Your employees will also respect you more, knowing that their boss is a hard worker and works for long hours. When you work hard, you have better chances to improve your business, product, services, and better your company, making more money.
11. When you work hard in business, there are lower chances of employees stealing money, and other people taking advantage of your company.
Employees in big companies know how to steal money once they gain enough experience.

12. A friend of mine owns a restaurant. When he is present at the restaurant, there is more profit than when he is away. His employees steal money when he is away. He eventually closed the restaurant, not having enough time to be there all the time. Another friend of mine is from Glendale, California, who owned five restaurants at the same time. He didn't have time to operate and run all five at the same time. He closed his restaurants because his employees were also

stealing money. This applies to many other businesses, not just restaurants. The more hands on and invested you are in your business, the less likely it will be for your employees to steal and take advantage of you.

13. I was once having dinner with one of my friends who is an engineer.
I was complaining to him that I am always busy and don't have time.
He told me that the way he looks at it, is that businessmen have a lot of free time, surrounded by girls, and on large yachts he got this image of businessmen from movies. I laughed. When a movie is made, they want the audience to know that the character in the film is a billionaire. The best way to show this is by showing the character in a mansion, or a luxurious yacht. Most of the movie goers are either young adults under the age of 24, or teenagers. The best way to tell these people that someone is rich, is by showing off their lavish lifestyle. When I was taking script-classes for my cinema course at USC, there were
requirements that included writing scripts for the audience to understand, and exciting stories to show descriptive imagery. For example, a billionaire having a large party on a yacht.

14. I once saw a program on 60 minutes during the 80s. It was about Maldives, which is a country located in the Indian ocean. 60 minutes was talking about the fact that the islands were so beautiful and that there were only 2 cars in the country at the time, and that their jail is an island. They made an interview with a German, who was in jail for 17 years. He said that he was very happy in jail, and that he didn't want to leave the jail to go back to Germany. He said that he was very happy in this jail island. To him, it was like paradise. He swam in the sea every day, he ran every day, he laid out in the sun, and had good friends that he talked to every time.

Unfortunately for him, he served his sentence and had to return back to his country. The point here is that some people are happy in what they are doing even in jail so the same thing with a businessman, he is happy with working hard. Working hard is enjoyable and fun because he likes it and he is used to it.

15. Usually, businessmen will never stop to have fun and smell the roses. The majority are ambitious and driven by their goals and greed. They say that after we reach our goals, we will stop to smell the roses and have fun. They say that after three years we will reach our goals, and then have fun. Unfortunately, however, a lot of times it takes more than 3 years or even 10 years to reach their goals. This is why businessmen are always busy twenty-four hours a day, seven days a week.

16. Also, there is another type of businessman who has debts and financial problems who work very hard, that are driven by anxiety, and are very worried about their debts financial problems. They want to solve their problems and that type of businessman will say to his friends, 'I will stop to have fun and smell the roses after I solve my problems'. Unfortunately, it may take 5 years, or 10 years to solve his problems. So, this is why he is working hard.

17. Since my childhood, I always enjoyed travelling by airplanes. From the top, you can see everything. The cars, the ships, houses, and roads all look miniature and small. Also, I can see nature. I see the deserts, forests, oceans, lakes.
I enjoy going to the back window where the bathrooms are and placing my ear on the window. It sounds to me like music, like a waterfall. Later on, when I became a businessman, I was once travelling from Los Angeles California to Miami Florida for a business trip. I did not

enjoy my flight, however. A day earlier, one of my employees stole a lot of money and ran away. With the money my employee stole, a person could buy 3 or 4 expensive sports cars. I was sad and depressed during the flight. I was stressed and had many worries. I did not enjoy that flight from California to Florida. Even though, my business partner in Florida took me to a good restaurant and we had a good dinner, I did not enjoy it. Because I was depressed. The next day, I went for a walk along the beach in Florida, but I didn't enjoy the beach because I was depressed, sad, and had things on my mind.

18. when I used to do the laundry or wash my clothes in university. When I used to bring detergent to wash my clothes, some people would throw my clothes on the floor. What I did instead was leave my detergent on the machine and I would get my clothes. People would then steal my detergent. Then, when I leave my coins and get the detergent, they would steal my coins. Relatively speaking, it was a big problem. I solved this problem by washing my clothes late at night when no one is there, even to wash your clothes you have to work hard.

19. A businessman must work 24 hours a day and seven days a week. He must always focus on his work and think about it day and night.

20. Some people are lazy and are escaping the reality of life by watching video games, watching TV, wasting time with many things. But if you really want to be successful in business, you have to spend your time on your business only.

21. Working hard is very important, no matter how smart you are and no matter how many talents you may have, without working hard nothing will happen.

22. There was a person in Africa who decided to sell eggs, he started to wake up early every morning at 4 am and started to visit small villages on his donkey to buy the eggs from the people for a cheap price and sell it to the people in the city for a higher price.

This man became well known for the other villages then he bought a car to go more villages, in order to collect more eggs from the people.

Finally, this man started to work with foreign currencies and shares.

Then he became a billionaire even though he was not an educated person.

23. Sometimes you must do things you don't like, like working hard on something and pushing yourself even when you are not in the mood for it. You have to work hard and get things done. Sometimes a person is not getting enough sleep but he has to work hard and get things done.

    Sometimes a person is not in the mood to do certain things but he has to do the research and get it done. Sometimes you have to put up with people, there are a lot of people that are rude and not nice to be around but you have to put up with bad people and rude people sometimes.

24. The last thing and the important thing for success is waking up early in the morning because you can get a lot of things done at that time. In other cultures, they think that there are more blessings when working in the morning. When you work in the morning, most of the people are there to work with in the market. This is a normal thing. But when you wake up late and at noon and for example start your working day at 12 noon, even if you are working long hours until midnight, you will be missing things. Some of the people that start work late are weird not normal. So, working late when starting at daytime will never substitute for

working early in the morning. If you don't believe me, start your day early at six in the morning till six in the evening and see how many things you accomplish compared to starting work at 12 pm to midnight.

Try starting your working hours at 6am for a month then try starting your working hours at 12 and you will see the difference.

25. Always reading books is good for you to have more knowledge about business and to keep up to date because many successful billionaires and multi-millionaires are always reading books and its always a good habit.

Chapter 7
Bravery and Risk-taking

Business is a risk. You have to be brave enough to take a decision, to start a business or new line of business. Because a lot of people hesitate to take the decision, they are cowards. Just make a decision and be positive. All things will work for you. Business is an opportunity. The opportunity will not wait for you. So, don't miss it. Like missing the train or missing the boat. Because the train is not going to wait for you. The boat will not wait for you either. I know a lot of people who are not brave and are afraid to take risks in business. They had a dream to be rich for the last 25 years, but they kept hesitating. Because they are afraid and scared to take a risk. I know a lot of people who hesitate when I tell them to buy shares, or to buy gold, or even real-estate. I tell them to buy it now, while they keep thinking about it. They cannot make a decision they are not brave enough to make a decision. The same thing happens when I tell them to sell their shares, their gold, or real-estate. They hesitate to do so. They are simply not brave enough and are too scared to make a decision. Because everybody is afraid to lose their money. A year later, they regret that they didn't listen to me, and they lost the opportunity. This is business.

Business is a risk, a calculated risk. If you want to be a businessman, you must start now, and take a decision now. You must be brave to have the ability to take a risk and make a decision. Because, that opportunity will not return. Start with any small business that you have experience and are comfortable with, and things will work out for you. If you keep telling yourself tomorrow, the time will fly by. One year will turn into 5, 5 will turn into 10, and you will see yourself not having donc anything, and regret for the rest of your life.

1. A friend of mine told me that he was once very fat and was always planning on losing weight. But he never got started. The time goes by, a month to 2, 2 months to a year. One day he had a plan to go with one of his friends to dinner. So, he told his friend after they ordered dinner at the restaurant, that he is always planning on losing weight, but he kept postponing it. His friend told him that he had to stop then, and not eat his dinner that night. He told him, "If you eat tonight, you will never be able to go on a diet and start doing sports. If you keep postponing, you will never lose weight. There comes a point in your life where you have to make a decision. Now means now". His friend had the same problem a few years before that and is now in good shape.

2. Some people have the ideas for business, but they don't have the courage nor guts to start a business. They keep reading books and asking people about business for many years. The years pass by quickly, and after 15-20 years, they find themselves not accomplishing anything. I just suggest that you should start any small business that you know, related to your work and experience, with a small amount of money, and things will start working out for you. You will then attain the feeling and the experience of business. There are a lot of opportunities everywhere, but people cannot see it. Because people are afraid to make a decision. A successful person would be ready the second an opportunity presents itself.

3. A brave person is determined to take a decision, take a risk and start the business.

4. A billionaire was once interviewed on T.V. The broadcaster asked the billionaire, "What was the reason or factor behind your success, why are you different and more successful than others". The billionaire took out his checkbook and told the broadcaster that he will write a check for any amount

of money that he wished. The broadcaster was in shock, he didn't say anything. The billionaire said, "You see, you had the opportunity to take money from me yet you didn't take it. This is life, there are opportunities given to so many people, yet most don't take it.

5. There are a lot of rich people that said, whenever there is an opportunity, they take it to do business and make money. At the same time, their closest friends, or their brothers hesitate when the same opportunity comes to them. But, a few years later, they regret it. They missed the opportunity.

6. Sometimes, when an opportunity comes to a person and that opportunity is a good one to invest in and a safe one. That person can sell their land or car to invest, yet they are too afraid to invest because they are scared to do so. Even if you asked someone to come with you on a vacation, some people would hesitate, while others would go. I remember when I was a student in USC, I sometimes invited students to come with me to Hawaii, or snow skiing in Colorado or California. Some people would refuse, and other would go. I was paying for the hotels and covering all expenses. This is human nature. People are hesitant. Now, imagine the fear with business. Very few people are willing to invest in business. Most are not brave enough. I don't blame people. Some people do not have any experience or are uncomfortable with certain situations. They would be naturally hesitant to place their money on the line for something they do not know.

7. Some of my friends who are working as engineers in different companies, are used to taking orders from management and their bosses. They cannot think or act for themselves. They are not used to making decisions on their own. So, when you tell a person to invest money or sell/buy shares or gold, they are afraid. They are not used to taking

decisions on their own. This is different than a businessman, a businessman is used to taking his own decisions every day. A businessman takes risks every day.

8. My first project was related to amusement parks. I took a risk and sold my sports car, a corvette. I had to make a decision. I worked very hard for that project, but it failed. I gained something, however. Indirectly, I made a lot of contacts and connections. So, I did not regret selling my car and working on that project, because I felt I gained something.

9. The most important thing is to be self-determined and you insist on doing what you want no matter what, no matter how long it takes and how much it will cost, in terms of effort.

10. You must take a risk and do it because many people hesitate to take a risk. They will start thinking then waiting then worrying then doubting then waiting again and then the time will go by, many months and many years and nothing will happen.

11. Do anything and anything will lead to something else just take a chance even if you start working without a salary but if you stay where you are nothing will happen.

12. Just focus on your next step. Don't worry whether things will work for you. I Think when you were in the 9th grade you worried about highschooler and friends. Also, when you are in high school you are worried about university, if you could survive grades and make friends. After college you worried about work, job and friends.

13. Sometimes you see a stupid person with no education become rich. Maybe because this person is a brave person and started the business without a lot of thinking and

analyzing things and reading.
For example, if a clever person keeps listening to the news about the storm before he goes to the mountains for snow skiing, he will cancel his trip while a stupid and non-educated person will go to the mountains thinking that maybe the storm will stop.

14. Most of the successful businessmen say that taking a risk is very important and all of them agree on that.

15. Ideas become clearer when you work on them just start working on your ideas and things will work out for you, the same thing applies to projects.

16. You must leave your comfort zone in order to be successful in business. Some people don't have the courage to leave their comfort zone and some people are lazy they cannot leave their comfort zone.

17. Take a risk when you are young and don't have a family and kids, for this reason is always best to start a business when you are young and between the ages of 25 and 35 years old.

18. Everybody has a dream to be rich but the difference between people is that some are lazy and some are brave, some are lazy and not brave and will not try while the other person will go out of his comfort zone and go out of his way and try. If you will not try and take a risk, nothing will happen and you will stay poor. More risk more money.

19. Onassis the Greek billionaire was approached by a poor man selling cake then he told the poor man that he will flip the coin and asked him to look at this coin and take a guess if you win. Onassis said: I will give you all what I have of

money and cheques to you but if I win, you will give me your cake. The poor man replied: "I am a poor man and I have a family to feed and I cannot take a risk," then Onassis said "you were born a poor man selling cake and you die as a poor man selling cake because you don't want to take a risk.

20. The reason why people do not like to a risk is that:

1. They are afraid of failure.
2. Not the right time
3. People or friends will laugh at them and discourage them.
4. Not enough self confidence
5. Many other reasons

21. I remember at one time I had a professor at university for international relations who is specialized in Africa. He knows everything about Africa, the systems, the government, the rule and regulations and also the people and tribes and also has a lot of contacts and connections. Then I asked him why he doesn't want to be a businessman when Africa is a very rich continent with many minerals and diamonds so he can make a lot of money. I wishI had one percent of his knowledge about Africa. He replied by saying that he doesn't like to take a risk and he is happy the way he is, I knew he is a person that doesn't like to leave his comfort zone.

22. I remember at one time there was a conference for power and electricity and part of my business is in power and electricity so I saw a speaker there who has a PhD in electrical engineering and I was impressed by the way he gave his speeches and also that he knows everything about power and electricity. I wished that I knew one percent of his knowledge so that I can make money and improve my business. Then I started to follow him during the breaks just to get to know him and finally I had lunch with him then I asked him the same question: "why he doesn't use him knowledge to make money." He replied saying that he is happy the way he is and

does not want to take a risk or leave his comfort zone.
The same thing happened when I asked the professor for
23.macroeconomics and microeconomics. They know a lot about business and economics and was so amazed by their stories, they have so many stories to tell but when I asked them the same questions about why they don't use their knowledge to make money, they replied the same way saying that they do not want to take a risk or leave their comfort zone.

24.Howard Hughes, the American billionaire was always taking risks even though his advisers are asking him not to do so but he does not listen to them. He makes the decision. He is a decision maker because he is a courageous person and this is why he was a billionaire. He takes a risk.

25.You must stop dreaming. You must be brave and take a decision to enter the world of trade and business. A chinse proverb says, "he who is living his life only on dreaming, he will live his life sleeping."

26.Most people, around 80% of them don't like to leave the comfort zone because people are comfortable in their way of life and in what they are doing. They do not want to change.
1.The reason why people do not like to leave their comfort zone is because:
2. they do not like to change their way of life.
3. They do not have self-confidence. They feel that that they cannot do it and they are always giving excuses for other people's success.
4. They are lazy and want things the easy way.

27. Sometimes we see a person who is not very intelligent, is making good money and he is a successful businessman, because he is taking a risk without analyzing the subject for a long time. While a smart person who reads a lot and analyses

the subject will be hesitant to start a business, and he will not make money because he is afraid to take a risk.

28. Business is a risk so you must be brave to take a risk no matter what it takes and no matter how long it will take and you might go through some sufferings for example living without a salary for one year or even five years.

Chapter 8
Being Humble and Modest

1. To be humble and modest is a good thing because people like a person who is humble and modest, and not a person who is arrogant. There are some people who have good manners but are not humble.

2. They made a study about the greatest 1000 people in history throughout the world, that influenced the world today. Political leaders, religious leaders, inventors, businessmen. The study found that all the figures had two things in common. They were all humble and modest also had brilliant communication skills and good speakers.

3. When someone is humble and modest, it is so easy for the person to make friends. When a person makes friends, the person makes connections. Also, if people grow to love and appreciate a person, they give the person ideas and many other things. If you are humble and talk to educated people, such as doctors or engineers, you will learn a lot of things. They are the experts in what they do. They know much more than you do in certain subjects. They may give you ideas about your business that can help you make more money.

4. There are a lot of smart people who have good ideas and can give you advice about business, but they are poor or employees. They are not big managers or CEO's. Because they are not fortunate enough to have a managerial position. So, try to talk to them and listen to them. Do not be arrogant, you may learn something.

5. Once upon a time a lion lived in a jungle. The lion always took his afternoon nap under the shade of a big tree in the

bushes. One day, a small mouse saw the lion and decided to jump on his head to play. This annoyed the lion as he woke up from his nap. The lion was about to crush the little mouse to death when the mouse began pleading with the lion to spare his life.

He told the lion that if he spares his life, the mouse will help him in return someday.

The lion laughed and amused at the mouse's words and decided to spare his life.

One day when the lion was strolling through the jungle, he got caught in a hunter's net.

The lion begins to roar, pleading for help from anybody who might be passing by. The mouse who lived nearby heard the lion and rushed to help him.

With his sharp teeth, He freed the lion, and both of them fled the place. After a while, they reached the spot where they first met, and the lion thanked the mouse immensely for his help.

6. Everyone in the world is important. So, everyone can help you directly or indirectly. They can introduce you to other people. Those people can link you to another. This is called networking. I always use networking in my business. So, don't be arrogant.

7. In your work, you must always be well-informed about your competitors and business. Information is power. This is called business intelligence. Many successful businessmen and big corporations use business intelligence. If you are humble and honest, people will tell you things, people will help you. But, if you are arrogant, you will get nowhere.

8. My third project was my second successful project that made money related to shares and stock market. The ideas behind it started because I am a humble person. After I graduated from University, I had some time to sit with people I knew

in a coffee shop. Some of them are friends who are not very well-educated. One of my friends who knows me, sat with me and those people. He told me that I'm too good for them. He said that those people were not on my level and that I am too good for them. They were not as educated as me and were very lazy and unambitious unlike me. Because I am a humble person, I did not listen to him. Of course, most of my friends' conversations were not important.
The conversations were very shallow and insignificant. One day, one of my friends told me about a good idea. The idea was a way to generate money before entering the stock market. I was speaking to the person because I am humble, and he subsequently told me a great idea. I remember when I was in publishing, there was a poor and intelligent accountant, who used to work in the publishing company. He told me about banking and how to deal with banks. Because I was a humble person, I was sitting with him and ended up learning a lot.
Immediately I connected the two ideas of the two-different people. It gave me a smart idea. This helped me to start a business after a few months related to the stock market. This is how I made my money. The point here is that I made money from two average people because I was a humble person, socializing with unfortunate people.

9. There are three types of people in the world. People who make the news, people who talk about the news, and people who listen to the news. If you have a product to sell or a message to deliver, you have to talk to poor people first. They make up the majority of the world and can spread the word for you. All the important people in the world will know about your product or message, as well as the media. So be humble and talk to poor people.
10. I know a successful businessman who has a habit to have lunch with a different one of his employees every day. He

listens to this employee. If the employee has a suggestion to improve the company, this person would listen. So, this person's company is always progressing and growing. Not because of his ideas, but the ideas of his employees who are helping him. The point here is that he was humble and was listening to his employees during lunch.

11. When I was a student at USC, I took a memory course. It was a course about helping me to memorize subjects in exams. This was because my grades in class were not proficient. This course helped me a lot in improving my grades. It helped me in learning languages as well. I also came to realize that it helped me in my social life. I could memorize the names of people in big parties consisting of 200-300 people. So, people stared to like me when I remembered their names. The memory course is based off association, you relate a new thing to something you already know. The professor who taught me this course, memorized half a million phone numbers.

12. I noticed in my life only losers are arrogant.

13. There was a manufacturer in the United States which had about 3,000 employees where the owner of that business took a memory course to know and remember the names of the 3,000 employees and their wives and their kids. He is a humble person. Whenever he sees his employees in the manufacturing company, he shakes their hands and calls them by their names. He then asks them about their wives and their kids by name. This behavior made all the workers in the manufacturer to love the owner.
14. There are many big companies that did not improve their service and products over the years and started to lose money then through bankruptcy. This is because they thought there are the best and number one even though some employees

in those big companies suggested to members of the board some ideas. To improve their services and products like other small competitors but members of the board were arrogant and did not listen. Finally, they lost money and went through bankruptcy.

Chapter 9
Honesty and Credibility

1. Since the beginning of history, people like to deal with others who are honest and those they can trust.

2. Today, if you go to a restaurant and eat bad quality food, and get sick because of food poisoning, the reason is because the owner of the restaurant may have cheap and low quality food simply to save money. You will then no longer eat at that restaurant and tell your friends not to go to that restaurant.

3. If you ask for food delivery such as pizza from a restaurant. They will tell you that the pizza needs 30 minutes, while you are waiting for 1-2 hours. Every time you call the restaurant, they say that the food is almost there and that its on its way. This will result with you ordering from another restaurant and dealing with others.

4. If you have a broken car, and they want you to fix your car, and they tell you that it will only take 5 hours, and it will cost you 300 dollars, but then it took 3 days and charged you 950 dollars. You realized that they were fooling you. You will no longer trust them. You will tell your friends and others about it as well.

5. If you borrow money from your friends and not pay them back, your friends will no longer trust you.

6. If you lie to people, then people will not believe you any longer, and you will lose your credibility.

7. If you take a loan from the bank for your business, and you don't pay the bank their money on time, it will be a disaster and you will have a bad credit.

8. If you buy a watch from a store, thinking it is a new watch, only to realize that you were cheated and that it was a used watch, you will no longer trust that store and tell your friends about it as well.

9. The point here, is that you always have to maintain your good reputation because your reputation is like your treasure. If you try to cheat, sooner or later people will know. Same thing with when people have bad habits. People will know if that person has a bad habit. For instance, if someone were to lie or cheat people sooner or later, people will know. The Chinese have a saying, "If you don't want people to know, don't do it".

10. So, honesty and a good reputation is your treasure. Try to always maintain your reputation and the quality of your product and your company. Don't cheat to save money. Once you start cheating or selling people bad quality products or services, the word will spread in the market. People won't trust you, or trust your company, or trust your products. If there is a good company, and there was a change in the CEO of the company, and the new CEO lied or cheated, it would be a disaster.

11. There are always people who are ready to talk and spread the news. And people who are ready to listen to the news. They say there are three types of people. People who make the news, people who talk about the news, and people who listen to the news. So, if you start your small business, like a restaurant or a shop, you must be honest to people. Don't lie to them or cheat them. People are not stupid. People talk a lot. So, if you are honest, they will spread the word. Also, if you lie and cheat, they will spread the word as well. Try to always make your client happy by maintaining honesty and

credibility.

12. I have seen and heard of so many people who lie and cheat, thinking that they are smart, yet they lose everything. They lose their reputation, their money, their company, and their life becomes miserable.

13. I always travel around the world, and always like to stay in five start hotels such as Hilton, Sheraton, and intercontinental. Sometimes, I travel to a country for the first time. Even though in that country or city, there are good hotels, I always prefer to choose the hotels with a good reputation such as Hilton, Sheraton, Intercontinental, etc. This is because it is a guarantee that these hotels are clean and have good service. These hotels tend to maintain their reputation, honesty, and credibility over the years – They say, something you know is better than something you don't know

14. I have an uncle who is a billionaire. I once asked my cousin, who was running his father's business, what is the main reason or factor behind your company's success in business? He replied by saying, honesty and credibility. Because, when their business was booming in the 1960's, they started to borrow money from banks and used to pay back the banks on time. Sometimes, they did not have the cash or the money, so they ended up selling their property or anything else they had just to pay the banks back on time. Other people were wondering why they sold their properties just to make the banks happy. Thinking of the family as stupid. Then, banks started to trust the family, and give more loans, leading to the business growing ever so greatly. The banks trusted the family and the company. The family company kept their reputation clean by. And now, no matter how big the project, banks don't hesitate to finance

the company, because banks trust them.
Today, without asking the banks, the banks would approach the company, offering big loans because of the trust that has been built there.

15. At the beginning of the 20th century, before the discovery of oil, in Kuwait, Bahrain, Saudi Arabia, Abu Dhabi and Dubai, many people were involved in the pearl diving business. This was where pearl divers would dive for pearls in oysters/shells. Where they would give the pearls to merchants, and that merchant would give it to a bigger merchant who goes to India, to sell the pearl to Indian merchants. The story here is from a merchant from Dubai, who was honest and trustworthy. He had a good reputation amongst other merchants and other people. But, unfortunately, this merchant, on his way to India, had a stupid servant that made a mistake, who threw the pearl into the sea. This was because the merchant put the pearl in an old and dirty piece of cloth next to trash can in his room. The servant proceeded to throw the bin into the Sea, or Indian Ocean. When the merchant came back to his room, he didn't see the pearl. He then asked the servant about the pearls. He told him that he didn't know that there were pearls. He told him that he threw the cloth into the bin, not knowing that there was a pearls in there. The merchant then told the servant not to tell anyone about what happened. The merchant lost the pearls and his money. But still, he had something. He had his good reputation. So, when the merchant arrived in India, he went to see the other merchants from Kuwait, Saudi Arabia, and other countries, he persuaded with them to loan him a pearl, indoor to bargain with the Indian merchant for a high price. Because, one merchant who sells the pearl, would be able to control the price and market he would have the bargaining power. The merchant was able to control the pearl market like monopoly.

Finally, this merchant sold all the pearls for high prices, with a good profit. He then returned the money to the other merchants who trusted him. Now, this honest person started to have money once again, and was able to maintain his reputation. The point here is that the other merchants knew the merchant had a good reputation, they trusted him and gave him their pearls.

16. People give loans to people they trust. Same thing with banks, they give loans to companies they trust. So, when people see that you are paying them back, they trust you more. Seeing is believing. People like to deal with supermarkets, stores, and companies they can trust.

17. A long time ago, during my summer vacation in Europe, one of my stupid employees promised a person, who owns a small company which is doing services and selling products to the hotels. And that I can be his partner, thinking that it is easy and quick money. So, when I came back from Europe, I noticed that the man is ready to work with hotels and already brought another person with him who is working with another company that is doing services for hotels and already contacted a hotel to start working together. I noticed that the first man is not honest and likes to cheat and lie. While the other person is honest and a good person. The only thing that they have in common is that they are both poor and are in the same line of business. Doing services for the hotels. Then, I had a meeting with them and with the hotel manager, and I mentioned that I am not interested in hotel businesses. I said that I didn't want to be involved with both men, neither the honest man, or the cheat. This is because it is not in my line of business. 12 years later, I met a hotel manager who told me that the nice honest person, became very rich, and his company became very famous in the market. About the other person who is a bad guy that is not

honest and likes to cheat, he lost his money and disappeared.

18. Today, big companies and corporations try to maintain a good reputation, because they get affected easily in the stock market, and end up losing a lot of money.

a) For example, if an airplane has an accident in the sky, the next day the manufacturer of that type of airplane's shares in the stock market will fall dramatically and will lose a lot of money. The media will also talk about it.

b) If an oil company did drilling and in result of that, there was a lot of pollution, the media will talk about it. The shares of the oil company in the stock market will fall.

c) If a ship sank in the sea due to technical problems, the media will talk about it. As a result, the manufacturer of the ship, or the company in charge of inspection will be affected negatively and lose money in the stock market.

19. When I was in my freshman year in the university of southern California, I always tried not to have bounced checks. Suppose I wrote a check for something, I always tried to have enough money in my bank to avoid bounce checks. Sometimes, I would go to the bank, early in the morning, before the bank opens at 8am, to deposit the money into my account. So, I will maintain good credit and a good reputation with the bank. In that year, the bank started to give students with good credit, a credit card. They gave me a visa card with 200 dollars limit. Because I pay the bank on time, after six months, they gave me MasterCard, increasing the limit to 400 dollars. A year later, they increased the limit to 500 dollars. As time goes on, I ended up attaining golden cards with the bank, resulting in higher limits.

Then I started to know the name of the game; when you are honest, the banks will give you more money and loans for your business.

20. After I started my second project in publishing, I started to have more income, and the bank noticed that I am honest and active. The banks started to give me more facilities. Later on, when I was in the stock market business. My third project, which was in the stock market, the banks trusted me even more, and gave me even more facilities and loans. I then started to laugh and said, "Now I am a completely different person, when I was a student at the university, I used to ask my friends to lend me 200 or 300 dollars. Now without asking, banks will offer me loans in millions". This is because I know what banks want, they just want to deal with a person that they can trust, a person who has honesty and credibility.

21. I know some brokers in real estate and brokers in the stock market. They are always poor because they always try to cheat and take advantage of the client, the clients are not stupid so when they notice that the brokers are not honest, they stop dealing with them. So, when I ask the brokers "why are you doing this," he answers by saying that he has a lot of debts and it is an opportunity to make money.

22. In Sweden, there is a story about a businessman of Egyptian and Swedish nationality. At the beginning of the 1980s, he took command of a small biotech company, Fermenta, which he quickly turned into one of the success stories of Stockholm stock exchange. El Sayed soon became Sweden's richest man and made the fortune of his employees and shareholders. A charismatic leader he was a favorite of media, and in December 1985 he was named "Swede of the year" by the TV news program Rapport. The following month, Fermenta announced a partnership with Swedish industrial giant Volvo. El Sayed was at the peak of his fame. Because he was a successful person some people start to call him a Doctor, which he seems to like the title of a

Doctor a lot. Unfortunately, once they conducted an interview with him on TV where a journalist asked him if he is a real Doctor, he lied and said yes. The broadcaster then asked him to show his certificate. He promised to prove it to them, he never did present his degree and kept promising and saying that he will show them next time. Then all the TV stations in Sweden kept asking if this person was truly a Doctor or not.

El Sayed was accused of lying about his academic qualification, and falsely claiming he was a Doctor.

Journalists who tried to verify these allegations discovered that according to some sources. El Sayed was never awarded a Doctor degree from California.

He was later sentenced to 6 years in prison for Fraud in different business.

23. Many managers make mistakes in big companies when they do not use the honest people they end up regretting. Unfortunately most of the people judge a person by his looks and his appearance like judging a book by its cover. Studies show that many young people and young men who look handsome and well dressed and young ladies who look beautiful and well-dressed have more chances to get jobs and be promoted.

24. So, when you try to choose employees for your company try to consider this: They are honest and loyal to the company. Usually in movies, the director or casting manager will always consider the appearance of the actors so that they have more creditability for the movie. The same way, you must consider yourself on how you look and how you are dressed or even your type of car etc.

25. People who lie and cheat will not last for too long.

Chapter 10
Persistence

1. Most people, especially employees are hard workers, not everyone however is persistent. Not persistent enough to work on weekends or days and nights.
   A persistent person who has the will and motivation to reach his goals overcomes all his challenges. Whenever there is a problem, he will be thinking about it day and night just to solve his problem. He will be focused on his work all the time. He will do the follow-up. He will be dedicated, focused, and concentrated on his business all the time, day and night, weekdays and weekends. So, you have to focus 100% on your business and your goals. Then, the business will be growing. It is like if you give a tree water every day, this tree after a while will be a big tree so you must have the discipline everyday to give water to your tree. The same thing will happen to you if you persist and have the discipline to work every day. Always think about the other options to solve the problems in your business. Based on the saying "find a way or make a way". For example, if you have a restaurant, not having a lot of customers, you can think about a solution which is to have one table or two tables, just to attract the attention of people on the street, or simply fitting more customers in your restaurant by doing that. He will do the follow up. For example, if he is short on cash and some other customer has to pay him, he will follow up and call them every day to get his money back.
   A persistent person is a person that never gives up because he has goals and ambition. When there are some bad years in business, and the income is little, a persistent person will think about making other plans or other things, just to make more money. Or he will lower his budget, just to survive. Because he wants to stay in that business. While other people

will give up and shut down or close their business. A persistent person will work hard, even if he is sick or tired. He will work hard because he loves his job and will be determined and insisting on reaching his goals, no matter what. Most of the billionaires were born poor, but because of persistence and determination they became rich. The main point here is the importance of consistency, and to follow up and facing the challenges, and overcoming your problems, or solving your problems. You will see a lot of rich families, who have a lot of spoiled kids who grow up to not care about their family's business not following up. Little by little, their business becomes weaker and weaker.

2. a. Persistent person who doesn't stop and doesn't take a day off.
   b. A person who doesn't get lazy.
   c. He doesn't get tired.
   d. A person who doesn't give up.

3. I just wanted to mention a story of an English family that borrowed a golden necklace for a party from their neighbor. Unfortunately, however, the lady lost the necklace during the party. Then, after the party, when she found out, she felt so bad and told her husband. They worked so hard to make the money needed to buy another necklace for their neighbor. After twenty years of working day and night, they bought a golden necklace for their neighbor. The neighbor said that they didn't have to work hard for it because the necklace they lost was fake. The point here because thefamily was persistent to make money for the price of the necklace finally they made it.

4. In the early 80s in the media, the newspapers and tv was talking about the refugees from Vietnam that they called boat people. I was impressed and felt bad when I saw a girl from Vietnam, talking about her problems on Tv. She said that she

was working all day all night, to memorize all the words in the dictionary just to learn how to speak English, in order to attain the green card to live in the United States. She was crying, saying that she was studying so hard, 20 hours a day, not getting enough sleep. She was persistent and had a goal she wished to reach, learning English in such a short period of time, which was three months. I had a lot of respect for that girl and felt sorry for her.

5. There are a lot of foreign students in America, who went to university for four or five years that don't speak English, nor do they try to learn English. Also, there are a lot of people who are now living in the United States for the past 20 years or 30 years who do not know English, and have not tried hard to learn English. For this reason,
   I respect the Vietnamese girl I saw on tv, because of her persistence to learn English in such a short period of time- with in 3 months.

6. Napoleon - the French emperor was born in the island of Corsica, which is located close to Italy. The people there speak Italian, not French. Napoleon's family was speaking Italian, Napoleon himself was speaking French with an Italian accent. So, when Napoleon went to school in Paris, some students at school used to mock him and make fun of him. Because he is speaking French with an Italian accent. It was also because he was short, shorter than the average boys in his school. But, because he was persistent, a hard worker, and courageous, he became the emperor of France, and later the emperor of Europe.
   He was persistent and used to work 20 hours a day.

7. Students who aspire to be a doctor, or enter medical school, all study on weekends. Also, students who wish to become an architect have to work all day and night, because their

work is time consuming. I always see them down the hall on my floor, staying up all night, working on their projects.

8. I love snow skiing because I love nature and sports, I also like being far away from the city. Far away from pollution and crowded freeways.
   I like to be in the middle of the mountains, with nature.
   I enjoy seeing houses covered with snow, and trees covered with snow. For this reason I always go to mammoth mountain in California, which is the highest mountain on the mainland or in the lower 48 states. There is always snow, even on the Fourth of July when people are celebrating the day of independence. Some people are funny and crazy on the Fourth of July, snow skiing in their shorts or tuxedos. One winter, I went to mammoth mountain for the weekend. There were about 32 people in the cabin I was staying at. They were all there for snow skiing on the weekend. All of them had to go back to work in Los Angeles after the weekend. Unfortunately however, on Sunday night there was suddenly a big storm. Only 8 people decided to go to the airport in the morning. the next day in the morning, the storm did not stop and it was cold and chilly, when we woke up at 5 o'clock the snow was still falling. So, only 3 of us woke up and tried to go to the airport. I was one of them. 3 of us decided to go to the nearby telephone booth. We had to walk in the snow. The telephone booth was very far from our cabin. We had to walk a very long distance. It was so cold and freezing, my ear became red. But, we have to reach a telephone booth in order to call the airport, to check if whether the airplane is coming that day. So, we kept trying to call the airport from 5:30 until 6:15. We tried to call the airport every 5 minutes, but there was no answer. We were three people. Because it was so cold, we all kept trying to get into the telephone booth. It was warmer inside. Finally, at 6:15 someone at the airport answered our phone call, and said that there is a good chance that the airplane will come,

and arrive at 7. So, we were happy and excited, we went back to our cabin and went to the airport. We were only 3 out of 32 people of the cabin who made it to go back to Los Angeles. Because we are persistent and that we have the will to wake up early in the morning and to try when there is no hope that we will be able to go back. Two of my collogues wanted to go back to their work, and I wanted to return to my classes in university on Monday. This story shows you, that only for one day, or 3 people out of 32 people or 10 percent people are persistent. This is only for one day, but how about a businessman or a merchant, requiring you to be persistent for 10 years or 30 years. The main point here once you are persistent and determined you can achieve your goal.

9. You might think that life is boring for a persistent person, but it's not.
   Especially if you see a person sitting in his shop day and night.
   Weekdays and weekends. But, to that person it is a lot of fun, because he is used to it.I remember that I once travelled to several Asian countries. I saw a man who was sitting in his shop and asked if he ever got bored. He said that he enjoyed it and said that "I am making money and am enjoying the challenges" I asked if he had any friends, and he responded by saying that he had many friends, and that they always came to talk to him in his shop. I then asked him if he ever got bored. He said that he only got bored when there is a national holiday and that he has to close the shop and sit in his house. He told me that he was once invited with some of his friends to a different city, and that he was so bored when he was with them. The only time he felt happy was when he came to his shop again. The point here that the life of a merchant or a businessman is not a boring life, once he starts making money and gets used to a certain way of life he will think it is fun.

10. I always work on weekends and try to finish the work that I did not finish on the weekdays. I also always try to meet people on the weekends. Also, when I travel to Europe or Hawaii during my vacations, I'm always on my phone trying to set up contacts for hours. Sometimes, I don't get enough time to get enough sleep, even if I take a nap, I have to wake up quickly for an appointment or make some phone calls, because I am a persistent person. Sometimes I see a persistent person who will be working hard, even though he is tired, sad and depressed. No matter what, if he is in a good mood or bad mood, he will work, even if he is sick or tired.

11. You will fail the first time but don't give up don't quit. All the famous people did not quit but most people don't know that Thomas Edison made one thousand experiments for the bulb light.

12. Don't give up. Sometimes when one door is closed another door will open for you so maybe it is good for you that the first door is closed so don't give up and keep trying.

13. Mercedes- Benz is one of the biggest premium car manufacturers in the world and is a well-known name today. But it's been a long journey for the automaker to reach this level. The car company went through many hardships, mergers, and immense struggles to reach the level that it is today. The story of Mercedes Benz the German luxury car, it is started with Carl Benz a German engineer who is recognized as the inventor of the gasoline- powered automobile. Carl Benz was born Karl Friedrich Michael Vaillant on 25 November 1844 in Mühlburg, now a borough of Karlsruhe, Baden-Württemberg, which is part of modern Germany. His parents were Josephine Vaillant and a locomotive driver, Johann Georg Benz, whom she married a few months later. According to German law, the child

acquired the name «Benz» by legal marriage of his parents. When he was two years old, his father died of pneumonia, and his name was changed to Karl Friedrich Benz in remembrance of his father. Despite living in near poverty, his mother strove to give him a good education. Benz attended the local school in Karlsruhe and was a prodigious student. Following his formal education, Benz had seven years of professional training in several companies. In 1871, at the age of twenty-seven, Benz joined August Ritter, in launching the Iron Foundry and Mechanical Workshop in Mannheim, later renamed Factory for Machines for Sheet-metal Working. The enterprise's first year went very badly. Ritter turned out to be unreliable, and the business's tools were impounded. The difficulty was overcome when Benz's fiancée, Bertha Ringer, bought out Ritter's share in the company using her dowry. On January 1886, Karl Benz filed a patent application for his "motor car with gas engine operation" but subsequently was met with great skepticism from general public.

14. Most successful people have failed many times. Your failure will teach you things in different way then you will understand the problem. The author of Harry Potter, J.K Rowling was rejected 12 times and at the 13th time, her book was accepted by the publisher.

15. There was man named Tom who had a very bad childhood and he has many different kinds of jobs, also lost money many times but because he is persistent, at the end he was very successful and established Domino's Pizza. He became successful because he is a persistent person.

Chapter 11
Sacrifice

1. Without sacrifice, nothing will happen because the key to success is to sacrifice.

2. Most people do not want to sacrifice. This is because making money is not easy, because sometimes, you have to work day and night, and must also sometimes work on weekends and many people want to sometimes come home for their families but the people who are sacrificing do not have the time to come home because they are working hard in their office or dedicating their time to their work.

3. The proverb is saying. **you can't make an omelette** without breaking eggs In order to achieve something, it is inevitable and necessary that some mistakes are made or some sacrifices must occur.

4. A lot of rich people after making money will become sick because they sacrificed their time, their hours of sleep, their health, their family, their wife because making money is not easy.

5. I think sacrifice is the key to success. You have to sacrifice your sleep, you want to sacrifice by not going on vacations, sometimes you have to save your money to not go on vacations and sometimes you don't have the time, this is why when you start your business you have to sacrifice, you sacrifice your holidays and your travelling. Also, you have to sacrifice by not seeing your friends by not going to their parties or their weddings but sometimes you have to go out of your way and travel for your business and for your contacts and connections.

Sometimes you have to sacrifice by selling your car and by living without your car or sacrifice by selling some of your belongings. By selling your belongings I mean selling something that you cherish, like a necklace that remind you of your childhood.

6. Steve Jobs, the CEO of Apple used to sleep on the floor of his friend's dorm room. Also, he returned coke bottles for food money, and got weekly free meals at the local Harekrishna Buddhist temple.

7. Sometimes you sacrifice by not eating well because you are always in a hurry, and you don't have time to eat a good hot meal. When you start your business sometimes you may not have enough money to eat because you will be spending your money for things on your business and to start your business. Also, after you start your business and your business is growing during the good years but suddenly your business will slow and you might have debts. In that case, you must lower you budget and sacrifice and stop living in luxury in order to survive. In that case, you might not have enough money to eat good food.

8. If you read stories about a lot of successful people in history in the world of trade and business they went through a lot of sacrifices, so don't feel bad you are not the only one.

9. Even if you want to meet important people and establish contacts and further your connections you must sometimes meet someone on their terms. For instance, if a person woke up early and wanted to go on a walk, it is important for you to wake up early and walk with them. If a person stays up late at night, you must also push yourself to stay awake to meet them.

10. Let me tell you about a very poor person who does not make enough money. He once said that he needed money so bad. He needed my help. I asked him to introduce me to someone he knows and if I were to make a deal with that person, I will pay him. I wanted him to go with me on my terms, so when I am available because I am a very busy person. The first time I called him, when I was ready for him, he said that he is going to dinner and watch a movie with his family. The second time I called him a month later, he said that he was on his way to have a haircut, the third time I called him after another month, he told me that he was going to the tailor and shopping. The point here is that this guy does not want to sacrifice. I am a nice person that wanted to help him and gave him the time, but he was not ready to sacrifice.

11. This is another story of a person from the Middle East. There was a person who was a very good student at university and got good grades but wasn't able to get a job after he graduated. His classmates faced the same problem. This man wanted to work at a bank. He went to a bank and told them that he will work for them for free just to get the experience. He got that job to work for free in that bank. What he did because he liked his job was waking up early in the morning and was at work earlier than other employees. He also stayed late after all the other employees left to continue to work and learn. His friends thought that he was stupid because he worked hard for no salary. After six months his colleagues and manager started to like him and gave him a permanent job. Because they noticed that he was interested, liked his job, and was a hard worker. He got offered a job because he sacrificed unlike his friends who didn't work hard and didn't get a job.

12. People should sacrifice luxurious things such as having a nice car or maybe not even having a car at all. Instead of

drinking tea and coffee at the café, he should minimize this once a week to save money. When someone has debts and has to sacrifice by not having a luxurious life like he used to not having a big car or a big apartment. Not going to the coffee shop just to save money etc.

13. Sometimes when you want to meet a new person and that person likes fishing and gets seasick you must still go if it is important to you.
14. Earlier in the book, I mentioned a Greek billionaire named Onassis. His business was maritime and shipping. He owned a lot of cargo ships around the world. He once saw a poor person selling cakes and cookies at the beach. Onassis offered him a deal, "Give me all the cakes and cookies you have, and I will give you everything I have in my pockets – whether that be cheques or cash." The poor person said, "I am a poor person and have a few kids and a family to feed, I cannot take a risk and sacrifice like this." Onassis replied, "You are a poor person who will always be poor." He said this because he saw that this man did not like to sacrifice.

15. A lot of people that start their business go through a lot of suffering and have to wait until their business grows. They do not have salaries. They sacrifice a lot and go through a lot of pain and suffering. Their business is not making money for a while. It depends how long it takes to grow. It may take one year, or maybe five years.

16. A person who sacrifices will look at things in a different way, saying "I will sacrifice and let go of all luxury to gain prestige and become rich and famous." A person who does not sacrifice will say, "why should I bother myself and work hard by sacrificing going through a lot of pain and suffering if I will get nothing". The difference between the two people is that the first person sees the result at the end, the second

person only sees the pain and suffering at the beginning.

17. Sometimes you will see a lot of weird people who sacrificed when they were young or when they were students in college and those people became very successful. Because those weird people have a goal in their mind, they did not care if they sleep on the floor or they don't have housing or they don't go to parties at college and most of the time you will see them wearing jeans. They are always working hard for school and studying and they are working hard on school nights and on the weekends and during Christmas holidays or Spring Break and sometimes they have part time jobs. Those people were not living the average life for students.

18. There was a cook working for a rich person in the Middle East, he was working for him for a long time then that rich person became richer and had a bigger house and thought about hiring a new second cook. The young cook did not respect the old cook so they had a few fights. At the end, the old cook was complaining to his boss (the rich person) but the rich person did not care,he was not fair. So he felt very bad and decided to quit and not to work as a cook anymore, he thought about establishing his own business but the only thing he knows is about food, tea and coffee. So he started to sell tea and coffee and some types of food because this is the only thing he knows. He opened a shop in the neighborhood and he ended up working until midnight and also at the same time opening his shop early in the morning at 5am. He sacrificed by not getting enough sleep but he started to make money because the people in the neighborhood they knew that this shop is the only shop open early morning and closes late at night so they started to go to his shop late at night. Also, people who wake up early in the morning buy things from him in the morning. This person, since he was poor, he did not have enough money to eat three

meals a day so because he did not have enough money, he was only eating one meal a day. This person started sacrificing his health since he was not getting enough sleep. At the same time, this person wanted to save money, so he only ate cheap food like bread and tea.

He was stingy and wanted to save as much money as he could to expand his shop and grow his business.

After a few years, when he started making money, he started to think about the real estate business because he remembers his rich boss and his rich friends were always talking about real estate.

By listening to them to for many years, he had many ideas and knowledge about real estate. This guy got lucky after the rising prices of oil in that country during the 70's and there was a big demand for real estate because so many people from all over the world came to work there so over the years this guy became a billionaire then he went into the banking business then owned a bank. So, the point here is that when he started he sacrificed a lot.

Chapter 12
To love your job

1. Usually when someone loves his job and interested in it also has a goal in his life to reach. He will be very eager and ambitious to achieve that goal. You will see that he is focusing on what he is doing, and he is not wasting his time in a party or a football game because he knows what he is doing, and he has a goal to reach. It is not just the money, you have got to have something inside you, that makes you love your job, and very keen to be in the world of business, and enjoying it, and being ready for the challenges. Because anybody who loves his job will enjoy working hard and taking the challenges. Then, in the long run, he will have the experience, and the talent, and the skills and the knowledge in his job. He will also feel guilty if he goes to a party or a football game. When a man loves his job, he does very well in his job, and can work harder working for a long time without looking at his watch, time or mobile.

2. The same thing about a student who loves his classes he will try to not miss his classes. I remember when I was in university, I always liked going to my psychology class because I love that class so much. And sometimes, even when it is rainy, and the freeway is risky between Newport beach and Los Angeles because of heavy rain and there are a lot of car accidents. But I still insist on going to USC to attend my psychology class.

3. I remember when I was a student at USC, one of my favorite classes was a psychology class. I really loved that class. At thc timc, I was commuting from New Port Beach in California to Los Angeles California. At that time, there was so much heavy rain, but I was still driving my car because I

don't want to miss it. Because I love my class and am interested in studying psychology. I saw a lot of people having car accidents on the road, it was so dangerous, but I always insist on going to my psychology class.

4. Some people are not interested in business, but they just love money. You can tell because they are not ready to work hard, and they do not like to read books about business, or articles in the newspapers about business. Rather, they like to read books about history, politics, religion, etc.... They read articles about sports, politics, etc.... but not about business. Also, when they are with a group of friends, they talk about different subjects. When one of them talk about business, they are not interested to listen and want them to change the subject and talk about something else. Also, when there is a program on TV about business, they might change the channel to watch sports, or anything else.
   I know some people like that, who try to open businesses, but they failed, because they do not know anything about business, and they are not interested and are not willing to work hard. They just like money like everyone else. They don't want to learn about business.

5. Students who aspire to be a doctor, or enter medical school, all study on weekends. Also, students who wish to become an architect have to work all day and night, because their work is time consuming. I always see them down the hall on my floor, staying up all night, working on their projects.

6. I know a person in Asia who owns a shop. He is always in his shop day and night, even on the weekends. So, I asked him, "don't you get bored sitting in your shop every day?" He said, "No, I am enjoying what I am doing "Then I asked him, "don't you have friends you can socialize with?" He said that his friends always visit him in his shop. And he

talks with them and laughs with them. Then, I asked him, "When is your worst day of the year?" He said it is during the holiday when he closes his shop. He feels bored. Even when he goes on a picnic, or to another city with his friends. He does not feel good until he comes back to his shop. Then, I asked him, what makes him feel good about his business. He said, when he makes money, he feels good because he was born poor. When the boys he grew up with are still poor, so he feels that he accomplished something in his life. Also, he feels good when he goes to a different city to buy more goods and merchandise, he buys it on credit because they trust him. Every year they increase the limit for him. Also, banks kept increasing the limit for him every year, because his business is growing. This made him happy.

7. There was a beautiful girl at my university, all the boys like her. Then, she met a boy who she liked very much, she wanted to marry him. He refused to marry her because he is not ready for it. He has goals in his life that he wishes to reach. He is very ambitious and eager to reach his goals. He wants to be rich and famous. She said that she does not care about the money. She will marry him, even if he does not have the basic money for living. Then I told her, that she cannot change his personality and his way of thinking mentality, because he is very ambitious person, and has goals and dreams and not be like an ordinary person. So, she would have to wait until he accomplishes some of his dreams, so maybe after 10 years, or even after 20 years. I then told her, that this young man has big goals and big dreams and big challenges in his life. He wanted to be rich and famous, he loves his job and he is interested to be rich, so his priority will be above love and getting married.

8. There are a lot of people who were born poor, and had dreams of being rich, because they used to watch films in the theatres about the lives of rich people. They wanted to live

the same kind of life. When they grow up and become rich businessmen, they don't mind working for long hours every day.

9. I then told her, that this young man has big goals and big dreams and big challenges in his life. He wanted to be rich and famous, he loves his job and he is interested to be rich, so his priority will be above love and getting married.

10. I always do my paperwork's on weekends. So, a businessman cannot work without paperwork's and reading reports. For this reason, I must work on weekends. Also, some people who are important to my work, I cannot see them on weekdays, since I do not have any open appointments on the weekdays, so I see them on the weekends. So, this is why businessmen are working on the weekends. A lot of my friends who are not businessmen, say "You must have fun on weekends", they do not know that businessmen are always working on weekends.

11. Of course, there will always be something in your job that you do not like.
But this is life. Everyone has something in his job that he does not like.

12. Businessmen love their job because of the following reasons:
a. A businessman does not have a boss or someone to report to. An employee would sometimes have a boss that makes his life miserable.
b. Because a businessman is free – he can go to work whenever he wants and can leave his office at whatever time he wants. He has a flexible schedule and timing.
c. There are higher chances that he can make much more money than an average employee.

d. Businessmen think that their job is more interesting, challenging, and not boring like an average employee.
e. An employee will do the same kind of work every day, but a businessman has different kind of work every day.
f. Everyday a businessman would meet different kinds of people. While an employee would be meeting the same kind of people every day.
g. An employee stays in the same place/office every day. A businessman on the other hand goes to different places every day.

13. In business it is always interesting because you start to know different things.
14. Sometimes when you are a businessman, you can accomplish some of your dreams. For example, you throw a very big party for your wife's birthday, inviting hundreds of people, exactly like what you see in movies.Or you throw a party on a big boat for your son's birthday, inviting hundreds of people. Or renting a large airplane and travelling around the world. You can live like a king for one day. But, for an employee, it is a dream that he cannot do.

15. A businessman always thinks of an employee as narrowminded, always talking about his job and his boss, while a businessman knows many things and has a wider horizon.
16. The son of a businessman starts from where his father ends his business.

Suppose a businessman made 200 million, his son would inherit that money, and continue that business. But, the son of the employee, would start from where the father started.

17. The problem with the work of a businessman, and the advantage of an employee is the amount of risk in business. The chances are 9/10 if a person starts his business, will lose.

So, an employee has more of a secure job. But if the businessman makes it, it is a risk to take. It is like the saying "Is it better to be a living mouse, or a dead lion?"

18. A businessman who loses his money and goes through bankruptcy loses everything. His life will be miserable. He might end up losing his company, his house, his car, and possibly his wife. A lot of times, when a man loses everything, there are problems with his wife, and this results in family problems, ending up in a divorce.

19. An employee can also have fun on weekends and go on picnics and go to the movies with his family or his friends, or attend wedding parties, or some other social parties, while a businessman cannot enjoy life, he works 24 hours, 7 days a week.

20. A businessman always has problems with his health, like diabetes, blood pressure, etc. because of working hard all the time, as well as the strain of stress.

21. If you want to be successful in anything, you have to love it. If you love engineering, you can study engineering and do well in
engineering and you will be reading a lot of books about engineering and will continue reading about updates concerning engineering and you will be asking a lot of questions just to learn more about engineering. Same thing, if you love chemistry, you will study chemistry and look at it as a hobby and do well in it and you will be reading a lot of books about it and read about the new things and updates concerning chemistry and you will ask a lot of questions about chemistry. It will be like a hobby for you. Same thing, if you like movies you will always be watching movies and reading about movies and you will be good in it. So if you

like your job in the world of trade and business you will work hard and you will not feel that you are working for long hours because you love your job and if you are reading books about it, you will find that reading the books are very interesting like a hobby and you will be asking a lot of questions. So, the point here is that you have to passionate for what you are doing. If you are passionate and interested you will work hard and you will have self-discipline, you will be able to work early in the morning to work hard in order to do well in your job. Even if it is a rainy day or a snowy day with snow on the road, you will go to your work because you love your work and because you are passionate. So by loving what you doing, you will not care how many hours a day you are working, you job will be fun for you and not a boring job.

22. Also, if you love your job, you will sacrifice a lot for your job. You will not get enough sleep, you will not get enough food, you will miss out on your friends' parties and your friends weddings because you are passionate about your job and what you are doing, you don't mind even sacrificing by selling your car and not living in a nice house or apartments and not going on vacations. You will put up also with some people who have bad manners whom you meet when you are working hard on that type of business because you love your job. For example, if you have a goal to start a restaurant business or a chain of restaurants and you are working as a waiter to just get the experience , you will encounter and meet clients with bad manners. Even in the oil business where you are someone working on the drilling rig or a refinery to gain experience, you will encounter a lot of people who have bad manners. Also you will start to smell the gases and the bad smell of oil or oil products.

23. So when you love your job you will work hard and be passionate to learn more about it and never give up but the people who don't like their business and are not interested, they give up quickly.

24. Sometimes there are a lot of young people who inherited money from their parents but because they are not interested and not passionate. They are not interested to listen to investors or the people that work at their company and they don't work hard because they would rather spend a lot of their time doing fun things like parties and they don't like to work hard and in the long run they lose most of their wealth or they lose everything. They are not even interested to listen to you when you talk about business, when you talk about business, they ask you to change the subject because to them talking about business and making money is boring to them. They would rather talk about more fun things like parties, movies etc.

25. There is a difference between a person who loves money and the person who loves his job. Normally it is very common everybody loves money but not everybody is interested and passionate to work for money, to work for long hours day and night for money. Many people like to just get money in the easy way, and this doesn't happen.

26. It is always easy to have dreams and ideas about making money, but it is not easy to find a person who is very interested and very passionate to work hard for making money.

Chapter 13

Optimism and Positive thinking

1. They say, that where there is a hope there is life. When you have hope, and are optimistic, you will work harder, you will never give up, and things will work out for you. Most people of the world are optimistic. Unfortunately, however, when someone had a bad experience in life, or a bad childhood, will always be pessimistic and have a negative outlook on life. This is due to the fact that he either had a bad childhood, or bad experiences in his life. When there is hope, it keeps us working and expecting the best. Everyone always expects that the best day of his life is yet to come.

2. Speaking about myself, I am always optimistic and have a positive thinking. If I go to the airport and there is bad traffic, I always say that "I will catch the airplane and I will fly", and I eventually make it. Whenever I am having a meeting with someone and I am late, I have a feeling that things will still be okay and work for me. This always happens, everything always turns out right. Even if this doesn't happen, and bad things happen to me, I stay positive and know that good things will come out of it. Because I know a lot of things in life when bad things happen, in the long run, it is good for you. For example, if I go seeing someone and he is not there, and I end up meeting his secretary or someone else in the same floor, and that person becomes my best friend, and that person helps me with work. Or, if I meet the secretary of that person, she tells me what to do differently next time. This is why I am always optimistic.

3. I mentioned earlier in this book, that my friend told me that when you plant apples you get oranges, and when you plant tomatoes, you get onions. Some things in life aren't clear.

For example, Christopher Columbus' plan was to travel to India, however, he discovered the Americas. The same thing happens to a lot of inventors and scientists. Darwin for example was a lazy and spoiled boy in school, then when he heard that some people were going around the world on a ship, he decided to go with them. His father told him that he is a loser, and after a few months in the sea, you will go and tell the people you are with to send you back home, because you don't want to continue with them. Darwin then went to his uncle to persuade his father to let him go on that ship. The uncle tried to persuade his father, but his father said that "Darwin is a loser, and is not good for anything, he is useless" His uncle responded," Since he is useless, you are not benefiting from him here, let him go".

4. Life will be boring if things will happen the way you plan it. So, when there are a lot of surprises in life, then life will not be boring. Life is full of surprises, which makes life interesting and not boring.

5. I always think positively. So, I believe that things will either work for me immediately, or things will work for me in a different way, like I said, when you plant apples, you get oranges. Or just as the second story goes with Christopher Columbus, where when looking for another route to India, he found America. Or just as the third story, where things first look like a problem but turn into a blessing. In my life, many bad things happened to me and it turned out to be good in the long run. When I look back at it, I am happy that such things happen to me. I am saying this based on books that I have read on a great number of people, where the same things happened to them in the past. Or, based older people I met that always say that the bad things that happened to them always look back and think of the negative and bad things as being good for them. Since my early childhood, I used to

read a lot of stories and history books. I noticed that nothing is impossible if you have the will and the patience. Those stories that I read in my childhood encouraged me to always be optimistic and be positive. It helped me a lot later in my business. If you do not believe me, then just ask your uncle, aunt, mother, or father or any elderly person, they will tell you the same and a lot of stories about things that happened to them. There is a saying that I truly believe in, which is that with ever dark cloud, there is a silver lining. Many stories like that happened to me, where it sounds like a big problem at first, only to turn out to be a blessing. This has happened to me hundreds of times. The main point here is that if you want to start a business, then you have to be optimistic, no matter what. If you are not thinking positively, then think of another job not related to business.

6. Let me tell you a story that happened to me when I was in high school. I remember when I was in 9th, 10th, and 11th grade, we would make a study group during the finals. So, I would find some of my friends to study with. I always tried to study with smart students in my group
because it encouraged me to study, and I can talk with the students when I get bored. I was always looking for smart students, 4.0 students who study well, because they are serious people who will motivate and push me to study all the time.
Unfortunately, however, when I was in 12th grade, all the smart students were taken, and would not take me into their groups because their groups would already reach their limit. It was too late and I did not find any smart students to study with. I felt very bad at that time. I had no other choice but to study with a lazy student who was not serious about school. He was not getting good grades and when I started studying with him, I used to go with him to eat at Kentucky Fried Chicken and take study breaks quite frequently. When I found this person, I did not get mad, I just thought of

myself as unlucky. Then, I indirectly noticed that the student was very sociable and had a lot of friends. So, through him and his friends, I met a lot of key and important people. This friend today, who became a billionaire. Today, when I look back at it, I think of myself as a very lucky person because I met this guy, and I learned a lot of things from him related to business.

7. During my freshman year at USC, I was an entrepreneur working on my first business project. This project was related to amusement parks and I failed. At first, I was unhappy and very frustrated because I thought I wasted my time and my money. But later on, I noticed that I was a very lucky person because during that year, in the summertime, this project made me visit some people every day and one of them was a nice person with a big heart who was later on very helpful to me for many years.

8. The main point here is that you should be optimistic, and have positive thoughts, not pessimistic with negative thoughts. Don't talk with people who are pessimistic and think negatively because they will discourage you to do any kind of business, and they will make big things out of little problems. Stay away from such people.

9. Because I think positively, I never give up. When I am aiming for an A and get a B in college, I say that it's alright since a B is better than a C. When I get a C I say that it is better than a D.

10. Many times, I am trying to catch an airplane in the airport or a ship in the harbor, or a train in the train-station, and the taxi driver keeps telling me that there I'm not going to make it, but most of the time, I make it in the last minute.

11. Now, because of my experience, whenever a bad thing happens to me, I know for sure, that something good will come out of this. Whether it be after one week or even after one year. The main point here is to never give up and be positive.

12. When someone is not optimistic, he will not try hard and give up easily, a person like that will never do any kind of business in his life.

13. When I was a student in University, I decided to go snow skiing for spring break in Lake Tahoe, California. My ex-roommate was from Chicago. He didn't have the money to go anywhere during spring break. I felt sorry for him. I told him, lets fly to Lake Tahoe, and I will pay for his ticket. He said no, he doesn't want me to pay for his ticket. But, if I am driving my car, he will go with me because his uncle is there in Lake Tahoe and has a cabin. I told him that I am a rich student, and that buying a ticket for him is no big deal. But he refused. I felt sorry for him because he is younger than me. I was a junior and he was a freshman. I considered him like my little brother. Finally, because I had no alternative, I had to drive my car and go with him until we reached Lake Tahoe. There, I had fun going skiing every day. Unfortunately, during the weekend, before school started, something happened. There was a very big snowstorm. A day earlier, I told my ex-roommate if he was ready to go back to university. He said that he was advised by his uncle not to return, because they were expecting a big storm. Since I am an optimistic person, I insisted on going back to Los Angeles because I do not like missing my classes I decided to go and drive my car because I am an optimistic person. There was a big storm at night, and in the morning, there was snow everywhere. I didn't know where my car was. There were so many cars covered in snow. I got a shovel and started

looking for my car. I shoveled the first car and saw that it wasn't mine, I then continued on the second, which was also not mine. After I shoveled the third car, it turned out to be my car. It was not an easy job shoveling the snow and looking for my car. I then started my car, and had another problem. The chains on the tires broke. So, I had to stop between the cold weather and the snow falling, and put the chains back. The weather was too cold. I had to take the gloves off my hands. Whenever I stopped. My hands were freezing every time I took them off, so I would quickly put them back on. I would try again and again, but my hands were freezing. Finally, I was able to put the chains on the tire, and go on my way. Because I am a persistent person, I never gave up. Then, I started to climb the mountains, the road was very narrow, and the mountains started to get higher and higher, and the visibility worsened to zero. I could not see the narrow road, which made the journey that much more dangerous and difficult. One misstep and my car would have fallen, and I would have died. I was following the car Infront of me. I was following its rear lights. If that car made a mistake going right or left, I would have made the same mistake. I was doing this for a long time. Finally, we reached an exit, and we saw a good hotel. When I went into the hotel, it was crowded with people, and was lucky that I was able to find the last room in the hotel. I was so happy and relieved that I was able to find a room in the middle of nowhere in the mountains. Also, I was very happy after taking a hot shower and saw that snow was falling all around me. It was a very beautiful moment. And later on, at night, I sat in a fireplace in the lobby of that hotel. To me, that day and night was like a fantasy/ a good adventure I will never forget. The next day I continued my trip, and everything was okay. I was eager to go back to university, and not miss any of my classes, especially my geology classes that I love.

14. If you are optimistic, you will never give up. If you are optimistic, you will believe the best is yet to come or a miracle will happen to you. If you are optimistic, you will know that the other people who made it before you are not better than you and you know that one day you will be lucky like the others, exactly like the saying "every dog has its day". If you are optimistic, you know that failure is the process of being successful so if you are optimistic, you will never give up. You might fail a few times but at the end you will know how to become successful because failure will teach you how to become successful. If you are optimistic, you know things will change and wait and good things will happen to you. People who are not optimistic think life is not fair but actually life is fair in the long run so be optimistic and be ready for the right time and the right moments. The others who are not optimistic, they will never think that way.

15. J.K Rowling, the woman who wrote Harry Potter, failed many times but at the end she won, her book became successful, and she made money because she didn't give up.

16. Robert Bolt, the scriptwriter who wrote Lawrence of Arabia; at the beginning of his life, he wrote many scripts and he failed but he didn't give up. He had to leave school for a while because he didn't have money. He ended up working at the post office for a year. He didn't like his job but later on, he wrote a script about the daily life of a man working at the post office. This script was his first successful script and made him famous because he lived that life of the postman and knew how to write it in details.

17. If you read the history of many leaders, many inventors, many famous people, they won and they became successful because they because were optimistic and have hope and

they didn't give up. For example, Edison, when he invented the lamp, he wanted to sell his product. He tried many times to make it economical and available to the public and he failed many times but at the end he invented the right thing and it was very economical for the public. Same thing with a lot of big business men and very big companies, they failed but at the end they made money and their companies became very big companies.

18. Also for example, the American president Abraham Lincoln failed many times but he didn't give up.

19. Pessimistic people and people who are not optimistic, they think there are no chances to make money and the opportunities are fake and you cannot compete with the other and the others are just lucky people and they are not and there are no other chances in the world to make money but in reality there are always chances and opportunities for new businesses and new rich people.

20. There is a short story I want to tell, there was a man who had an Ox in his field doing the job for him and then one day the Ox died, he didn't know what to do. To him it was the end of the world and then the people at his village told him to go see the wise person in his village so he went to see him. He told them that this is good for you. After a while, he saw a horse and he brought a horse to his field, the horse was faster so he became happier then at one time, his 17 year old boy was riding the horse and he fell down and broke his arm and he was very disappointed. The people in the village told him to go to see the wise man at the top of the mountain, he went to him and the wise man told him that maybe this is good for you. A few months later, there was a war and they drafted all the young people except this person because he had a broken

arm. So the point here is whenever bad things happens to you, don't give up maybe the bad thing that is happening to you is good for you in the long run.

21. If a person was trying really hard to be a manager at the age of 30 years but he became a manager at the age of 45 years, maybe if you ask him if he has regrets, he would say no because he gained experience and understood a lot of things at work so how he became a good manager and know how to deal with his employees. But he was a good manager and knows how to deal with his employees but if he was a manager when he was at the age of 30 he would be like an idiot. He will consider himself lucky that he did not become the same thing with a rich businessman maybe he worked hard to become a billionaire at the age of 30 years, he would not be able to invest his money in the right way at the age of 30 and he would maybe lose his money easily and he will not know back then how to enjoy his money so now he considers himself a lucky person when he became rich at the age of 50 where he has more experience in his life and in business.
I believe even when something goes wrong for a person may be there is a hidden luck or treasure for him. For example, if a person loses his job and becomes sad suddenly, he might come up with an idea of selling anything. It is happening to a lot of people who lost there jobs then they became successful in the world of trade and business.

REGRETS

Since I am an optimistic person and I believe in fate, I want to mention that no matter what happens to me, I do not feel bad and have no regrets. People who believe in fate usually don't panic when things go wrong and don't have regrets so they are happy people.

There are many lessons I have learned in life people may think of them as regrets but they are things I always think back on to better myself.

1. I trusted and consulted my secrets to my friends who shared the information I told them, later realizing that they are not real or good friends but fake ones.

2. I was too nice to some people and trusted people when it came to money and my business and they ended up stealing from me thinking that I am a naïve person.

3. I helped and sacrificed so much for some people and they never appreciated it.

4. There were some people who were nice to me and were good friends and was supposed to spend more time with them, but unfortunately, I could not since I was always busy. I was supposed to continue my contact with them during high school, university, and even work.

5. When I was in Japan, I was in a 5-Star Hotel and left my Rolex watch in my suitcase which was open. When I came back to my room, I saw that the watch was gone. I was not careful and it got stolen. I learned not to trust 5 star hoteles.

6. For my graduation picture for the USC yearbook, I spent a lot of time choosing the right picture. After the yearbook came out, I saw that I just looked at it once, and no one looked at my picture but me. It was a waste of time. But I learned that people dont care about your picture or your graduation.

7. Since I had many stamps, I wasted a few days organizing my stamps in an album. No one even looked at them, it was a waste of time.

8. My coin collection was also a big waste of time. I wasted a few days organizing my coins.

9. I used to do a lot of sports and at certain times during my life, I would stop for months on end because I was very busy, ending up getting sick and having illnesses which wasted my time as I was going to the hospital repeatedly. One of these sicknesses was diabetes.

10. Many small companies approached me to work with them, and I felt like they were too small for me. They were generating much less than the larger companies I was used to. These days however, uring Covid-19, it is the small companies that are the only ones generating money, instead of the larger companies and they are much easier to secure deals with.

11. I was naïve and made a mistake when I told some of my friends how much I make. Never specify how much money you generate or deal with. The less fortunate will envy you and the bad people will try to take advantage of you. If you are making less than expectations, some rich people will look down at you and spread the word because people always talk.

12. I wasted my money on a lot of things I did not need and was not important. But now I learned how to save my money.

13. I took a lot of pictures for the USC Yearbook and never took a look at it; I was very picky with the pictures I took and wasted a lot of time on it.

14. I was always in a hurry and did not stop to smell the roses and there are a lot of people who are good people who I am supposed to spend time with but I am always busy and always in a hurry so I did not stop and spend time with them.

15. There are a lot of things I did not know when I was young, I wish I knew at least 10% of those things.

16. I missed a lot of golden opportunities because I was not ready at that time.

17. I was a happy student at USC for 14 years, I wish I was still there and wish I spent 30 years in college.

18. One of my regrets that some friends did not appreciate me even though I was nice to them and I am supposed to leave them immediately and not give them chances. I thought they would change but they never changed.

19. When I was at USC, I took many courses and I thought people will be interested to ask me questions about the many courses I have learned about at the University. But this did not happen, I noticed that people are not that interested in knowledge and education. They became jealous of me because they had noticed that I am more educated than them.

20. If I had a chance to be a student at USC for 30 years instead of 14 years, then I would be even happier. I would learn a lot of things every day and have less worries because a business man has more worries than a student.

21. At one time I regretted, when I travelled to Singapore, Hong Kong, Thailand and South Korea because I did not enjoy it very much because I did not have enough money with me. But now when I look back, I am happy because I look at it as it was adventures to travel to those countries and I love adventures because since my childhood I used to read a lot of comics books and stories about adventures. Also I feel I learned about the lives of people in those countries.

Chapter 14

Contacts and Connections

1. They say that it is not what you know, it is who you know.

2. Contacts and connections are like miracles. They make anything impossible, possible.

3. Some people measure a person's value or power based on how many people he knows and how many contacts and connections he has.
   A persons worth is measured by how many contacts and connectionshe has.

4. You can transfer and use the amount of contacts and connections into money. If you know how to use it in the right way. It is exactly like when you have gold, sell it, and exchange it into cash. This is how theimportance of contacts and connections are.

5. Many people use and utilize their contacts and connections into making money. They know hundreds or thousands of people, and know some of the key people and powerful people. All people are important in different levels.
   The powerful and the higher class of people are very important, also the middle class people, as well as the key people in the lower class are important. So, everyone is important and can help you, so don't underestimate people. The more people you know, the better off it is for you. But, try to concentrate on key people, who are more important than the others. The name of the game is how to meet people and make contacts and connections.
   Because, not everybody has the talent and the skills of meeting people and making contacts and connections. I

noticed and I heard since my childhood, that many people made money from contacts and connections. For example, a person who has contacts and connections gets promoted from his job quickly, and gets a better salary than his colleagues. A car dealer who knows more people can sell more cars than the other car dealer who doesn't know many people. You can sell more cars and make more money than a person who doesn't know many people. A broker or dealer in the stock market who knows more people can make more money than a broker who doesn't know as many people.

6. If you read stories about people who made money in many businesses, you will find contacts and connections with a lot of very rich people. There are many stories such as this everywhere in the world.

7. I'm sure that you know a lot of people who got good jobs because they know someone or know some people. This is the same thing in business, if you know people, then your business will grow quickly. There are a lot of people everywhere around the world, who became rich because of their contacts and connections.

8. For every kind of business, people always need contacts and connections.I learned the importance of connections and how it can help you make money at the age of 18 when I was in high school. I used to go camping and fishing with my friends in high school. At one time, my cousin told me that he has a used car worth 4000 dollars. And he told me, that I must sell it for more than 4000, and any amount for more than 4000 is for me. My cousin told me that I always go fishing and camping with my friends, ask your friends if anyone would want to buy your car. So, you are going to have to use your contacts and connections. So, my friends told their fathers about the used car. One of my friends father,

told one of his friends about this car, and we finally sold this car for 4,300 dollars. Then, I became very happy because I made 300 dollars. This was quite a lot of money at the time. I remember that with that money I bought a very good camera and a lot of other things. The most important things I realized the important of contacts and connections, since with little effort you can make some money.

9. I remember at one time during my freshman year at USC during Christmas holiday, I was travelling to the Philippines and Thailand and some other asian countries. On the way back, during high-season (since it was Christmas time) they put me on the waiting list, since the plane was full. I wanted to travel back to California from the Philippians. I was on the waiting list for the flight and arrived at the airport five hours before the flight. There at the airport, I saw a young Filipino man working at the counter in the airlines, and started talking to him for a long time, since he was a friendly person and I am a friendly man. He was telling me that his sister graduated from the same university I attend, USC. So, we started talking about football games and other things about Los Angeles. After talking to him for a while, I was wondering if there was any way I could get back to Los Angeles since I was still worried about not getting a seat back to California. So, when I told that person that I was worried about not getting a seat back to California since the flight was full during Christmas time in the holidays, he told me, "Don't worry, you will be the first one to get a seat on the airplane", I replied by saying "Wow, this is like a miracle". Even at that age, I knew that contacts and connections can make miracles. There are a lot of stories about contacts and connections that help people reach the top and help people make money. There are a lot of important and key people in every kind of business who can help you, so you must search for them because knowing the right

people will make your business easy, and help you make a lot of money.

10. Also, during my freshman year at USC, I used to go to the cafeteria to eat my lunch, where all kinds of students go and eat their lunch, with all types of the students they know. At one time, I heard them talking about a director and a producer – a USC alumni - who has no money but started financing his first film from the help of the students who he knew that graduated earlier from USC. And since he was in touch with them after they graduated and was still at college, he used his contacts and connections to finance his first film. The most important thing was his first film which was a hit, he then started to make more movies and then he started to produce and direct more films and then he became rich and famous.

11. A lot of rich people don't like to admit that they became rich because of their contacts and connections. They will keep telling you that it is because of their hard work. If you try to do a study and research however, you will find that at one point in their lives, or at a lot of times, they had a lot of contacts and connections through high school friends, family friends, college friends, or work friends. At the same time, there are a lot of people around the world who are very hard workers, very smart, but because they were born in the countryside or in bad neighborhoods, they are not lucky enough to have the right contacts and connections because they are surrounded by poor people or people with no contacts and connections.When I was a student in USC in freshmen year, I asked a lot of students who lived with me in the dorms what made them come to USC and why they chose USC. Some of them answered that their reasoning was because USC was a prestigious university and very famous, other students told me that it was because USC was strong in

their major such as architecture, cinema, electrical engineering, business etc.... A lot of students told me however, that USC had a lot of good alumni and a lot of good connections, wanting to get good jobs once they graduate.

12. I noticed since my early childhood, that my billionaire uncle brother of my mother – had a lot of connections and contacts. When you connect some of his stories about his contacts and connections, you will notice that many of his contacts and connections made him a lot of money. Of course he was a hard worker and sociable, but his connections helped him a lot. At the same time, the connection of his father and mother helped him a lot.

13. Some people think of connections as a part time job, or extra points in classes. No, it is wrong, in order to get contacts and connections, you must spend time and money on it. If you spend five hours a day on studying, then you should spend three hours a day on contacts and connections, then, it will grow over time. It is like when you have a tree planted in a vase, you must give it water every day. This is the same with friends, staying close to them and constantly being present-visit them and talk to them. How about when you have ten big vases in your house, it means you will have many trees in your house. And you have to give them a lot of water. Spend time to let them grow and eventually, give you the fruits of your labor.

14. Some people believe that contacts and connections are simply luck. No, it is not luck, you must work on it and it will grow.

15. Someone may say that they have no time to search for

friends or key people. At the same time however, you will see that the same person is watching tv five hours a day, playing video games for two hours a day, and on social media for three hours a day. You can minimize these things instead of spending 7 hours a day, and spend 30 minutes on that, and using 5 hours for establishing connections and meeting with people. The point here is that if you want something, you must sacrifice something else in order to let your contacts and connections grow, which they will over time.

16. I remember when I took several political science classes, the professor told us to read newspapers such as the Los Angeles times every day and we will get 5 extra points – in order to encourage students to find out what is happening in the world politically. This was also to know about different countries of the world, and to know who their prime minister was, who their minister of foreign affairs was, and who the president was. There would then be a quiz related to that subject. But to me, to get contacts and connections, it is like taking a hard course in college, like physics, chemistry, and not like reading newspapers for an extra five points. Because, I am taking the matter of contacts and connections very seriously. This is exactly like taking hard courses like physics and chemistry. A lot of stupid people believe that I got contacts and connections because I am a lucky person, they don't know that I earned it, because I put a lot of effort and time and money. I remember that when I was at university, I was a member of the society of petroleum engineers -SPE-. I sometimes went to faraway places such as Bakersfield California or San Francisco California, where I had to drive my car for 15 hours and stay at a hotel or motel for 2 nights, just to meet people in the oil industry.
    I was spending money for the accommodation and gas, while I was still a student on a low budget. I would rather stay in Los Angeles and spend money going out to movies with my friends.

17. Sometimes in life, you don't have much of a choice. Either having fun, or having contacts and connections. I have hundreds of stories that happened to me like that. I travelled to many places across the United States and across the world, just to get contacts and connections. And I put a lot of time, effort, and money into it. It was not easy.

18. I was also subscribed to a lot of geological magazines. At that time I wanted to know everything besides my school books. But, at the same time, contacts and connections play a big part in my life. At the same time, I must admit that without the education and the knowledge, I will not be able to start my business.

19. It is a social skill which requires a lot of time money and effort to meet friends. It also depends on your potential and ability. The key for this is networking. This means that one person will introduce you to another person. Also, a chain of people introducing you to each other, until you reach your goal or the person you want to meet. For example, person A will introduce you to person B, and person B will introduce you to
person C, and so on until you reach person Z. Of course, this process will take a lot of time and effort, maybe even costing you money. Sometimes when you invite people to lunch or coffee, you have to pay for it. Or, when you visit a person in another city, you have to pay for your transportation. You have to be patient, because it may take you a longer time than what you are planning to meet the right people.

20. The best way in networking is you let Mr A introduce you to Mr B who will introduce you to Mr C, all the way to Mr Z. Sometimes it will take a long time to reach Mr Z but eventually you will reach him and this is called networking, someone will introduce you to the other person.

21. Also, you have to go to the right places to meet the right people. For example, parties, football games, events, gyms, swimming pools, wedding parties and funerals etc..

22. In case you want to start your business, contacts and connections will help you to raise funds and money. Many young people when they started their business, they took money from their friends because they had plenty of friends.

23. Some people are lucky because they inherited money from their rich parents. You may say that there is no chance for me. No, there is still a chance to make money from your contacts and connections. If you have a charming and social able personality to meet people, and use networking to know more people.

24. In the world of trade and business. You must always maintain a good relationship with your clients. You must call them and visit them just to improve the relation. Send the greeting's during the holidays and be in touch with them. So, contacts and connections are like trees. You must irrigate contacts and connections like water every week, not just once a year.

25. Today you can also do networking with the social media.

Chapter 15

Dealing with people

1. Dealing with people is a skill and a talent, it is also an art. Not everyone has it. Dealing with people, communicating with people, understanding people is very important. A lot of people got very rich and promoted, because they know how to deal with people. A lot of successful people who have the skill of how to deal with people became rich, even employees that know how to deal with people and their bosses, will become promoted by their bosses. If he is a businessman, he will make a lot of money. People who have the skill and talent of dealing with people will have a lot of doors opened for them. Their businesses grow very quickly, in a short period of time, since they know how to deal with people and make contacts and connections. A lot of people got very rich because of their contacts and connections. A lot of people got promoted in their jobs because they know how to deal with people, especially their bosses and because of their contacts and connections. Dealing with people in the right way, will make you have your contacts and connections. The most successful people in history became successful because they knew how to deal with people.

2. You must know how to deal with people in order to sell your products and services. The most important thing, is how to approach people. How to get to know people. How to convince people. And, how to let people accept your personality and ideas. And how to make people like you.

3. You must know how to deal with people based on the level of their mind. Because, dealing with men, is different than dealing with women. Dealing with educated people is

different than dealing with non-educated people. Dealing with bosses and big managers is different than dealing with average employees. Dealing with kids is different than dealing with adults. Dealing with rich people is different than dealing with poor people. The same can be said about dealing with people from different cultures and countries.

4. You have to know how to deal with different kinds of people, this is psychology, so don't blame people for the way they are because circumstances made them this way. So, there are different kinds of people: A. The stingy people B. The Arrogant people C. The educated people D. non-educated people E. Technical people that focus on numbers only also math's and science F. people that like to brag and show off G. Rich people H. Poor people I. Some people who are rude and have no manners.

5. So, our planet Earth is full of all kinds of people, so you need to know how to deal with them and try to focus on what they are interested in, just imagine they are your clients or customers, so you have to know how to deal with them. Also, dealing with nice people is different than dealing with bad people or thieves.

6. You always need to know how to deal with people to sell your product or do marketing with him. If there is a genius inventor who invented a good invention, he must know how to deal with people to know how to sell his great invention. Maybe, he is good in inventing things, but he is not good in marketing it. So, he must rely on himself to sell his product, or find a smart person who knows how to deal with people to sell his product.

7. The same thing with a good author, if he writes a good book, but he cannot sell a publisher, he must know how to deal

with people in order to find a publisher to publish his book. An author must also know people in order to raise money for his book. The same thing can be said for any businessman who wishes to sell his product or services, he must know how to deal with people.

8. I wanted to mention something here, a person who reads his books all the time, and does well in school, is called a book smart person. In a way, a nerd.It is the type of person, who always gets very high grades. Getting 100 in physics, chemistry, and math. He knows how to do well in exams and he knows how to study. This type of person is called book smart. He always reads books, and works on papers and is on the internet and focuses on his books and work. There are two types of people, book smart and street smart. Book smart is the type of person who always reads books and has a lot of knowledge. If he is a student, he knows how to study for an exam, and can get straight A's. This person is always focused on studying and reading books. Some people may call him a nerd. Also, he always talks about knowledge, science, computers etc.… After graduating from university, he will work as an engineer for example, he will be a hard worker focusing on his job and will always be talking about his work and engineering. In a lot of cases, in work, he is not going to get promoted, because he does not know how to make his boss happy. There are a lot of people who do not have the basics about meeting people or dealing with people. Even those who are very well educated and have a PhD cannot approach people and he cannot start a conversation with people and he doesn't know how to use the right time, right place, and correct approach.

9. A street smart person is a very socialable person who has a lot of friends, and a lot of girlfriends who knows how to talk to people. And, he knows how to convince people and

persuade people, sometimes he is quick on his feet, and makes tricks to meet people, he can even convince people to invest in his company, he is good in communication and socializing and dealing with people. Also, he knows how to act and how to behave. And, how to approach people in the right time and the right place, also cunning and knows how to make people happy. This is due to the fact that has a good sense of humor and has a lot of stories to tell and always likes to tell people what they like to hear, and at the same time, respects people. So, he has contacts and connections because he knows the right and the key people.
Maybe, he is a hard worker, instead of working 8 hours a day, he might work 15 hours a day. When he goes to college, his grades are averaging at C or D or even worse. If he works as an employee, he will be promoted quickly because he knows how to deal with his boss and make his boss happy. For example, if his boss is talking about fishing, he will be talking about fishing, if his boss is talking about basketball games, he will be talking to his boss about basketball games. On a rainy day, if he sees his boss watching the rain, and he has papers for his boss to sign them. Instead of asking his boss to sign the papers, he will be talking about the rain. There are a lot of street smart people who have no education – not going to school nor college in some parts of the world, but they are very rich, because they know how to deal with people and talk to people and make people happy. I travelled around the world a lot and I met a lot of people who are not educated, but they are rich because they are street smart and they know how to deal with people.

10. A street smart person knows how to deal with people at a certain time, or call them at a certain time or visit people at the right place, right time with the correct approach.

11. When Stephen Spielberg was still up and coming and not

yet the famous director and filmmaker we know today, he was a young man who got to know the people in Hollywood. He makes contacts and connection so he went on a tour to universal studios. He jumped off the tourist train and started rolling down the hill then found himself in the middle of the studio and then he kept walking in the streets of the studio like the other studio so the other people there thought he works there. He started talking to people pretending that he worked their with them just to get to know them. At the end of the day, on his way out, he wanted the security person to recognize him so he started to sing and wave his hands and making a scene just to get the attention of the security guard. Of course, this guy thought this guy was weird or funny or crazy but he recognized him. So, the next day, in the morning, Spielberg came back to the studio and started singing and waving his arms and making a scene again. The security person recognized him and thought he was one of the employees in the studio. He started coming every day in the studio and started making contact and connections with the people there at Universal studios.

12. If you try to re-trace and investigate the successful people, you will find that they have the education and the knowledge, but they also have the social skills and they know how to deal with people in order to deliver their products or their invention to the people or in order to reach their goals.

13. Most of the big managers get promoted quickly because they know how to deal with their bosses and at the same time, know how to deal with people. Most of the world leaders in history know how to deal with people.

14. Unfortunately people will judge you by your appearance, your clothes, the way you look and the way you talk, and

they will not try to look inside you. So, for this reason you must act like an actor. Just change your personality for a few days just to get to know somebody or to get along with some people for a few days.

15. A street smart person – a person who talks a lot, who is cunning, and uses tricks and quick on his feet. They are also sweet talkers, and they know how to make their bosses happy, and know how to get to know people. A lot of street smart people don't usually get good grades at school yet a lot of times, they make money or become good leaders.
I remember when I was in university, my chemistry tutor used to tell me that those who get A's go for research and development, and those who get B's go for teaching, and those who get C's get the money. There are a lot of people around the world who are not educated, but they are street smart, and they became successful businessmen and leaders, because they are street smart.

16. There was an engineer working in an oil company who decided to quit his job and work on his own, so he started to work from his house in Europe. He started to do design for a big company because they gave him little work so he kept working from his house doing small scale work. After a while, that big company contacted him and asked if he could do a bigger job for them, but they said the management wanted to make sure that the man had an office. However, this man didn't have enough money to have his own office and was working from his house. Then, he came up with a good idea; he rented an office only for one day. When the people from the big company came to look at the office, they believed that he had an office. They wrote in their report that he had an office so they started to give him a lot of work on a bigger scale. Then, this man's business started to grow and finally he made a big company. It is now a well known

company in Europe.

17. A situation could be made that if a billionaire or important person was in a hospital, and the doctor may want to get close to him by giving him a book as a gift. He might give him a book in a subject that he is not interested in, such as science or astronomy. However, the driver of the ambulance in the hospital, who is a street-smart person, might get to know the driver of the billionaire. The driver of the billionaire who has known his boss for many years, would know what the billionare likes to read, for example, history books, and would tell him what kind of books he likes to read, or what kind of fruits or candies he likes to have as a gift. Then the driver of the ambulance will give the billionaire a history book and the fruits or candy that he likes as a gift. Later, the driver will keep visiting the billionaire's house. There is a saying that goes, "give the fish what the fish wants to eat, not what you want to eat". In this situation, the doctor may like science, and science books, and he thought that the billionaire likes the same.

18. When you talk to people in order to do some marketing in order to sell your product and ideas, try to convince people and motivate people. Convincing people and motivating people is a skill that not everybody has, only street mart people know how to deal with people. Some people try to call you, but they never leave their name and phone number but smart people when they call, they leave their names and phone numbers because they know how to deal with people. Some people know how to call at the right time and some stupid people, they call at the wrong time. Some people know how to approach people at the right time and the right place, those are the street-smart people. The stupid people try to approach people at the wrong time when they are mad or busy and also approach people at the wrong place.

19. I once went to the gym, and I saw an important person running on a treadmill. I went straight to my car and got my running shoes and shorts. I got on a treadmill next to him, and I acted like I did not know how to use the machine. He was graceful enough to show me how it worked. After we finished from exercising, I thanked him a lot and I apologized for bothering him. I told him that the last time I used the gym, was when I was a student in California. He asked me where I studied. I told him I was a student in USC. I asked him the same, and he went to a university in Minnesota. After that, every time I met him, we would talk about our lives in university, and we became good friends.

20. During the 7th century, the governor of Egypt, named Amr bin Alas was a smart military leader in the Middle East. He later became the governor of Egypt. He once wanted to invade a heavily defended enemy fort. He decided to infiltrate the fort rather than let one of his men do it. This was because Amr did not trust his men to describe the situation in the fort as detailed as he needed it to be, because he wanted more information, and information and knowledge is power. Amr worked as a person selling water and acted like a very poor man in the fort for many weeks, until he got all the information he needed. Once he returned to his army, he created a plan to overrun the fort and he conquered it. The point here is that information is very important, and the smart leader knows how to get the information.

21. In today's business, every manufacturer wants more information about their competitors and other manufacturers. For example, Toyota's car industry knows everything about the General Motors industry, and at the same time General Motors knows everything about Toyota. This is called business intelligence. The same thing can be

said about the aviation industry.
Boeing knows everything about Airbus, and Airbus knows everything about Boeing. Same thing about telephone, Samsung knows about Nokia, and Nokia knows about Samsung. There are many people in each company that serve the competing company and give them information about their rivals and the industry. Because every company and manufacturer wants to know about their competitors. This is called business intelligence. The people who give information are called business consultants.

22. There was a family that used to come to the pool a lot. A smart person wanted to get to know the father of that family. His wife and son used to swim and stay by the pool frequently. His son was quite a troublemaker and used to jump in the pool – causing quite the mess. He thought that the best way to get to know the father was to get to know the mother. He stood up by the pool while reading a book deliberately. He got closer and closer to the son while the boy was jumping into the pool. The man grew close enough to the boy that once he jumped into the pool, the splash got his book wet. The man complained to the boy, and the boy told him that this was a pool, not a library. He laughed and used that as an opportunity and an excuse to talk to his mother. He approached his mother, and told her that her son was quite the comedian and troublemaker. He told her that he told him that this was a swimming pool and not a library. She said that her son was rude, but she repeatedly tells him to respect people and not be rude to people. He told her that he found him funny, and that when he was his age, he used to jump into the swimming pool all day. He then started to talk to his mother about his childhood, becoming good friends in the process. And in the long run, she introduced him to her husband, and he created a business connection with him.

23. The famous Mongol Emperor, Genghis Khan, took over and ruled most of Asia. He ruled more land than anyone else in history. When he died, he left a large and vast empire for his sons and his grandsons. Then, his grandsons started to divide the empire. Some of his grandsons who lived among Muslims converted to Islamic religion Islam. From the dynasty of Genghis Khan, came the emperor Akbar of India the most powerful emperor in the history of India. At that time, Pakistan and Bangladesh was a part of India. Sometimes, King Akbar went alone in the streets of his empire wearing normal clothes, to see what his people are doing and what they are talking about and what their feelings were. He did this without the people knowing that he was the King. People did not know how the king looked like because there were no newspapers or cameras that revealed his appearance. At one time, King Akbar asked the Muslim merchants why they don't go to Mecca as pilgrims. They replied that they did not have the money for it because they were paying a lot of taxes, so they do not have much money left for them. Then, the next day, King Akbar decided to stop most taxes. So, all the people of India started celebrating, and singing and dancing for King Akbar. So, Hindus, Muslims, Christians, and all people love King Akbar because he reduced taxes. The main point here is that King Akbar knew how to deal with his people, the Indians. He knew what people wanted. The grandson of King Akbar is named Shah Jahan, the man who built the Taj Mahal for his wife, Mumtaz in the city of Agra. The last point that I wanted to mention is that is the same thing in business, where one must know what his customers and clients want in the market. This is the same thing as to what Jeff Bezos did with Amazon, where he knew people wanted a service that could offer packaged delivery and products all across the world.

24. There was a hotel in Europe that was losing money, so a smart person bought this hotel, and just did a few changes and started to make good money. All he did was add mirrors everywhere. He put mirrors on each floor everywhere. Because he knows that most women like mirrors. Then, a lot of women started asking their husbands to take them to this hotel. So, the rumors and gossip spread, and all the women who traveled, started bragging to their friends about the hotel. Women kept asking their husbands to go to the hotel. The hotel eventually became booked all year round. The owner then increased the price, yet the hotel was still always full. The prestige of the hotel increased, and the word of mouth spread, making all interested in staying in the hotel.

25. Today in the stock market, a lot of people rely on rumors and exaggeration for the stock market to go up. Those people make money by selling their shares. A lot of people make millions relying on gossip and exaggeration in the stock market. Of course, the media play a large part in this, always exaggerating things, this is their job. Some people think they are smart the way they spread rumors and make money.

26. There was a person who was desperate for money and wanted to sell his house for four million dollars. The buyer realized that the seller was extremely tense and nervous by looking at his body language. The seller wanted to sell the house for four million, but the buyer was offering two million dollars. The owner of the house said that the house is worth fourth million. The buyer gave him his phone number and told him to call him when he decided on selling for two million. The next day, the seller called him to settle it for three million dollars, but the buyer refused, he insisted on two million. A week later, the seller agreed on selling his house for two million, thus making the deal. The main point

is that the buyer understood the body language from talking to this person and looking at his reaction, knew that he was desperate for money and knew that he could purchase the house for half the price.

27. There was a man who owned a shop for gifts and souvenirs located in a very popular town close to the beach, where a lot of tourists come. The owner of the shop is not making money, he is losing money, and was putting a sign that said you could purchase anything in his shop for half the price. He didn't make money, and another smart person bought the shop, and changed the number on the sighn board, saying that you should hurry and buy the product for two times its original price. That gained a lot of attention with the tourists', believing that this price was only going to rise. The shop sold all of their products, and the owner made a lot of money in the process. The point here is that the new owner of the shop is smart in marketing and knows the mentality of most of the people.

28. There are many ways and many tricks to meet people but unfortunately there are some people who use bad tricks to meet other people. When I took some political science courses at USC, we learned some of Machiavelli's theories like consequentialism. Niccolo Machiavelli, an Italian diplomat and author wrote a book during the 16th century called The Prince- which is not based on morals and I don't agree with him. One of his theories that the goals justify the means which means a person can do anything illegal or legal in order to reach his goals. A person must consider his morals and the feelings of others before using any tricks because some people who have no morals they think like the Machiavelli who said that the ends justify the means. This means that if you have a goal, whatever you do to reach your goals, no matter how bad what you are doing is okay as long

as you are going to achieve your goal.

29. I once sent two of my employees to an oil company. I asked them to go at a certain time to meet a certain person there. Because that person is quite moody, but he is friendly in the afternoon after he gets most of his work done. Unfortunately, my two employees are not street smarts. Even though I told them to go in the afternoon, they decided to go in the early morning just to get the job done, when that person still has a lot of work to do and is in a bad mood and stressed. He got mad at them and kicked them out of his office. They don't know how to deal with people. They are not street smart, and they did not listen to me, as I know that the best time to meet that man is in the afternoon when he is in a good mood. After that I went to see him in the afternoon, and I got things done.

30. I remember that I used to go to a good seafood restaurant for dinner, because they have a good menu and I used to give good tips to the waiters. I noticed that there was a waiter who was nice to me at first. He was nice, however, after a while, he said he does not want tips, he said that he wants to be rich like me. I laughed because I thought he was funny and I knew that he does not have the factors of success that are mentioned in this book. Later on, whenever I gave him a tip, he said that he doesn't want money or tips, he just wanted to be my partner. After a while, he kept saying that I thought he was very rude and annoying, I then told his manager not to let that waiter serve me or talk to me. Because, this person is annoying, rude, and does not know how to approach people and deal with people.

31. It is always good to be known and be recognized by other people. There are a lot of human beings that like to attract attention, the same way some students like to ask questions in the classroom to attract attention. Just like my time in the dorms, where people would create drama such as a food

fight, just for people to recognize them, because a lot of people like recognition. People like it when others remember their names. This is human nature. The same thing can be said with companies, companies want to be famous, and for everyone to know their trademark, logo, and name. They pay a lot of money for advertisement and just to be known by the public. It is always good when a manager of a company visits his clients, it's good for his clients to remember his name, recognize his company's name, the same thing is the case for the secretary of the client, where that secretary would talk to the one for the manager there, to know who you are. Or, even for the people in the reception. So, it is always good to know the people in that building, so you do not walk in like a ghost, and no one recognizes or knows you. I always stop for one minute to talk to the secretary for one minute about any subject she likes, especially if she is bilingual. This is because I am good in languages. Because next time she will know who I am.

32. Some new companies, when they sell their products, they sell it for a little cheaper price, just for them to be known and recognized in the market. Or a big construction company might decrease the cost of a project for them to get the project and possible be well known. Just imagine, that there is a new pizzeria opened, and wanted everyone to know them. They do this by putting a low price. For example, if the market has a pizza for 7 dollars, this new pizzeria will sell theirs for 5 dollars. Within a few months, they will be known. They might not make good money, but they will be recognized in the market.
33. I love my doctor in California, even though he is a busy person and has a lot of patients. In the first five minutes of seeing him, he always talks about social things, and asks about my trips to Europe or my Snow Skiing trip in Colorado. So, I always think of him as a friend not just a

doctor.

34. I have a friend who is a billionaire. Something good about him, even though he is in a meeting, in the middle of his meeting, he would come and see me for three minutes or five minutes and go back to his meeting. He knows how to deal with people and make them happy.

35. When a key person or a friend is ready to invite you for a cup of tea or lunch, do not tell them that you are an extremely busy person. Just to show them that you are an important and busy person. Other people do not care how busy you are, just try to make time for them. Or at least, stop for three minutes and talk to them, or say that soon we can have lunch, it is better than to say I am in a hurry.

36. Finally, I would like to mention that a lot of times, you may meet a key person in a place such a hotel lobby, elevator, or anywhere, and you may not be in a position to talk to them because you are busy or are going to a meeting. This is wrong, when you see an important person, the best thing to do is to talk to him for at least a minute and not show that you are busy or are in a hurry. When this key, or an important person is able to talk to you, use that to your benefit and talk to that person, don't show him that you are too busy for him and cannot talk, because a lot of people who do not have self-confidence want people to think that they are too busy for them and cannot talk to those people. This is an opportunity and may not happen to you again. That one minute might create a good impression for you. They say that the first impression creates a lasting impression.

37. There are 5 categories of people in the world. The first type of people are the very rich and the billionaires. They have a combination of being both book smart and street smart. But they are very rare. Those people, because they have the

education and the knowledge of dealing with people along with strong contacts and connections.
Sometimes, those people inherited the money because their parents or family knew how to deal with people.
For example, John D. Rockefeller who formed standard oil in 1863 he know how to deal with people Most rich people and billionaires are from the first category described. Today, less than half a million people control over 60 percent of the world's wealth and their estimated wealth is in the trillions.

38. The second type of people are the small millionaires who have some contacts and connections, and knows how to deal with people.
Additionally, they could have inherited their wealth from their parents who also know how to deal with people. In terms of business, they make good money selling their services or products.

39. The third type of people are the upper-middleclass. Those are the educated people who are doctors, engineers, professionals, small businessmen, and people with good jobs who are making good money. But they are not very rich, because they have little contacts and connections, They are also lacking some of the factors mentioned in this book.

40. The fourth type of people are the average ordinary people, and average merchants and average store owners, and employees, the ones that you see everywhere and every day. Those are the middleclass people, they are lacking most of the factors mentioned in this book.

The fifth type of people are the poor people. They don't have the education, They are not street smart, they don't have contact and connections, or contacts and connections. Most people within this group are workers, laborers, farmers, and make up the majority of the world, are very poor and eat one meal a day. The point here is the more you know how to deal with people the more chances you have to make money

Networking

1. The most important thing I learned at USC was networking. Networking at USC taught me how to contact and build connections later on for my business. Having the skill of meeting new people also made me able to know the key people everywhere.

2. A key person is an important person who will open the door for you. He is the person who will help you to reach the important person or to reach your goal or target. For example, a good friend of an important person is a key person, a wife of an important person is a key person, a secretary of a manager is a key person, the neighbor of an important person can also be a key person.

3. During my freshman year at USC, many girls who lived with us in the dorm building would go home to visit their parents on weekends because their parents lived about an hour drive away from the university in orange county and Newport beach. When the girls came back to our dorm building on Sunday night with their luggage, all the guys on my floor tried to help them carry the luggage of the beautiful girls and wouldn't help the average normal girls. I then noticed that they would help an average looking girl Cathy with her luggage and everybody was trying to talk to her and be nice to her. At that time, I was naïve and did not know why. Later on, I realized that this girl Cathy was a good friend and roommate of the most beautiful girl in our building. So, this girl Cathy is the key person who can introduce them to the beautiful girl and can also tell her friend about the guys

on my floor. For example, Thomas is a good tennis player, George is a handsome guy, John has a nice car, etc.

4. Networking also helps in meeting different people, for example, actors and directors know each other. Directors know producers, also, directors know camera men. Because, they are in the same line of business, they know each other, and they were introduced to each other. They know each other because of networking.

5. The most important thing is to take the subject seriously, the same time you spend on your work. You must spend time on meeting new
   people. Most of the people do not know this, and this is why they have no contacts nor connections. For example, if you are a student, and spend five hours a day to do your homework, you must spend five hours a day to meet people and visit other students. This is what I did when I was in college. And people asked me how I knew all the students. The reason why is because I don't sit all day in my room, watching TV with my roommate, or arguing or talking to my roommate or neighbors all day like many other students on my floor do. I was more like a social butterfly at the university, and now I am a social butterfly at my work.
   I don't sit in my office all day like other people. I always spend time to visit people related to my job. They then introduce me to their friends and colleagues. I do not think of visiting people as wasting time, it is a part of my job. This is how I know everyone in the industry – related to my work and job. Many people always ask me how I know everyone. The reason is simply because I spend my time on it, while other people waste their time watching TV and on social media (WhatsApp, Twitter, Instagram, etc…) or playing cards with their friends. I don't have the time for all the things I just mentioned. Someone may ask me, "Why are you

isolating yourself from the world?". I reply by saying that "I am not, whenever there is something happening in the world, either in the news or on social media, someone will tell me, since I am always in contact with others, and someone will always tell me". Concerning sports, I rather go on a walk or swim, rather on sitting in my room and watching sports on the TV or reading the sports section on the newspaper. Sometimes a person may say that my life is boring. Rather, I believe it is the opposite, since I am always in contact with others, and love talking to people.

6. A smart person once wished to get close to a key person who was an important person to him for his business. The problem was that he was not very friendly. He used the opportunity to get to know his wife. She was an English lady. She was very much into arts. He used his own knowledge from university and specific courses about art pieces and artists such as Picasso, Michael Angelo, and Leonardo Da Vinci to have a solid conversation with her. She was very happy to talk to him about art and artists. After getting to know her and being friends with her, she eventually introduced him to her husband, and they got to establish a business connection between each other. Once he became closer to the family, her husband introduced him to his colleagues and other partners on his floor in his company. He then ended up knowing everyone on his floor. This is what they call networking which is when person A will introduce you to person B, and that person B will introduce you to person C etc.

7. The best way in networking is you let Mr A introduce you to Mr B who will introduce you to Mr C, all the way to Mr Z. Sometimes it will take a long time to reach Mr Z but eventually you will reach it and this is called networking, someone will introduce you to the other person.

8. Companies which are building hotels, by letting managers of a certain company, introduce you to managers of another company in the same line of business. A hotel would use a company to build their property. The company that they use would know other companies that build the doors, and windows. All the companies involved would know each other since they are in the same industry.
9. I don't play golf – it is a good sport, but it is time consuming. It takes time to get ready, and it is a long drive to get to the golf courses.
   However, I once heard that several key people who I wanted to get to know were playing golf. I don't play golf and was not interested to learn how to play golf, even though I used to walk on the golf courses quite often since they were beautiful places to walk by, especially by sunset. I once had to meet certain key people who always go to the golf club to play golf. I then started to go to the golf club to take lessons and learn how to play golf. To me, it was very time consuming to drive to the golf course, change my clothes, and get ready, but I had to do it to meet those certain people. After a while, I started to meet the key
   people.
   After that, I started to have tea, coffee, and lunch with them. Once they became my friends, I stopped playing golf.

10. I once met an Italian person with his wife at the beach and started speaking Italian with him. Then, after a while, he started to introduce me to one of his Italian friends who introduced me to a lot of companies in Italy related to my business in the oil and gas business.

11. The best way to meet a lot of people is through networking which means somebody will introduce you to someone else and the other person will introduce you to others. But always

remember to have good manners when you talk to people and give people good complements because everybody likes to hear good complements but your complements have to be true. For example, if somebody is hard working you tell him "I respect you because you are a hard working person". If somebody tells you a story about himself and what he did when he was travelling, tell him "wow you are a smart person that thought of something others did not think about etc." If he tells you a joke, tell him you like his jokes and sense of humor. I know you may think it is easy to give compliments but it is not. There are a lot of rude people where when they meet people they just say rude things to people or they never give compliments to people. Also, always remembers to tell people what they want to hear. If somebody likes to talk about sports and basketball, talk to him about sports and basketball. If somebody likes to talk about travelling, talk to him about travelling.

12. When I was a student at USC, many actors, producers, dirсctors, and script writers came to our classroom to give speeches, and they always talked about networking and how they got their first job. At the same time, the head and vice-president of movie studios such as paramount, Columbia, all said after graduating from University with a degree in cinema started to work in the mailroom at the movie studios just to get to know people and get connections. They began from the bottom. They then started to meet people when they delivered mail to them. They then worked their way up, until they became managers, and finally, after many years, they became the head of studio production.

13. Many of my classmates when I was in university, tried to work in the summer after they graduated as PA's – personal assistants. This was to bring coffee and tea to cameramen, photographer, actors, producers, and directors in the movie

industry. After a while, he will be familiar with the movie industry and how it works. After a few months, he will start to know the people in the movie industry very well, by serving tea and coffee to them. After a few years he will work as a camera man, eventually working as a director and as an assistant director. By serving people in the crew, he will get to know others as they introduce him to others, which is another example of networking.

Finally, a cameraman will introduce him to another cameraman in another company, where he will be able to get a job and work his way up until he becomes a director or producer. This method does not only apply to the cinema business, but to any industry like oil and gas or car manufacturing. Networking starting from scratch and being able to apply it anywhere.

How to Make Friends

1. People love compliments and attention. Always try to give people true, honest compliments. Suppose one of your classmates in school is very bad in math and sciences but is good in history. People don't like criticism, so don't say that he's bad in math. Instead, say that he's good in history. This is a true compliment. He will be happy and like you. If somebody is not good at any of his classes but is good at asking unique, thought-provoking questions. Pay him a compliment regarding his questions and he will like you. When you see somebody who is short and skinny, don't tell him he's short and skinny just tell him he's skinny. The main point here is to pay people compliments and not to criticize them.If somebody is a hard worker, but he's stupid, just say the good thing about him. Something like "I respect you a lot because you are a hard worker."People love others to call them by their names. So always try to memorize people's

names. A lot of successful people memorize the names of their employees and the people they deal with.

2. Talk to people about subjects they enjoy talking about. If they like sports, talk to them about sports. If they like movies, talk to them about movies. They say "give the fish what the fish likes to eat, not what you like to eat".

3. Try to have self-confidence when you talk to people. The more confident you are, the more people you will meet. Keep in mind that other people are not 'better' than you, they are just different. You may have your own problems but others might have more problems than you do. Have confidence in yourself. Most people don't have self confidence so they always need compliments.

4. The nature of human beings is that they are sociable and like to make friends. So, try to approach people and talk to them. But, be careful, you must approach them at the right time and the right place with a good approach.

5. Always listen to others when they talk about their problems or things that they want to talk about. Try not to talk about yourself, because people enjoy talking about their feelings. People like people who pay attention to them. Encourage them to talk about themselves.

6. Every human being thinks he is an important person. Let him talk about what he thinks he is good in. Everybody thinks or considers that their cold, headache, or fever is more important than a war or earthquake or flood somewhere else. So, give a chance to the person to talk about his problems, his feelings, or his hobbies because everybody has something to say and a story to tell. Some people make a mistake- they just like to talk about themselves and don't give others a

chance to talk.

7. Don't irritate people or annoy them by bragging about yourself. Don't mention things about yourself that other people don't have. For example, don't talk about your expensive car to someone who doesn't even have a car or has a cheap car. If you have parents, don't talk about them in front of an orphan. If you went to a famous university, don't flaunt these things in front of a person who went to small college or people that don't have an education as they may feel bad or start to envy you. If you go on vacations a lot but this person has never travelled, don't talk about your holidays. Don't tell a crippled person or an unhealthy person how good your health is and how you can run for five miles a day.

8. Don't argue a lot with people. Try to avoid argument. Don't interrupt people when they talk. When someone starts arguing with you, just say "Okay. You won, I lost". They will be happy.

9. Don't be rude or pushy when you ask a person for a favor.

10. Don't embarrass people in public, even if it's a joke. Don't say that someone has funny shoes, for example. And don't embarrass a person in front of his friends Try to always talk to people about simple things they understand because people don't like to hear things they don't understand. Don't talk about science in front of non-educated people. They'll think you're a boring person. Don't talk to people about complicated subjects they don't understand.

11. If you make a mistake and say something bad about somebody, apologize and acknowledge that you hurt his feelings.
12. Always have a smile on your face when you meet people.

If you have a frown on your face, people will think that you don't like them or are looking down on them.

Psychology

1. Psychology helped me to know more about people and to understand people and their behavior. It is easy for me to discover whether or not a person is a nice or mean person by asking a few questions. It is exactly like when a school teacher asks questions during exams. He knows about the student and his level. For example, it is exactly like when you see a person who has muscles and expect him to do a lot of sports. If you ask him how he has muscles, he will tell you that he goes to the gym every day and lifts weights. The same thing with a person who is very rude, not nice, and very aggressive. When asking about his childhood, you will know why. In university, I studied psycho analysis – which means we studied the childhood of a person, his parents, his father, his mother, and his environment, and his history, and how he grew up. His childhood in details, and all his life story. His marginality, and his problems, his level of education, and whether or not the person dropped out of school as well as many other things.

2. Speaking about my roommate, the one from California, he was fatherless. His father died when he was a child, and his mother was very poor. He went to high school in a very bad neighborhood in California. The boys in his high school were very aggressive. They fought a lot and cursed each other out quite often. They beat him up which is why he was aggressive and defensive. The boy however had a scholarship from the University. I then knew that this boy had no manners.He was very aggressive and very rude because he did not have a good childhood, had no father, no

car, and no money.

3. When I see him sleeping, I would not turn the lights on, however, whenever he saw me sleeping, he would turn the lights on. He swore at me proactively, lacking any class. I then decided that if I were to ever communicate with my roommate, I would use a piece of paper. He did the same, and we communicated entirely through the use of writing for the whole year.

4. At the same year, there was a boy on our floor who was very rude and aggressive. I noticed that this boy was a friend of my roommate. The boy was from New York. Sometimes, when I would go to the bathroom, he threw my towels away. I knew he had a problem. The two visited one another quite often, sharing a similar trait, both not having good manners, they had something in common. At the end of the year, I decided to invite them to dinner, and go out with them to a movie.
   This was to see what was wrong with them and understand their problems. I realized that the boy from New York had quite a harsh childhood. He came from a homeless family, living on the streets of New York. This was because his father was a hippy from the sixties and the seventies, who used to live on the streets of New York with his mother. When this boy was a child, he was always scared, living in a dangerous place in the streets of New York. He was very poor, and until today he does not feel secure, not even owning a car nor having any money. He attended the University on a scholarship.

5. I knew a beautiful girl who was nice and had very good manners. She had a personality like a princess. I knew that she likes certain kinds of foods from a certain restaurant. Every time I would go to that restaurant with my friends, I

bring her some of the food from that restaurant that she likes. When I bring the food to her, she waited for me outside the building, even on a rainy night ignoring the rain and cold. She was not like the other girls who waited in their rooms for food. I then became very curious to meet her parents. Also, when I met her parents, I was impressed. Her father was friendly and a nice person, he was a gentleman. At one time, he had a lot of money yet lost it, regardless, he continued to be a nice person. Her mother was a nice lady, very friendly. When I talked to them during dinner, I knew that their daughter had a very nice childhood. This is why she became such a nice girl, with good manners, like a princess.

6. When I was studying at the University of Southern California (USC), I was living in the dorms. I had many good roommates, however.

7. One of the most important classes of all time in my opinion is psychology class, more specifically psycho-analysis classes. This is about analyzing the personality of a person and to know why the person is a nice person, why he is rude, why he is a bad person, and why this person became a criminal. You always need psychology to deal with people, clients, partners, employees, and even your friends and all kinds of people. We do that by studying his childhood and the way that he was brought up. The most important thing is to gain information about the person by reading about him or asking him questions. It is exactly like when a teacher asks many questions in an exam. By asking questions, the teacher will know the abilities of the student and their level of understanding and knowledge. For example, if there are 30 questions in a math, physics, or history exam, then the professor will know about the student. But, in psychology we ask questions about the parents, childhood, and problems/ difficulties of the kid in his childhood. His history,

marginality (a person who grew up in a society that treats him different, he doesn't have things others have. Examples of these marginalities:

a. If all the boys are tall and he is short.
b. If he has no parents and all the other people have parents.
c. If his father died when he was young and everyone else has a father.
d. He is very poor and everyone around him is rich.
e. If everyone goes to school but he doesn't.
f. If he has an accent because of his ethnic and cultural background and no one around him does.
g. If a person is crippled and everyone else can run and play.
h. If someone is unattractive and blind but everyone else was born normally.
i. If he used to be mistreated and abused in his childhood where his parents used to beat him up every day.
j. If a boy is cross eyed, the people in his school will make fun of him because he is cross eyed. He has a small marginality as he is cross eyed while all the other students' eyes are okay. But, if he is half blind, then he has a big marginality. Then, more students will tease him and will be rude and mean to him so he will have a bigger marginality. Another example is if another boy in his childhood, his parents are divorced, that is a small marginality. But, if the mother is dead, and he has no mother, then that is a big marginality. If both of is parents are dead, that is a very big marginality. Usually, when a person has more marginalities and problems in his childhood, later in life, they become mean people, and not nice. The less marginalities and problems a person has in his childhood, the higher the chances of him being a nicer person.

7. Everyone in the world has one or two marginalities and a problem they were born with it or had it since their childhood some are much more serious than others. Sometimes it is good for a person to have one or two

marginalities in his childhood because it will give him the incentive to work hard and become successful.
However, sometimes when there are a lot of problems and marginalities with a person, it is more likely for them to turn out as a bad person and a criminal. Be careful because he might be a thief, will try to lie to you and cheat you and he's not a nice person and you cannot trust him and cannot be your close friend.

8. A lot of people think that everyone is acting like him or thinking like him. Everyone is different because they have different history, different parents, and a different childhood. They think that everyone will think like them or act like them. An honest person will think that everyone is honest. An educated person thinks that everyone is educated like him. If someone is interested in a specific thing, he will believe that everyone is interested in the same thing. In reality this is not the case, not everyone would be interested in what he likes. Sometimes a person thinks that he can convince another person easily without knowing the psycho analysis of the person and how the other person thinks.
Sometimes parents can't even convince their kids to behave and do certain things. For example, parents may tell their kids to play sports and not to play video games all day. If parents cannot convince their kids, how can you convince a random person to buy your products, invest in your business, be a partner, or loan you money.

9. Sometimes you will find students who grew up in a family where his family has a lot of education, and they encourage him to go to a really good school and amazing education. Or a poor person who is really struggling and wishes the best for his family and accepts the challenge of going to a big university with a lot of ambition. Someone will wonder why

the spoiled boy is spoken to differently who doesn't like the challenge or work and study hard – not committed to going to a good or strong university.

10. Unfortunately, bad people are everywhere. No matter how nice you are to them they will not appreciate you. If they work for you as employees, they will steal money from your company and you might end up with financial problems and bankruptcy. If they are your clients, they will not give you your money after you sell them products or sell them services. Even as friends, sooner or later you find they are not good friends. If you study the basic psychology, you will know why some people are not nice people.

11. I remember when I once had roommates living with me in university housing. I was living in student housing with three other students at the same apartment. My roommate a tall and big man from Colorado and I and in the next room, two guys from California. The two people from California were nerds who were busy with schoolwork all the time.
    I invited my roommate to lunch and kept asking indirect questions during lunch. He was a former football player who had a car accident and a bad childhood. Within an hour, I knew that he was a mean person and a bad person very aggressive. So, when I came back, I told the other guys sharing the other apartment with us that the big guy from Colorado is very mean and is not a nice person. They replied, "how can you judge a person within an hour, it is not fair to judge people so quickly". I told them this guy is a bad person and an evil person because I took many courses in psychology and I know how to judge people. They told me that it was my problem and I had to deal with it, they said that they did not want to interfere in my problems or his problems. He had a girlfriend that he used to bring to our apartment. He and his girlfriend used to watch on the TV

and watch what they liked. After a while, the other guys felt uncomfortable since they were not allowed to watch the TV shows that they like. A second problem is that after he ate, he never washed the dishes. The kitchen started to smell bad, so the other guy used to clean the dishes for him. The third problem was that the other guys did not have enough self-confidence when there was a girl around. They could not go to the bathroom and take a shower or feel comfortable. They would typically sleep shirtless and in shorts, but since there was a girl around, they did not feel comfortable wearing those types of clothes as they fear the girl may see them when they wake up. The fourth problem occurred when he started sleeping with his girlfriend. I shared a bunkbed with him, and while they were sleeping together, I was unsure whether or not we were in the middle of an earthquake. I was afraid and started to worry because the bed was shaking. It was only after, that I realized what had actually happened and was fed up with his disrespectful behavior. In the long run, our room stated to smell bad and was not allowing me to open the window for ventilation. Every time I tried to talk to him, he would tell me to shut up. The same thing would happen when the other two guys in the apartment would try to talk to him, he would tell them to shut up. Because he was bigger and taller than us, he felt like he was the boss of our apartment. Since I am a patient person and can put up with the pain and sufferings and can wait. I wanted the other guys to learn a lesson since I told them about him since the beginning and did not listen to me. The other guys started to call their parents every day. They then went to university housing to complain about this guy. Then, their life became miserable. The manager in USC housing was not able to enter the room for more than a minute because of the bad smell. The reason why I have to put up with my bad roommate and the bad smell in my room for 6 months. Because I had no choice since the university housing is much cheaper, I had to sacrifice because back then I didn't have enough money, I was on a budget. Also living far away from the university would be time consuming in driving for hours. When I told them from the first day that this guy was a bad person, they did not believe me. The reason I knew that he was a bad person because I studied psychology.

12. Psychology is very important in the world of trade and business, because, you have to know the mentality of the other person to tell him your ideas. You also have to know the mentality and psychology of them when dealing with them in business. I have seen so many people who are not honest, and cheap people, in the world of trade and business. So, when I tell people about them, they do not believe me. After five years, ten years, or sometimes even twenty years, they know that I am right. A lot of people who do not understand psychology make mistakes because when they see a bad person or a thief or a liar thinks that they can change him. They do not know that it is hard to change the person's personality. It is like changing an orange into an apple. If you see a spoiled boy who does not like to study a lot, one will ask why you do not study in Harvard or Stanford. They do not know that this boy grew up spoiled and did not put an effort to study will never think about going to a hard university and think about studying or working hard. If a boss sees one of his employees who lies to clients and tries telling him that lying is not good, he will not know that the employee was lying all his life. Also, if a boss sees that one of his employees is rude to clients and tries to tell him that it is not good to be rude to clients, does not know that this guy was rude to people all his life.

13. There is a story of a scorpion who wants to cross a river to

the other bank of the river. The scorpion asks the frog to carry him to the other bank of the river. The frog told the scorpion, "I'm willing to help you and carry you to the other side of the river, but I am afraid that you might sting me since you are a scorpion". The scorpion, replied by saying how am I going to sting someone who is helping me and doing me a favor. The frog asked the scorpion to promise not to sting him. The scorpion promised the frog not to sting him. The frog carried the scorpion to the other side of the river on his back. When they reached there, the scorpion stung the frog, the frog then said, why did you sting me, you promised me not to sting me. Then the scorpion replied, "I am a scorpion, this is by habit, and I cannot change my habit."

14. Some people who don't know psychology when they see a rich person they approach him to borrow little money from him and he refuses. They don't know that this person when he was young or in his childhood was very poor and he used to wash cars or work very hard for little money or had a bad job where he made only five dollars. So, if you ask him to lend you $100, it is still a big amount of money to him even if he is a billionaire. This is because he still remembers his bad childhood. He still remembers when he was insulted in his childhood during work, also he had to work had for little money. Most of rich people were born poor and this is why they are stingy and not generous.
15. Short stories in brief about two famous people in history: Joseph Stalin and Adolf Hitler.

First on **Joseph Stalin:**

1. He was born on December 18, 1878, in Georgia in the Caucasus, for this reason he speaks Russian with an accent.
2. His father was a cobbler so was fixing shoes for a living. His family was very poor since they used to work for food and

not for a salary. Two of his older brothers died.

3. His father, who to come home drunk, used to beat him every day at the age of 10. When people in his neighborhood used to see a kid crying, they knew this was Joseph. His skin was blue from the beatings.
4. He had an accident at the age of 6 when he was hit with a wagon. For that reason he had an injury in his left arm throughout his life which is why he wearing jackets in most of the photographs of him so that he can cover his arm.
5. When he was at the age of 5, he had smallpox decease. For the rest of his life, he had bad scarring on his face.
6. He was a short man in comparison to the majority of people in Russia.
7. His mother sent him to a church school which he did not like. He was then kicked out of school and never earned a degree.
8. He joined a secret group who are against the government so he was in jail many times.
9. The point here is that Joseph Stalin had a very bad life which is why he became a bad person.

Second on **Adolf Hitler:**

a. He was born on April 20, 1889, in Austria.
b. His father was illegitimate and he was a very mean person and was rude to him and his mother. Adolf Hitler did not like his father. His father used to beat him up and his mother.
c. His father used to work for the state customs service.
d. He lost his father when he was at the age of 14.
e. Hitler's mother was suffering from cancer so he was doing the cleaning and cooking in the house from a young age.
f. Later on, while he was still young, his mother died.
g. Soon after, he used to shovel snow and carry luggage at train stations.
h. Hitler did not finish his high school. His dream in life was to be a painter but he wasn't accepted into art school.
i. Sometimes on Sunday, he used to stand in line at the church

just so he could get a piece of bread and soup to eat.

j. Adolf was very short in comparison to the majority of men in Germany.
k. He tried to go find a job in Vienna but was not able to find a job.
l. Hitler joined the army just to find a place to stay and food to eat.
m. During World War I he was injured and it was a shock for him that
Germany lost the war.
n. The point here is that because Adolf Hitler had a very bad childhood, and a lot of marginalities, this is why he became a bad person.

My Advice

1. Be careful when you meet someone that had a very bad childhood or had a lot of marginalities. If they work for you, they might steal from you. Also, do not try to select people who had a bad childhood or have a lot of marginalities as friends.

2. Sometimes there are some people who are jealous of you, and do not like you. No matter how nice you are to them, they will never like you because they are bad people. Do not worry about such people because there are very few people like this.

Understanding People

You must understand people in order to sell them products and services.
There are gaps and because of these gaps between people, people don't understand each other and the communication and understanding between people will be very bad.
The Gaps Are:

1. Gender gap – men do not understand women because the mentality of men is different than the mentality of women. This is why there is a high divorce rate and there are always misunderstandings and fighting between men and women. An example of that: I know somebody who invited some girls for dinner at valentine's day to leave at 7 o'clock to dinner. The nice girl was late and he got very mad at her and he doesn't know why she's late. She was late for more than an hour. He told her he would leave without her. Then, he asked what's wrong and she said she changed her dress many times. From a white dress, then a green dress, then a red dress. Finally, she chose the black dress. . changing her mind what to wear numerous times. All this while the man is waiting and begins to get frustrated – not understanding that a woman cares about how she dresses and looks. The guy laughed at her because guys don't think that way- they don't keep changing their clothes. They are supposed to be there at 7, however, it will take longer for the girl to get ready because the girl's mentality is different than a man's mentality. Most men have a completely different mentality than women. This is why there is such a high divorce rate and why relationships between a boy and his girlfriend do not last that long.

2. Status gap- Rich people think differently than poorer and less fortunate people. This is because rich people think of prestige image and reputation, and what people think of them and try to impress people, for instance, driving luxurious cars or living in a big house in a nice neighborhood or going to eat in a famous restaurants, staying in 5 star hotels. While the poor people are thinking of their daily expenses, simple things, and how to survive. There is quite a difference of perspective and a gap between the rich and the poor in this aspect. Rich people always think of prestige image and how

others talk about them showing off in a sense. While poor people are thinking of the basic things like food, transportation, and paying their rent.

A. I once invited a poor person to a nice restaurant because he was nice to me for many years. During dinner, I asked if he liked the food. He replied "It is very expensive" I repeated the question 3 times "Did you like the food?" He kept responding with "It is very expensive". He made me very mad because I just wanted to know if he likes that kind of food or not. However, his mentality is different than mine. He did not answer my question - whether the food was good or not. I was thinking that if he does not like the taste of the food, we will go somewhere else. He kept answering that the food is very expensive. He finally told me that the food is good. The communication with him was so bad, he didn't understand me and I didn't understand him.

B. There is another story, during one of my trips, I met an educated
person but he was a poor person, and I used to talk to him about many different subjects every time I saw him –
I enjoyed talking with him. I once invited him to dinner; to a nice and big restaurant. I ordered good dishes for him. Instead of talking to me, he kept talking about wasting food, and wasting my money. All night, he kept talking about the same subject. To me, that night was a boring night, the reason why was because this boring person is not used to going to nice restaurants with good food and many different dishes. I was trying to be nice to him and wanted to enjoy the meal with me, however, he has a different mentality and was only thinking about money and wasting money.

C. A person with good manners who was raised in a good

respected family will not understand a rude person who don't have manners and was raised in a family where everybody is shouting at each other without respect.

D. Little money is not important to rich people, so sometimes rich people don't know that little money is very important for poor people, for example. If a rich person promise a poor that he will give him a little money for his work or lend him a little money the poor person will be waiting for the money for days and weeks and trying to be patient while the rich person did not care or forgot about it or the rich person will go on a vacation and delaying the payment until he come back from his vacation, this behavior will make the poor person hates the rich person who does not have a feeling for him and his suffering.

3. Cultural gap – people who grew up in different countries with different values and different cultures they do not understand the people in other countries when they travel for work or leisure due to a cultural gap. There may be misunderstanding. Because, that person from a different country is used to the norms in his own country. People from different countries and different cultures have different values, different mentalities, and different habits. Sometimes the things you think are important are not important to them. And the things you think are small, they think they are a big deal.

a. I remember during the 1970s at USC, there was a coed international dorm for students. They keep one student from one country to live with an American student and sometimes there would be misunderstandings between them. Once, there was an American girl living with a Japanese girl in the dorm and there were always bickering over small things.
At one time, the American girl hit the Japanese girl in the knees and said that it was revenge for pearl harbor.

b. It is always important to know the basics of everything, if you do not understand the basics of a culture for instance, you will not be able to understand a joke. For example, I once spoke to a Russian girl who traveled to the United States on vacation. I asked her what her impression was of the United States, she said that the people there are very nice and friendly, but they do not understand our jokes.

4. Generation gap it is the difference between the way a father and his son think. Sometimes, you will see misunderstanding between a boy and his father, because the father is thinking exactly as how people used to think 50 years ago.

5. Education gap educated people don't understand non educated people. Communication and understanding are hindrances due to these educational gaps.

Education Gap and Non-Educated People

1. Everybody thinks that other people are like them. A nice person will think that other people are nice and an honest person will think that others are honest. A rich person thinks that others are rich and a poor person thinks that others are poor. For this reason, I wanted to mention that an educated person thinks that a non-education person thinks like him or understands things like him. The majority of people in the world are not educated as only 7% of the world population have a university degree. In this case, you have to deal with them.

2. Since this chapter is about dealing with people, I wanted to mention the education gap and how non-educated people think and how their mentality is like. On the case of your

business, some of your clients are not educated, or you might end up working with some people who are not educated, or having a partner that is not educated. Or some employees in your company that is not educated like drivers or even a maid in your house. Because, non-educated people are everywhere.
Especially that only 7% of the world population have a university degree. The point here is that non educated people are the majority of people in the world and you have to deal with them.

3. Since the gaps which are mentioned above like gender gap, cultural gap, status gap are known to most of the people, I just want to explain more about the education gap because I noticed that many people don't think it is very important.

4. The point here is don't get mad at them and don't laugh at them because they aren't as privileged with education. They are just like kids who don't understand a lot of things. Be patient; to explain things to them and be patient because they don't understand things the way you do. The pressure of poverty and bad circumstances make those people not educated and narrow minded.

5. Even if you try to explain things related to geography and the climate of the world, he will not understand you, because he does not know the basic things about the sun and the solar system. I remember I once travelled to Greece with one of my friends. I saw a man on a donkey, I wanted to take a picture of me riding a donkey, so I offered this uneducated person some money, he refused. I offered him more and more money and he kept refusing. I offered 10 Dollars at first, he refused, then 20 Dollars and he refused, finally I offered him 30 Dollars and he got mad at me. He thought I wanted to buy his donkey. A non-educated person has a different mentality.

If you tell him A, he will think that you are telling him B. If you tell him C, he will think you are telling him D. This man got mad at me and thought I wanted to buy the donkey. The problem is that it is hard to argue with a non-educated person because of his different mentality.

6. Many things in life happen that you don't have a choice of. Sometimes you have to borrow money from a non educated person. It is always good to know how they are thinking and their mentality. Some of my friends in the University of Southern California's business school wanted to make a small business and were borrowing money from the students, around 70-100$ each. They ended up borrowing 5000$ from a gardener from South-America who lives close to their apartment.

a. The mentality of a non-educated person is different. He looks at things in a different way than you do.
b. His imagination is different.
c. His thinking is different.
d. His hobbies are different.
e. He evaluates things in a different way.
f. He thinks money is everything and doesn't know the importance of education. He always chooses friends who are not educated like him because he understands them and feels comfortable with them.
   A proverb says "birds of a feather flock together".

7. He doesn't know the difference between an educated person and a non-educated person, because, he doesn't know chemistry, physics, geology, history, geography, or sociology and cannot ask questions in such subjects, so he cannot ask people. So, for this reason, all people look the same to him, so he will not know how to choose the right people for his company.

8. Maybe he can see the difference in people by looking at their clothes or the cars that they are driving.

9. He does not like knowledge. He will run away when people start talking about knowledge and is not interested in knowledge.
   You cannot explain to them things in business, economics, psychology, sociology, communication, political science, international relations, and many other things. Their mentality is different, they will not understand you and will argue with you in a different way.

10. Sometimes, he will receive basic knowledge late in his life and will be talking about it like it is a new thing not knowing that we already knew this when we were in middle or high school.

11. He does not know the importance of the sun or solar system. He does not know that the sun is behind the rain, evaporation, snow, wind, and rivers. He thinks the sun is only for tanning and to get vitamin D. He doesn't know that it is the sun that generates the wind, rain, seasons, and all life on earth.

12. A lot of them are shallow and like to imitate people without thinking. If they see that a pilot started a training school, he might open a training school as well. He doesn't know that the pilot has a lot of experience in flying and knows every little thing about flying schools. The same thing, he might see a doctor open a hospital, he might imitate him and open a hospital too. He would open a hospital without thinking. Without knowing the details or secrets of medical business. He doesn't know that every profession has a lot of hidden

secrets.

13. He does not know the importance of things. If you ask him why the sun is important, he will tell you that the sun is only important for a sun tan or getting vitamin D. If you tell someone who wants to go to Norway or Sweden, he will not understand you. If you explain that the weather is cold because it is country to the north pole, he doesn't know that the north pole is very cold. If you tell him that the weather in high mountains or high altitude is cold, he will not understand. If you tell him that in all deserts of the world, the weather is cold at night, and hot in daytime, he will not understand. If you explain the history of the Roman empire to him, he will not understand. When you try to talk to him about the economy, that next year it will be bad for specific reasons, he will not fully understand. When it comes to science, it is much worse. It becomes very difficult for him to understand as he has no background at all.

14. One time, a non educated person tried to go to mount Everest in Nepal. He noticed that it is so hard to get oxygen at the top of high mountains. He doesn't know that I learned this at school when I was 12 years old.

15. I remember I was once in Bahrain airport in the Middle East, I saw some workers from an Asian country who were not educated rushing to the gate of the departure that lead to the airplane, after the announcement for the flight.
Suddenly, all the non educated workers rushed all together at the same time, pushing each other, causing a big problem like a bottlenecking at the gate. They were pushing each other very aggressively and they were trying to get there first. The people working on the plane wanted the workers to make a line so they get into the airplane smoothly and easily so they can pick up their boarding pass from each

passenger. The security working at the airport and the people on the plane were trying to tell them not to worry and that all the workers will find their seat. The non-educated workers believe that if they do not board quickly, the plane will leave them and they won't find a seat. They do not know that the seats have numbers and that the plane won't fly if there is even a single passenger missing.

16. There was once a non-educated person who wanted to travel from London's Heathrow airport but he does not speak English. So, he told the young lady who works at the counter for the airlines to inform him of the boarding time, because he cannot read the boarding times on the display. So, he ended up spending three days sleeping on the chair in the airport because the lady forgot to tell him of his flight. The bottom line here, is that if you deal with anyone who is not educated, you have to understand his level of education. Because everyone has a different level of education, a person who finished third grade is different than a person who finished sixth grade, and a person who finished ninth grade is different than a person who finished twelfth grade.

17. I remember I once met a man who finished 9th grade and asked why he didn't finish high school and go to university. He replied, he doesn't think going to university is very important because he thinks that it is a waste of time to learn a subject like mathematics. He doesn't know that mathematics, or math, is the key for all sciences and knowledge of our world today. This is due to the simple fact that no data can be drafted without mathematics. No industries or discoveries can happen without mathematics. There will be no internet, computers, or cellphones without mathematics. There will be no space discovery without mathematics. There would be no medical manufacturers without mathematics. There will be no bridges

or roads without mathematics.
This means that there will be no cars on highways or in cities without mathematics. All that we see around us petrochemical plants for instance are all based on mathematics. Wherever you look; cars, ships, airplanes, etc. are all based on mathematics. All modern things that we see in today's life are all based on mathematics. Even liquid bottles Coca Cola, Water, different juices, are all based on it. He does not know the importance of math. He doesn't know that all the car manufactures, TV manufactures, medical manufactures, are run by mathematicians and based on mathematics.

18. A non-educated person cannot explain things because he is not used to writing a report and is not used to writing an exam. A student puts more effort and more thorough answers in his examinations in order to get a better grade. Many times, when you ask a non-educated person a question, he doesn't know how to explain things and how to give you a full answer. I remember I once asked someone from an Asian country about the people in his neighboring country. He said that they were people not knowing how to explain.
I wanted to know how they acted and behaved, but the person did not know what to say. I once asked a taxi driver from an Asian country about a famous king in their country's history. He said that he was watching a series on television about him. I asked the driver to explain about the series but he told me it is a long story. I asked him to tell me anything about it, yet he was not able to explain.
19. He doesn't know the importance of education. He looks at things from his own point of view and his own perspective. He doesn't like knowledge and is not interested. He does not like introductions to things because he is not used to introductions and classrooms, and introductions in classrooms. So, when you open a topic about

something, he will interrupt you and will argue with you in the introduction because he is not used to classrooms telling you to get to the point. Once you get to the point, he will not understand you because he does not have the background of the subject.

20. He cannot accept new ideas about business or anything. Also, It is very hard to convince him in business or many other things. I once met a person from the middle east. He told me that he has been to Germany. So, when I told him that I spoke German, he was so surprised, because he said that he was in the hospital for sixth months and was trying to learn the German language but was not able to. I laughed. This person was not educated and did not know the basics to learn a language. It was obvious that this man did not go to school or university, so he did not study languages before, and he does not know how to study any language, and doesn't know that to study a language, he has to study the basic words and nouns. Once you know the basics, everything will be easy.

21. When you tell him something he is so shallow and not deep. For example, if there is a big business party for big business people and that day you did not meet the right people or make a business deal, he might think that you are sad or depressed because you did not like the cake or the food in the party.

22. He has no vision in a lot of things. Even if you explain something like salaries, bonuses, he does not think with 360 degrees, it will be hard for him to understand. Even if you see somebody who finished the 9th grade and you tell the non educated people that this person is not an educated person, he will say no, he is a very educated person because everything is relative. It is like a five year old boy who thinks that his 11 year old brother is a big boy.

23. If you have a non-educated driver, he will interrupt you while you are reading in the car as he is not experienced with such things like reading. He thinks money is everything, he does not know the importance of education.

24. Socially, they have different hobbies and different interests.

25. Because they do not understand many things, they think that everyone is like them, they ask stupid questions and do not know that the question is very stupid. It reminded me of the movie, born
yesterday by Melanie Grifith. The bottom line is that you should not get mad at people who are not educated because for certain reasons, they did not get the chance to go to school like you do.

26. A lot of times, when you explain things to them about education and knowledge and Science, they will ask you how you knew about such things. Because the non educated person does not know a lot of things and thinks you are like him.

27. If you tell him you learned communication and body language at college and you can understand the intention of the person or if the person is lying to you from his eye contact and his body language he will not believe you or he might think that you use black magic. Also, if you tell him you learned psychology and you can do psychoanalysis of people he will tell you okay do psychoanalysis for that person who is walking in the street. He does not know that in order to do psychoanalysis, we need some information about the history of the person and his childhood and some information about his parents.
28. If you argue with a non-educated person for ten minutes,

you will discover that he is not educated. It is not wise to argue with them in front of people because they will think that you are insulting them and start shouting at you, saying bad things about your shoes, clothes and face or even about your family your father and your mother. He does not know how to choose his employees if he starts a business possibly putting the wrong employee in the wrong place. He cannot see the difference between educated people and non-educated people.

29. It is so easy to find out whether or not a person is educated. Because, when you ask them questions, they do not know how to answer even the most basic questions. When they do end up answering, their answers may be wrong. The way they talk is a bit off as well where you can tell if they are educated or not.

30. It is so easy to tell when a French person speaks English that he has a French accent. At the same time, it is easy to notice if a person is not educated. If he looks like a duck, walks like a duck, talks like a duck, then he is a duck.

31. A non-educated person has a lot of free time and does not know how to use his time. He might watch TV his mind is empty. This is how he notices things and remember things he doesn't have much on his mind. He doesn't have a goal or target in his life. He has simple ambitions. He doesn't have a goal for higher education or to attain a PhD or to travel to another country to study or write a book. He doesn't have goals in life.

32. He is not interested in education or knowledge. If he is sitting with a group of people and if they say the highest mountain in the world is mount Everest or the second highest mountain in the world is k2 in Pakistan, he will not be interested to know this because he doesn't like education. He

will think this is a boring subject. If this is the case, then he will talk to the person next to him in his group about a different subject, or he will call one of his friends.

33. Even if you keep giving him many lectures and information about many things for many years in history, sociology, geology, etc, and one day you ask him did you learn something from me he will reply, no I did not learn anything from you because he does not appreciate knowledge and education.

34. The educated person's mind is focused on thoughts, ideas, and theories while non educated people will focus on talking about people or to wear nice shoes and clothes. Sometimes, the educated person will forget to wear nice shoes and nice clothes because he is thinking about something more important. For example, in the story of Archimedes the great scientist who lived in Syracuse on the island of Sicily in the 3rd century was asked by the king to find out if the crown given to him by a goldsmith was pure gold or not. The king threatened Archimedes to solve the problem so Archimedes was thinking about it all the time. One day, when Archimedes was in the bathtub naked, he realized that the water displaced by his body was equal to the weight of his body. His discovery made Archimedes running in the streets naked and shouting "eureka! eureka!" which means "I have it! I have it!" in Greek. He went to the king and informed him that the crown was not pure gold. Archimedes discovered the principle of buoyancy. Because of that, we know how ships can float in the sea. His discovery was helpful to all people throughout history and until today. He had important things on his mind that made him forget that he was running down the streets naked without clothes.

35. The educated CEO or the educated general manager for

example, will come to work wearing a suit without a tie because he forgot the tie because he was thinking about meeting with the bank manager that morning. Because in the meeting, he will be discussing $200 million dollar loans for his company. Because he was wondering how to convince the manager and his team from the bank, he did not remember his tie. While the non-educated driver noticed that his boss did not wear a tie that day because the driver doesn't have many things on his mind. The problem here is that the driver thinks that his boss is stupid because his boss forgot to wear his tie. He doesn't know his boss has bigger things on his mind that day.

36. I remember once a non-educated person told me he's going to Paris, France. He wanted me to write him the most important words that are used every day in France. I wasted thirty minutes of my time. He went to France for a few weeks. When he came back from his trip, I asked him if the French words I wrote for him were useful. He answered "no" because he lost the piece of paper with the French words. I was surprised because to me, when I learn new words in any language, I write it down on a piece of paper and put it in my wallet with my money. To me, knowledge and education are as important as money. After that, I transfer the words into a special notebook for that language.

37. I remember at one time I told a non-educated businessman that I was planning to make a short movie. He asked me, with a big surprise on his face, "where can you bring actors for your movies?" He didn't know that in Los Angeles, there are a lot of agencies that represent actors and actresses with their pictures and experiences who are ready to act in movies. This is just an example of non-educated people asking silly questions.

38. One time, there was a non-educated manager who was promoted into the managerial role because he knew how to deal with people and his boss. However, when he tried to give a speech, while all people were waiting for him, he started to tremble and blush. Panicked and embarrassed in front of all the people, he wasn't able to finish his speech. The problem is that this person didn't know that there are courses of speech communication that he can take to give speeches.

39. He is thinking is only about material things and money and how to save money. His ultimate goal is to have a house, a car, and get married.

40. He liked to imitate people without thinking. For example, if he saw a doctor making money from building a hospital, he will build a hospital, he doesn't know that the doctor knows a lot of the important things about hospital business. Then, he will lose money. Or, if he notices that someone opens a private school or private university then he will imitate him without thinking and lose money.

41. A lot of times when you try to explain certain things to him, he will not understand you because he does not have the same background. Even if you repeat what you said, he will not understand you. They say, hearing is not listening. Educated people make a mistake when they meet an uneducated person, solely due to the fact that they wear the same clothes as them, or drive a nice car like them. So, even if you repeat things to your client many times, he will not understand you. He does not have the background or the basic knowledge to understand you even if you repeat it many times to him. Just imagine if you take a non-educated person to chemistry class or physics class at any university,

he will not understand what the professor is talking about. The same thing can be said about a non-educated person about a business. For example, oil and gas business, solar energy business, he will not understand you. Because he doesn't know physics, and chemistry.

42. Everything will surprise him. I remember on one of my trips to Asia, the taxi driver wanted to show me that there is water that comes out of the ground onto the surface. I told him that this water must be very hot. He was surprised and asked how I knew. To me, it was very simple since I learned it in my geology classes the deeper you go into the Earth and towards the core of the Earth, the hotter it will get and the temperature will be very high. This is why volcanoes bring out hot rocks and lava. Another person who is not educated told me he was surprised when he noticed there was a freshwater lagoon on an island surrounded by seawater. He doesn't know that there is a break or fault in the Earth formation under the island and that formation has fresh water. To me, those things are so simple because I learned it in my geology classes but to them, it is so surprising. The same thing if you talk to non-educated people about business or the economy; they will not understand you easily.

43. It is very easy to tell whether or not a person is educated, because, he is not interested to receive any information nor knowledge. He will either run away from the topic or subject, or he will ask you to change the topic. You can also tell by looking at his eyes or body language, that he is not interested to listen. Even if you give him a book to read, he will not read it. Even if he accompanies you to a seminar or a lecture, he will concentrate on the lecturers shoes, face, watch, or pants instead of listening to him.

44. Since he is not used to classrooms or university, he is not a

good listener he does not know that there is an introduction to the subject, so he will interrupt you and will not wait until you get to the point. He does not know that the professor will spend hours or days on the introduction before getting to the subject. If you try to tell him about the subject right away without himknowing the background since he asked you to skip over, he will not understand you.

45. For example, if you try to explain history, WW2 for instance, he will not know the background, and will not know the history about WW1 and the basic history of Europe so he will not understand you fully when you talk about WW2.

46. He doesn't know the importance of education. Even if he sends his son to school, he is just sending his son to school to find a job, since he believes that money is everything. I remember I once traveled to the Maldives in 1985, there I was talking to a waiter because whenever I travel, I like to talk to the people in order to know about the culture of the country. He was working as a waiter when I asked him about his dream in life. He told me that his dream in life was to be a cook.

47. He thinks that an educated person is stupid because he realized that an educated person cannot remember nor notice things. For example, since an educated person has many things in his mind, he may not remember little things nor notice little things.

48. My driver is a good driver. He believes he is the best driver in the world. He never gets speeding tickets nor fines, but he does not know that Mercedes cars are made in Germany, nor that Toyota is made in Japan, Ford is made in the United States.

49. He does not have a vision at all. He never read history books and does not have the background. He is shallow, not deep, he analyzes things in a different way. He has no plan for his life. He cannot even enjoy life. For example if he travel on an airline he will not read books on the airplane he will think traveling is boring, so if he travels to a country where they have museums he will never try to visit the museums, if I go to a city where there are a lot of theaters he will never try to go to a theater, if he visit a country where there are a lot of snow and high mountains he will never try to go snow skiing, even if he stayed in a five star hotel he will never try to go to the gym or the swimming pool in the hotel.

50. He drives cars and travel on airplanes and does not know who is Isaac Newton, and does not know Newtons law of motion. Meanwhile I learned of him in my physics class.

51. Some of the non educated people they travel to London they walk around Piccadilly in the city center of London where there are a lot of theaters and don't know Shakespeare who wrote Hamlet and Romeo and Juliet.

52. He writes numbers and does not know that they are the Arabic numerals and zero discovered by indians.

53. If you ask him to write one page of any topic of his choosing, he will not be able to write that one page. Or if you ask him to write one page so he will not forget it, he does not know how to write one page because he is not used to do so. Even if you try to tell him and help him write it, he may lose that page one day.

54. He is shallow, and just likes to imitate people not knowing the background of things. I remember there was a lifeguard in the swimming pool from one of the Asian countries he was

very impressed when he saw me talking in different languages to the tourists of other nationalities. He said that he wanted to be like me, speaking in many different languages. I told him that it is not that easy, spending 14 years in college that cost me a lot of money. I also took a memory course where I learned to memorize things, and I knew that practicing the language is very important. Since I am an educated person, I can talk to anyone in a different language about a topic he or she likes such as economics, cinema, history, and many others. He does not realize that he needs education to talk to these people about the subjects they like, such as history economics sociology etc. Without education, people would find you boring and not talk to you. Learning a language requires practice, and usually,educated people do not get along with those who are not educated. The bottom line here is that a non educated person likes to imitate other people and this person wanted to imitate me to speak languages, he does not know that there is something beyond that. If they see that a doctor is making money by owning a hospital, they would also build a hospital to try and make money.

55. The non-educated person does not know how to do research because he did not do it in university. I remember I once had to write about the French emperor Napoleon Bonaparte for my political science class.
I had to read and go through countless books, around twenty books.

56. A non-educated person is exactly like that – having zero awareness towards his surroundings and cannot understand why certain things happen.
57. He doesn't know if the economy is going to be bad or worse next year or why the economy is going to be better next year. And he does not know what the media is talking about

global warming and carbon emission is or what the problem of fossil fuels.

58. Finally, I wanted to mention something important, that there are a lot of people around the world who bought their degrees or certificates and diplomas, or were cheating it at college and do not consider them as educated people, or they went to very small colleges with very low standards. Those people remind me of actors in movies. Sometimes, you see an actor who plays a white robe and uses the same gadgets doctors use in their clinics, however, he is not a doctor, he is an actor. If you asked him specific things about medicine, he will not know how to answer. The same thing would occur if he was playing an engineer or architect- he would not be able to answer. This is why I do not consider those who bought their college degrees, or were cheating during their exams as educated. As it is very easy to tell that they are not educated.

59. Once you ask them a simple question about the subjects that they studied, they do not know how to answer your questions.

60. You can tell that they are not interested in knowledge nor learning. Once you speak to them in a subject such as science, physics, chemistry, geology or economy, psychology, political science, communication, international relation, sociology, business, accounting, and many things, they will run away. Or they will ask you why you talk about something we don't understand. Even though for me it is something simple or normal because I always talk about these subjects with my educated friends.

61. He has a simple way of thinking and has a different mentality, like the non-educated people. For example if you tell a non educated person that the area of Brazil is greater

than the area of Mexico he will tell you how do you know, did you measure it with a ruler or rope. The same thing if you tell a non educated person that the distance between the earth an the moon is about 239,000 miles he will say did you fly to the moon and measure it with a rope. Also he cannot explain things like the educated people, a non educated person when he talk he talks out of continuity like saying 3,1,5,4,2 he will jump from one subject to another while the educated person his thoughts are in sequence 1,2,3,4,5. He will explain things like a school teacher, he will start with an introduction.

62. The minute you start arguing with him, within 5 or 10 minutes, you will find that he is a non-educated person.

63. It is so easy for me to tell if a person is educated or not. It is just like a French person speaking English and people can tell that he is speaking in a French accent, or does not have a wide vocabulary in the English language. So, those people who bought their degrees and are cheating are just fooling themselves because it is so easy for people to notice that they are not educated because they do not know much like the non-educated people. We don't look at the size or prestige of their degrees, but the level of knowledge and education the information in their mind. If we were to ask these people simple questions, they will not be able to answer. When you try to argue with them for 10 minutes, you will easily discover that they are not educated people by the way in which they argue. You will discover his mentality, and realize that his mentality is just as a non-educated person. The mentality of educated is completely different from non educated people as I mentioned earlier in this chapter. These types of people that cheat and bought their degrees are just like actors in a film. Just like when they wear surgical coats in a scene in the ER, they are just playing a role they are actors.

64. I also wished to mention that only knowing half of anything is dangerous. An example of that can be seen with the person

who had only finished 9th grade and said that mathematics is not important. Just imagine if kids listen to him and believe that mathematics is notimportant listening to his advice and not going to university and college.

65. Uneducated people have a different mentality and different way of thinking, they interpret and translate things in a different way for example A means B, C means D so you may reach a point where you cannot get along with them and cannot deal with them as clients, partners, or even employees who work for you. So, the communication and understanding them will be very hard, this is called education gap.

66. The non educated people think the educated person is stupid or crazy because they cannot accept his idea, uneducated people have different mentality and different way of thinking. So you may reach a point where you cannot get along with clients, partners because of education. For example in Italy during the 17th century an Italian astronomer, physicist, and engineer named Galileo who said earth was rotating daily and revolving around the sun. He was met with opposition from the catholic church. He spent the rest of his life under house arrest.

67. Most non educated people are shallow and not deep. For example, if an educated person talked to an important person nicely and gave that person a compliment and told him he knew his boss when he was a student at Stanford university, who also told him he has shares in Walt Disney. The non-educated person will try to imitate that person by giving compliments but will never mention about knowing the boss and Stanford university. The non educated person forgetting to mention the boss in a conversation when giving someone a compliment. Also forgetting the shares. The point here is that the educated person will use different

terms to convince the person also by mentioning that he is very rich and owns shares in Walt Disney. But the non educated person cannot see these things, because he's a shallow person. He does not know Stanford University and he does not know Walt Disney. Like inserting gold and money into a fruit basket, for example if he give somebody a fruit basket as a gift. The educated person will insert certain important words in his conversation the non educated person will not understand.

68. It is like giving the important person a fruit basket and inserting gold and money inside the fruit basket, while the non educated person will try to imitate the educated person by giving that important person a fruit basket only without gold and money because he cannot see the gold and the money in the other persons gift.

69. Another example is that if a non-educated person met some important people and became their friends by giving them compliments, he will try to meet those people and give them compliments. He did know that the educated person was giving them compliment but at the same time, he was talking to them about subjects they like to talk about. And most of the educated people have in common or the good old days at college. This is something the non-educated people would not realize because they are shallow.

70. So the same thing when it comes to business if the educated person build a hospital because he is a doctor and knows how to choose the right people for the hospital. The non-educated person might build a hospital, but he will not know how to choose the right people for it and not know how to run it and will have bad management.

71. The non educated person is like a kid. Maybe he's taller than you, or bigger than you, but there are many things he does not understand. He does not know the difference between big famous universities and small universities. Also he does not know that studying engineering is harder to study than economics. He doesn't understand things like you do so do not get mad at him when he makes mistakes. Even if you try to explain things to him, sometimes, he will not understand you because he just has a different mentality so try to explain things to him in a very simple way.

72. A non-educated person will say education is not important because he does not feel it, he does not understand the importance of education. He will say that for business you don't need education which is wrong. He will say that Mr X has no education but he has more money than Mr Y who has the education. He just respect people with money and power.

73. Unfortunately in life, many people need partners or some other help when they start a business because they require money. This is why some people have non educated partners as they might need money. Also, non-educated people sometimes have connections and know some people or they can help you with information. For example, if you wanted to meet a key person to your business, this non educated person may have seen him somewhere, in a golf course or a cafeteria. They can give you some news such as a car accident in the freeway so you avoid driving on that street. He may give you some important information. Some non educated people are street smart, they know how to act and behave and notice a lot of things like kids. I remember in YMCA in the summer camp, I was an instructor for young kids. One of the kids realized that I was wearing a blue sock on one foot and a green sock on the other foot.

74. Non-educated people can remember things. He can remember that last week, the waiter in the restaurant was wearing different shoes with different colors. He will notice how a person sits, how a person walks, talks, what a person wears, if he has a small or big office, a big wallet or a small wallet, a lot of money in his wallet, because he is impressed by certain things. Also, if you have non-educated people in your company or manufacturer or a big farm with many farmers working on it – a lot of workers and drivers and you wanted to meet your non educated employees, you have to know what they like.

A successful businessman needs to be popular by his own employees and know what they like and what to talk about. The businessman needs to talk to his employees and be friendly with them. Some of the things they like are talking about people. They know Mr. John has a beautiful wife, or Mr. John divorced his wife, or Mr. John got promoted, got a new car, got a new house, etc.. They like to talk about people. They also like to talk about religion even most of them don't know much about religion. Or they talk about politics but they do not know much about political science or international relations. Some of them like to talk about sports and like to talk about certain sports. They talk about philosophy and of course, they love money and they love to talk about money because to them, money is everything.

Chapter 16
Generosity

1. People and companies always like to deal with someone who is generous. They do not like to deal with someone who is stingy and tough. Also, no one likes to serve a stingy person. When a manager is dealing with people and generous in payment, he will be loved by people, clients, and his employees. However, if a manager is tough and stingy, it will result in disaster. I am not talking about bribery; I am talking about generosity because I have come to realize that a lot of people are not generous. By doing that, they are missing a lot of opportunities.
   Today, there are a lot of people in the world who are losing millions every day, because they are not generous.
   In the beginning when you start your business, you must save money and be stingy but when the business starts to pick up, you can be generous with everything.

2. When I go to restaurants in California or in any restaurant in the world, I always give tips to the waiters. I also pay tips to the people in hotels. At the same time, I get good services in return for it. Because people love those who are generous, and not stingy people. People in restaurants and hotels, like to serve a generous person, not a stingy person. I always believe that you have to appreciate people and their services. Even with good words. By saying thank you. There are some people, who do not even like to say a good word or thank you to someone who serves them.

3. When I was living on campus in USC, we were four students sharing the same apartment with two bedrooms. Two students were from California, and one student was from

south America. We decided that one of us should clean the toilet once a week. We agreed on it, so I cleaned the toilet and so did the other two students from California.
The problem arose when it came to the student from South America. The student from South America is a nice person and friendly, and I always practice Spanish with him. The problem was that he refused to clean the toilet once a week. He said that for his entire life he had listened to the instructions of his older brothers and sisters, and thought that when he went to university, it would be a relief on him and no one will tell him what to do – he wanted to be like a free man. He decided not to clean the bathroom. The other two students from California were very upset and did not want the South American to live in the same room as them. I came up with an idea. I was afraid of getting a new roommate since I thought he might be a bad roommate. My idea was getting a maid once a week and paying her 20 dollars. By doing this, I solved the problem, and everyone was happy.

4. In some companies, after someone retires after many years, management has a farewell party for their employee. Unfortunately, this is not the case for all companies, and do not give them a thanking letter. This behavior makes the employee who served the company for many years feel bad inside. So, when I said generous, I did not mean to bribe people, I meant to appreciate what people are doing for you. Sometimes I realized that people who serve you and offer to help you, even friends who help you with something, are just waiting for a word of gratitude and appreciation, a simple thank you, yet many people do not tell them this and are disrespectful.

5. There was a restaurant that was delivering good food. There was a client who lives far from the restaurant. The driver asked his boss, why waste time and gas for someone who

lives far away, and it does not cover the cost of delivery for gas for the car. The boss, who has a lot of experience in business said that all will be fine. In a few months, the client hosted a big party in his house and ordered a lot of food from the same restaurant. Then, the owner of the big restaurant made a lot of money. He then questioned the driver, "you see what I meant? We will cover our costs". This was all because the owner of the restaurant was flexible and generous with the client. It is always good to be generous to your clients, by giving them discounts if you can. For example, if they buy three t-shirts from you, you give the fourth t-shirt for free. If they buy a car from you, you fill up their gas for free. At the same time, if you have a restaurant and buy extra food from you, you get them extra desert or cakes for free. At the same time, you also become generous with words, saying things such as, "we appreciate having made business with you, thank you."If you have a big construction company and are building a hotel for instance, and sub contracting companies to build the doors for the hotel, or building swimming pools for the hotel, try not to squeeze them, and not letting them make money, do not be stingy. Do not delay paying them their money.

Because the same way you like receiving your money quickly on time, so do they, they like to receive their money on time, because they need the money the same way you do.

6. In one of the Asian country's there was a rich man who went to the nightclubs Every night he got drunk along with a lot of girls.

At one time he wrote a check to one of the girls at the nightclub the check was for small amount of money approximately 1000 dollars but since he was drunk he made a mistake in writing the check where the numbers of the amount doesn't match the words so the next day the girl took the check to the bank but the check bounced and the bank refused to cash the check for her.

So that night that girl went to the same rich man at the nightclub and throw the check in front of everybody at the nightclub, insulting him and saying that the bank rejected his check because he had no money in his bank account.
This rich man became vary mad and he called the CEO of the bank immediately and he woke him up at 12 mid-night and he told the CEO that he will close his bank account and he will transfer the all of his money and millions to a different bank. Then the CEO of the bank immediately called the bank branch manager and told him to open the bank at 12 mid-night and bring the amount of approximately 2500 dollars from the safe in the bank and give the money as a gift to the girl. Then the branch manager who knew his rich client very well and he also knew the clients hobbies and which night clubs they go to. He called the Central bank and the police and he woke up some of the bank employees just to open the bank at that time. Then he went to the bank and took the money from the safe of the bank then he went to the night club and gave the girl approximately 2500 dollars as a gift from the bank which is much more than what she expected.
The point here is that the generosity of the bank made the girl happy and also made the client happy and of course the branch manager also was happy because he did not lose his rich client .

7. Giving bonuses to your employees based on their performance is a good habit. Whenever you make good money in that year, it is good to give your employees small bonuses to make them happy. At the same time, it is good to thank your employees, and tell them that you appreciate their work and their teamwork. Also, it is recommended to make parties for your employees once a year. And to also send some of your best employees to a vacation with their family.

8. Sometimes, a person has a good manager that works hard, has many connections, and makes money for the

company, when he asks for a raise in salary for only for 5 percent, when his boss refuses him, this employee or manager will go to another company and then, this company will lose his manager. It happens a lot, many companies lose a lot of money when their good managers leave for an increase in salary. They then replace these people with new managers who do not demand an increase in salary but are not good in management.
A company's entire structure might be destroyed if the CEO or manager was replaced, as he had a strong work ethic with many connections.

9. I know an owner of a construction company that generates millions every year because the company has a good CEO who runs the company very well and knows the people and market very well. He has the contacts and connections. He also has a lot of experience in his business. But one day, the smart CEO asked for a higher salary and more bonuses. The owner refused to give him what he wanted. He brought in a new CEO to run the company. The new CEO is not smart enough and does not know the market and does not have the contacts and the connections and the experience that the older CEO does. After a few years, this big company went bankrupt.

10. A situation can be seen with two people for instance. Person A would be an owner of big land that consists of oil who will argue with the drilling rig, and the cost of drilling per day. It takes him a long time to argue and negotiate the price. It may take many months, or even a year. While person B also has land that consists of a lot of oil, may rent a drilling rig immediately. By doing so, he will save a lot of time and money. The second person is a generous person. By doing that, he will be making more money. One year later, person A would attempt to contact the drilling rig, and they will tell

him that it is too late, because they already rented a drilling rig to person B for a higher price. These kinds of stories are always happening in the market, as the oil demand and prices always go up.

11. If there are two people are trying to build a mall person X and person Y. Person X will make a quick agreement and architect with a construction company quickly, and he will rent the shops in the mall quickly, and he will start making money. While, person Y that is also trying to build a mall, will start arguing with the architect and the construction company about the prices and negotiating with them about the construction costs. It might take him five years, or even seven years. He will miss the chance and opportunity to make millions, because he was stingy and not generous. He just likes to argue a lot.

12. A friend of mine does not talk much and he always tells me that he is busy, and every few years he changes his business. Unfortunately, he always loses money in his business, and moves to another business and he loses money there also. After thirty years of his experience in business, I asked him what he thought of business as a whole, or what he learned in those thirty years and why he is losing money. He replied by saying that he used to give his employees very low salaries to minimize the costs. Those employees are not professionals, he just hired them because he did not want to give them high salaries. He said that was his biggest mistake, not getting professional people to not give them high salaries. Even when he had a store for selling clothes, his salesmen do not talk much, and do not have the skill or talent to talk to his clients. He just hired them because he did not want to spend that much money on their salaries. He was stingy when it came to this.

13. Sometimes, if a person had a bad childhood and suffered a

lot during his childhood, for example his father died, was born in a bad neighborhood, he used to clean cars for less than a dollar. When he grows up and starts to make money, even if he becomes rich one day, he will still be a stingy person. People will wonder, how is this person so rich yet so stingy. People do not know about his past and the bad childhood of this man. At the same time, you will see the same stingy person, you may see that he has a spoiled son who grew up with money, and the people might notice that the son is more generous than the father, because the son did not suffer a lot in his childhood, unlike his father.

14. These are the things you must do when starting a business; pay your employees and give them bonuses. In one of the Asian countries there was a five-star hotel with a life guard at the swimming pool who works from the morning until 7 in the evening, many people were members and used the pool and facilities of the hotel. The problem was that the management refused to pay for another employee to work after 7 in the evening. Where there are many members who finish work late and by the time, they reach the health club it would be too late, and they would not be allowed to swim after 7 in the evening. This issue made many members cancel their memberships and went to another five-star hotel which caused the hotel to lose a lot of money. This happened because the first five-star hotel didn't have a generous and strategic management who was willing to pay extra money to hire another lifeguard.

15. When there is an auction for cars, anything after a few years the person can sell it for a higher price and make money because the person was generous at the beginning when buying it. At the same time, during the time he bought it, another individual would call him crazy for buying it.

16. I noticed many generous people who paid a lot of money for land or real estate, they made a lot of money after a few years while some stringy people who have the money refused to buy it by saying it is very expensive lost the opportunity.

17. A friend of mine who is very well educated studied at the University of Minnesota. He always like to read about making money. He reads newspapers about finance. He is interested in business. He always talks about business, finances, big corporations, stocks, and shares. He does analysis and is a hard worker, he opened a big store for shoes then a big store of clothes, but his problem is that he is stingy and does not like to spend money.

18. In oil and gas, they need drilling rigs to drill for oil. Sometimes they negotiate for a year for the price of drilling of $60k or $80k then another oil company offers them more money than like $100k then the other company agreed to pay $80k after one year but it was too late.

19. When some companies try to build a building and keep negotiating the price of construction for a long time, he loses time. Even some construction companies don't like to deal with stringy people.

20. In the beginning when you start your business you must be stingy and save money but later on after your business starts growing, you must be more generous with your employees and you clients and you must pay your employees bonuses and start to hire good employees with skills and good personalities even if they ask for higher salaries.

21. A lot of times when there is an auction for cars or watches or anything, some generous people who do not hesitate to buy

despite the price, later on they start to make money but the people you hesitate to buy it at the auction, they never make money. Also, I noticed that many generous people who paid a lot of money for a piece of land or real estate they made a lot of money after a few years while some stingy people who hesitated to buy the same piece of land or real estate because they thought it was expensive, they lost the opportunity.

They lost this opportunity because they are not generous. One of my best friends who is very well educated and went to the University of Minnesota, he always likes to read books about making money and he also read newspapers about finance, he is always interested about business and talk about business, he always reads about big corporations, stocks, shares and does analysis. He is a hard worker, but he has a big problem he is stingy and he does not like to spend money, he doesn't like to pay high salaries to his employees, he always choses employees who are not qualified because he does not want to chose employees with high salaries. He opened a supermarket and lost money, he opened a shoe store and he lost money, he opened a big store for selling clothes and lost money. He opened many businesses and lost money After 30 years of experience I asked him what he learned, he said: "generosity is the key to success" but unfortunately, he was not aware of that when he started his business and now it is too late and because he was stingy, he always used to hire the wrong employees: the cheap and stupid employees.

22. There is an oil company who wants to drill for oil so they want to rent a drilling rig at a daily rate for a few months so they can drill for oil then produce oil. So they started to negotiate for a year for the price of renting the drilling rig. It took them a year to do that, they just wanted to bargain with the owner of the drilling rig to have a discount but after a year of negotiation, they decided to go for the drilling rig,

but it was too late since they found another company to use their drilling rig and at a higher rate. So this company lost the chance of selling oil for not being generous and by being stingy for looking at a discount and this is nothing compared to what would happen once they start to produce oil since the price of oil will cover all the costs of the renting the drilling rig.

23. The same thing, some companies when they try to build a building or a big mall, they start negotiating the price of construction for a long time and they lose time and opportunity. By doing that, they lose making money from renting the shops in the mall or from renting the space in the building. Even some construction companies do not like to deal with stingy people.

24. Most of the generos people their parents are generos.

Chapter 17
Flexibility

1. Flexibility is very important in your daily business. You must be flexible with people and have to be flexible with money when it is needed and not tough. You will notice in life there are certain people who are flexible and easy going when you ask them, they always say yes or okay. If you ask them to go with you to dinner, they will say yes, a movie - yes, a walk yes. Those are flexible people. At the same time in life, you will notice that there are certain people will always say no. If you ask them to go with you to dinner or a movie, they will say no, if you ask them to go to the gym with you they will always say no, even if you asked to go with them on a walk. This is their nature. The same thingwhen it comes to business. Some people are flexible some people are not. The great people are the flexible people.

2. Sometimes, you have to sell your car or your property quickly to buy shares or whenever you get a good opportunity to buy something quickly. So you have to be flexible to sell either your car or your property quickly, or when you have to pay your bank quickly to avoid bad credit.

3. I remember that when I was a student, I wanted to buy a sport car, wherever I went, all the car dealers wanted a large advanced down payment – they were not flexible with me. Finally, I found a big car dealer who was flexible with down payment, he said, "you can pay me the down payment within two months". Then I got so excited and bought the car, I asked him, "how can you do that? You are different

than the other car dealers". He replied, "because, we are the largest car dealer in the city of Los Angeles, we know how to deal with our clients, at the same time, we tell the bank what to do." The main point is that I bought the car from this car dealer because he was flexible with the down payment.

4. In a middle eastern country, there was a man who had a good falcon for hunting. He was staying in five-star hotels. He wanted to sell his falcon for 70 thousand dollars. Some people offered him 50 thousand dollars, and others offered him 60 thousand dollars. He was not flexible, he insisted on selling his good and expensive falcon for 70 thousand. One day, when he woke up in the morning, he noticed that his falcon was dead. He now had a big problem; he did not have enough money to pay the five-star hotel. The hotel then took legal action against him in court.

5. Sometimes a client will buy a product from a shop and there is something that he does not like about the product, and he comes back to the shop, and the owner of the shop is not flexible and will refuse to change the product for the buyer. The other person will spread the bad news. The bad news may ruin the reputation of the shop.

6. Some people are not flexible and are very stubborn. They are more likely not to be successful in business. They just like to say no, and they are hard people to deal with so when you are asking them to go with you to a movie, a dinner, to play tennis with you or go for a walk, they refuse and say no. Also, if it happens that you are with them at a restaurant, they will argue with the waiter why the dinner is expensive. Also, if you are with them at a supermarket, they will argue why a product is 10% more than last year and might refuse to pay.

7. During bad times, I tell my friends to sell their shares when their shares are going down. I tell them to minimize their losses and say that, losing five percent now, is better than losing 15 or 20 later. However, they are greedy, not flexible, and do not listen. After a short period of time, they lose a lot of money and some of them go bankrupt because they are not flexible.

8. Speaking about flexibilities, there are millions of people around the world that lose their money every day, because they miss their chances and their opportunities. For example, if someone bought gold and shares in the stock market, and the price of the gold and the shares went up in a few months, then it is good to sell them, just to make good money. It happened to me. I advised many of my friends to sell their gold and shares at the same time, but they are not flexible. Then, when the price of the shares and gold went down, they lost a lot of money, and regretted that they did not listen to me. They did not listen to me because they are not flexible and are greedy.

9. I once wanted to rent a house, all the owners of the houses wanted a big down payment. I finally found an owner of the house that there is no problem, and I can pay the down payment after one month. I then rented the house from him because he was flexible.

10. A lot of times, I see prices of shares going down, or the price of real estate going down because a crisis is coming. I told my friends to sell, since losing a little bit of money is better than losing a lot of money, but they refused since they are not flexible. A year later, for some reason, because they do not have enough cash, they end up selling their properties and shares for very little money, and they regret not listening to me.

11. A lot of people lost hundreds of millions during the 2008 crisis because they are not flexible.
12. A lot of times, the cost of gold goes up, their shares go up, and I tell my friends to sell their shares, some of them are greedy and want more, they lose their opportunity. I tell them to hit and run, but they do not listen. They are not flexible.

13. There was a Swedish American businessman who was the co founder of the Nordstrom department store chain mainly, for shoes.
    He emigrated to the United States at age of 16. Arriving in America with $5 to his name, he worked his way across the continent taking jobs on railways and in mines, lumber camps and shipyards, eventually arriving in Seattle, Washington in 1896. While working at a sawmill he read a newspaper account of discovery of gold in Klondike and headed to Alaska to make his fortune. He was flexible in selling his gold and his shares to move to the next stage of his business. Because he was flexible, he did not insist on selling it at a high price. Then he opened a shoe store with his partner.

14. The people in the world of trade and business think employees are stupid and narrow-minded people because they notice that when an employee starts talking they see that they have no experience. For example when a businessman rents his house he would be flexible with the payments and give him more time to pay. But if an employee has a house for rent he would take action against the tenant and try to prosecute him because he is not flexible. Where the house will be vacant for many years. The same thing if a businessman has gold or shares, he will sell the gold and the shares once it goes up just to make a little money because he is not greedy. While an employee has an investment in gold and shares, he will be greedy and refuse to sell his gold and

shares once it goes up assuming that it would go higher in the future. Because he is greedy, he will lose the opportunity.

15. Sometimes when things go wrong, and your company goes through financial problems and bankruptcy during the bad years of the economy. You have to be flexible to sell your cars, properties, house and assets in order to survive so you have to be flexible and take a proper decision. Also businessmen and merchants think employees don't have some of the factors of success mentioned in this book.

16. The most important thing is to have flexibility in your mentality and your mindset. Start thinking like a businessman or like a merchant and not like an employee. Usually after the age of 40 years, it is very hard to change someone's behavior or mindset. I noticed some people as employees, after retiring or about a few years before retirement, they start thinking about opening a shop or a business but their mentality and mindset is still that of an employee. They are exactly like kids who are living in their own world thinking about chocolate and ice cream.

17. I know a bank manager who always has meetings with bank businessmen and merchants. At one time, I decided to ask him if he ever thought about having his own business since he has a lot of years of experience in dealing with people in the world of trade and business. He replied that he is thinking about starting a business after seven years and after retirement because he wanted the money and the benefits of retirement first, so he has to wait for seven years. His answer shocked me on how his mentality and mindset was because he is thinking about his salaries and bonuses like employees. He is completely living in a different world, his meetings with businessmen and merchants for many years did not change him much. He does not know that if he waits for

another seven years, he will miss a lot of golden opportunities because the world will not wait for him and things are changing in the world every day, life is full of golden opportunities and this bank manager is still thinking about his salary and bonuses. Since my background is that I came from a business family, I never thought about salaries and bonuses even when I was a teenager or when I left the oil company working as a petroleum engineer. The salary and bonusses were not on my mind. A few years later I met that man, and he said it is too late for him to start his own business because he only thought about salary and bonuses for the time he worked in the bank.

18. I think about the result of my growing business in millions over the years. The bank manager focused on saving his salary and bonuses while I focus on investing money of business and other things in order to make more money. The main point here is to have the flexibility in your mentality and in your mind set.

19. Businessmen and merchants have different mindset than employees.
   Sometimes it is so hard to explain things to an average employee about the world of trade and business or the factors of success mentioned in this book because his mindset is not ready to absorb and understand things because there is no flexibility in his mind. Even if you repeat things to him many times because his mind in a different world and his reaction to you like he is from a different planet. So, for this reason many businessmen and merchants think that the other people are simple people and narrow-minded people.
20. An employee or a person who is not a businessman or merchant his mindset and his way of thinking and talking is completely different than a businessmen or merchant. His thinking is a reflection of his job and his daily work.

21. It is always good for a young man at the age of 25 to start his business when he is young because his mindset will be more flexible than an old man at the age of 50.

Chapter 18
Education

1. Education is power. Knowledge is power. Education will help you to have more ideas, more imagination, more vision, and will make you see the future clearer and help you to know what to expect, because educated people have a vision, and an educated person has the knowledge and can understand when someone explains to him complicated business or business to do with technology, because his mind has a wide horizon. An educated person has the basic understanding of most subjects related to business and he can start any kind of business, so it is always easy for an educated person to understand the concept of a subject, even if you try to explain some ideas in business, and he can also research about any kind of business easily. This is because when he was in university, he was doing research to write a paper for his classes writing a paper requires a lot of research and reading a lot of books.

2. On the other hand, most uneducated people have a narrow mind that cannot research because they did not attend university and have never researched in their life. A study shows that only 7 percent of the world population attend university. An educated person has more chances to meet people and have more friends and more contacts and connections. I speak many different languages, and this has helped me to meet more people and have more contacts and connections. It is always easy for me to meet people and talk to them about the subjects they like to hear, such as history, geography, economy, cinema. Education will make someone have more potential and a strong background to be able to do many things.

3. Most of the billionaires are from countries of high level education.

4. Sometimes, a person may say that there are a lot of rich people who are not educated, the reason why is because I mentioned earlier in this book, they have the other factors of success, such as contacts and connections. The answer to that are that there very few rich people that are not educated, but have the other factors of success.
5. An educated person has the knowledge and can understand when someone explains it to him specially to do with technology because the educated person has the basic things to understand most of the subjects you can tell him, or it is easy for him to relate things or do research. He also has an open imagination for new business ideas. Because the educated person's horizon of thinking is large and wide. An educated person has basic understanding of most subjects about business. An educated person can talk about more subjects, is able to talk and meet more people, and has more ideas about business, also having more contacts and connections because he is knowledgeable and can talk to people about the subjects they like to talk about.

6. However, if there is a person who is not educated and inherited a lot of money, it is easier for you to convince him to do simple businesses, like restaurants, coffee shops, dry cleaner. Non-educated people cannot understand complicated business like the steel industry, oil and gas, solar energy.

7. You will also notice that only educated people do big businesses like Bill Gates who started Microsoft, Steve Jobs who began Apple, Jeff Bezos and Amazon, or Elon Musk and Tesla. Education made a lot of people rich. For example, Edison made a lot of money after building the first power station in New York which was the first power station in the

world. Also, the inventor of air conditioning Mr. Carrier. He was an engineer who invented the AC and made a lot of money. Thus, there are a lot of people who made money because of their education. There are a lot of rich people in African and Asian countries, they have little education, they became rich and multi-millionaires because they have more education than other people in their country who cannot read and write at all. Also, imagine Elon Musk only finished the fifth grade. Do you think he would be able to succeed in Tesla? Elon Musk succeeded in Tesla because he studied physics. Just think about it, if he didn't study physics but studied history, he won't be able to succeed in Tesla. Or, if Steve jobs didn't go to school at all. Or even Warren Buffet- if he didn't go to school or college, do you think he would be a billionaire? What would happen if Warren Buffet didn't go to college but instead went to work at a farm as a farmer. Do you think he would be a billionaire? Today, if you look at the poor people around the world, they are not educated. Also, poor countries tend to have low levels of education.

8. When I was a freshman at USC, I took an American business history course. This course helped me a lot to be ambitious and have big dreams. In this course, we studied about how the big businesses and famous entrepreneurs started their business. Just like Rockefeller in the Oil industry, Karangi in the Steel industry, and DuPont in chemicals and paintings.

9. A person may ask the question, there are a lot of successful people in business who have no education and famous scientists who were not good in school like Thomas Edison. Thomas Edison, who made the first power station in the world and made a lot of money. The answer to that is that there is an exception to everything. Those people are geniuses. They have the interest to learn on their own, who

also like to do research.

10. They are geniuses and very rare people. In my freshman year, there was a 10 year old girl in our university. Her IQ was 180, she was a genius. She attended some of the same classes as me like my chemistry and math class. She would get straight A's. They even made interviews with her on TV and in some newspapers as well because she was unique.

11. I know a doctor from the middle east who used to make money during the 1940's and 50's even though the people during that time were very poor. However, this person makes money when he treats the patients, and the poor patients that do not have money give him a goat, chicken, or some eggs as a gift.

12. The educated person has a strong background exactly like the story of the 3 pigs. The story says that the mother of the 3 pigs told the 3 pigs to go to the forest and live on their own, the first pig was very lazy and decided to make his house with straws. The second pig was lazy and decided to make his house with sticks, but the third pig was a hard worker and intelligent he decided to make his house with bricks because he wanted to have a strong house which can save him from danger, even though it will take a long time to build a house with bricks.

13. After some time a bad wolf came to the first house the house of straws. He started huffing and puffing and he blew the house away. Then he went to the second house with sticks. He started huffing and puffing then he blew the house away. But when the bad wolf went to the third house which was made out of bricks, he was not able to blow the house away.

14. Then the bad wolf climbs down the chimney but the intelligent pig made a large hot pot of water waiting for the bad wolf then the wolf started screaming in the large pot of water.

15. The point is that the third pig survived because his house is strong, it is made out of bricks. The same thing with the educated person has a strong background.

16. 12-In some poor countries in Africa and Asia you might meet some merchants or businessmen who are not educated, however, in comparison to other people in their community, maybe they finish fifth grade but they are more educated than the people in their community who did not go to school at all or maybe they know how to read and write while the others in the community don't know how to read and write– they hold more knowledge than the average person.

17. The more educated you are the better it is for you. There are a lot of educated people who studied engineering or economics or any other subject but did not study psychology that make mistakes when they talk to a non-educated person the same way they talk to an educated person. After a while, they realized that they made a mistake, and notice that the reaction of the person is the opposite. When you tell an educated person things, even if he does not know it, he can relate to it and do research. Also, he can understand and accept new ideas about business, and he can start any kind of business, because his mind has a wide horizon. So, it is always easy for an educated person to understand the concept of the subject. Even if you try to explain some ideas in business, for example, if he is in real-estate, he will understand you when you talk about oil and gas, or solar energy, or mining, or medicine.

18. The educated person who has the experience has a vision, he can see the future of his business, he may do a lot of research, read a lot of books, and can see in which direction his company is heading. He has a lot of business ideas and has the imagination and the vision for the future. There are always other opportunities for people to discover a new type of business and make money.

19. However, if the person is not educated, you may try to explain a business idea to him 20 times, he will never understand.
A non-educated person would not accept new ideas of business. He is narrow minded. Because the non-educated person has a completely different mentality than you. If you tell him about something, he will not believe you. If you tell him the star is bigger than the moon, he will not believe you. You will also be surprised that he does not know the simple things that you know. If you explain things to him about something twenty times, will not understand. For example, if you take an uneducated farmer to a physics or chemistry class in Harvard university or Stanford university and let him attend the class 20 times, he will never understand what the professor is talking about because he does not know the basics of chemistry or physics.

20. An educated person has the basic knowledge to understand people explaining subjects such as investments. An educated person can choose the right people for the right subject as advisors. They understand the qualities it takes to hold certain positions people with rich experience and qualifications. He will put the right person in the right job. An educated person can meet with a lot of people and can socialize with a lot of people easily, he will learn something from every person. On the other hand, most non educated people have a narrow mind that cannot do research because

they did not go to a university and did not do research in their life.

21. A study shows that only 7 percent of the world population attended university. They cannot understand the business when you give it to them, and cannot select the right people lacking both the knowledge and experience on the subject. If you explain to a non-educated person simple business ideas related to chemical engineering or
civil engineering, he will not understand you because he does not know the basic things about physics or chemistry.

22. Education is very important, even one course in university may change someone's life. For example, one of my female friends in university told me that her father was a music major but took one elective course in business. This one business course helped him to become a businessman.

How Education Helped Me

23. Education gave me the habit of reading since a young age. Educated people are used to reading books and they like to read books and have the habit of reading books. So, this habit of reading is helping them a lot to know about the world of trade and business also they will keep up with the technology and the new events in the world of trade and business. All the successful billionaires and businessmen no matter how busy they are they are reading books and they have the habit of reading books. For example, the billionaire Warren Buffet, he said that he used to read a lot when he was a little kid and this is why he started to know a lot about companies, shares etc. This habit is the one that helped him a lot. Education is the nutrition of the mind. Reading is very important to get new ideas for business. Reading books is very important in business, educated people enjoy reading books and have the habit of reading books because this is what they are doing

all their life in elementary school, high school and university while a non educated person thinks reading books is boring. There is a connection between learning and earning because ideas come from reading books. A lot of billionaires read one book per week. Exactly like a football players, tennis players and volleyball player who think jogging is easy and fun while a person who is not an athlete and lazy person will think sports is boring and even walking is boring.
Education will make you a better thinker and will make you have bigger dreams. It will make you think you can do it and that you can be a successful person because you already read a lot of books and have read a lot about successful people. So educated people always have the motivation. I think education made me a better thinker.

24. Education will give the potential and the ability to be successful. Also, education will give you the chance to have a good job and be promoted in your job.

Education helped me a lot, it was the reason for my success. Because I started my business from scratch.

Education helped me a lot for the following reasons:

1. What helped me a lot in my career as a businessman was mostly my career in education. Because first of all, studying geology and petroleum engineering made me able to work in the oil business.
   Studying communication made me understand the body language of people and understand what subjects people liked to talk about, it also made me understand if a person is lying or hiding something from his facial expression. For example, if someone is trying to sell me his car, I can tell if he is lying about the price of the car or if he is talking about certain products and is lying about how many people want the product, but he just wants to sell his product to me.

2. Education also helped me take a memory course that helped me memorize many things. People's names, street names, numbers, phone numbers, and many words in foreign languages. So, I started to talk about the subjects they liked to hear. I then started to have more friends and more contacts and connections. Also, when studying cinema and zooming in the lens on certain people made me understand the reactions of people and how they reacted to conversations. Focusing on the face of an individual and eye contacts was very important. I took many courses in psychology that made me know the certain behaviors of people and how they are thinking and the best way to approach them and not talk about the subjects they do not like to hear, because it will hurt their feelings. Education also helped me to speak many different languages. My ability to speak more languages helped me to meet more people and have more contacts and connections and I finally started to work with many different companies from different countries. Education helped me to avoid the financial problems of the financial crisis of 2008. Because the world financial crisis in 2008 was similar to the crisis that happened in 1929. I had already studied about the crisis in 1929 when I took courses in history, economics, political science, and cinema. Where watched movies and film in my cinema class about that period. In political science, we learned about President Roosevelt's efforts to solve the problem.

3. Education helped me learn the basics for everything (Physics, Biology, Chemistry, Math, Sociology, Engineering, Geography, History).
   Mathematics made me understand that logarithms led to inventions such as computers and all the technologies that we use in our daily lives. If there was no logarithm or mathematics, there would be no search engines, internet, computers, and so on. The people who don't study

mathematics don't understand the value of it. Those who use computers every day and send emails every day aren't aware of the mathematical basis of the technologies they rely on. It made it easy for me to understand the basics for most business ideas, because of the education that I possess. Living with students for a long time, exchanging ideas, made my mind filled with knowledge. Education made me have a wider horizon.

4. Education helped me to have a career in Oil and Gas. Without studying Geology and Engineering, it would not be possible for me to work in the Oil and Gas fields for five years, which made me know the business and projects of oil and gas at the same time made me know the people who worked in oil and gas.

5. Education helped me to learn languages this made it very easy to talk to people from different cultures and different nationalities which led me to deal with different companies from around the world.

6. Learning communication made it easy for me to understand people and their reactions, because of body language and their eye contact.
   It enabled me to know if someone was lying, telling the truth, or what subject people like to talk about and many other things.

7. When a student is away from his parents, he starts to learn how to rely on himself. I relied on myself, especially because I was away in university for 14 years. You will learn how to depend on yourself and make your own path in life. This made me a stronger person and a better person, to deal with all kinds of circumstances.

8. Psychology helped me a lot in understanding people due to psycho analysis. I understand why a specific person become a kind-hearted person, why another became a thief, and another a bad person.

9. Being a student, living in university housing for 14 years helped me a lot in understanding networking.

10. Made me develop the skill of writing since I was made to write so many papers and research in my classes. Thus later helped me in my business and also led me to write this book.

11. Living with students who were ambitious to be rich and famous for a long time, had an effect on me to be as ambitious as the other students. There was also a good class called American Business History, which talked about how the big companies started in the United States, had a positive effect on my ambition.

12. Education will make you learn the basics of everything because the basics are very important. The basics of physics, chemistry, biology, physiology,cinema, political science, history, math, geography,
economics, business.
Education helped me to have a vision, as most educated people have more of a vision than non-educated people.
A friend of mine who is an engineer once approached a rich businessman to sell him a business idea. He was complaining and told me that there was no success and if you try to explain something to a farmer or a non-educated person, will he understand? He said no. Then I asked him, if you give him books about engineering and the time to read the engineering books, do you think he will understand them? He said of course not, because he does not have the basics of physics, chemistry, and math to understand engineering.

I then told him that it is the same thing here, with the rich person. He does not have the basics to understand what you are talking about. Maybe it is easy for you to understand it but it is not easy for him.

13. Education helped me talk to all kinds of people, in all different kinds of professions, it helped a lot in meeting people and thus having contacts and connections.
For example, when I talk to engineers about engineering, they feel comfortable with me. When I ask them questions, they are happy to answer my questions as I boost their ego. They then become nice and friendly with me. This is the same thing as to when I talk to a doctor about something related to biology, since they know the subject. When I talk to a financial analyst or an economist about micro or macroeconomics, he becomes very happy to talk to me, and would be talking for many hours. This is how human beings are like. They always like speaking about things they enjoy and like and the subjects they know and stay away from things they do not know or are ignorant of. If you talk to an actor or producer about movie and film, they will be very happy to talk to you, they will then be your friend, especially if you talk about a movie script, acting, editing, then they will talk to you for many hours. When you talk to people that do not understand a specific subject, ignorant people, they get bored and lose interest they will ask you to change the subject, or they might leave you and go and talk to someone else. I have sometimes noticed a bank manager will try to approach a rich person who owns farms to invest money in copper or minerals. However, that person doesn't know of copper and minerals, so he gets bored, when you have the education, you can talk about many subjects and thus talk to many people, thereby having the contacts and connections. When a person in not educated, he does not have the basics to meet a lot of people and will end up

meeting fewer people.

14. When I started my career as a geologist and a petroleum engineer, I worked onshore and offshore where the drilling rigs and the oil tanks and the pipelines were. I started to know the real problems of the oil industry, also I started to know the mentality of the people, how they think, and how to approach them. Later on, I chose to become a businessman in the oil and gas industry, because it is something I know and something I experienced before, and something I feel comfortable with, whenever someone explains something about oil and gas projects, I understand them quickly since I was there, I know what they are talking about and know the basics of the oil and gas industry. I know the people and the mentality of the people, how to reach the right people to get more information about the subject. To me, the oil industry is a good business because it is worth hundreds of millions and billions of dollars. Being involved in any little thing is worth a lot of money. Working there, made me understand the mentality of the people in the oil and gas industry.

15. Education helped me to understand mathematics and the importance of mathematics because all industrial and manufacturers are based on mathematics. The importance of mathematics is exactly like the importance of discovering paper – an enormous aide to human civilization. A long time ago, the people used to write on goat skin, cow skin, rock, and wood. It was so hard for people to write books. This only changed until the Arabs, who went to China, discovered that the Chinese had been using paper for thousands of years. The Chinese had been keeping it a secret –disclosing the information of paper inorder for other nations not to know about it. When the Arabs had traveled to China preaching Islam after the death of Prophet Muhammad (Peace Be Upon Him) in 633 AD, they had discovered the papers and brought

it back with them to the middle east in order to print the Holy Quran. From the middle east, the Europeans had discovered paper and used them to print their own. I also wished to mention that the Arabs had established the Arabian numerical system, the same numbers we use and see today where most the countries of the world are using the same system, as well as the value of 0.

16. Education helped me to learn many languages. Education and being in university for a very long time made me learn many languages. This made things easier on me once I traveled. Also, it helped me in my business, at the same time, languages helped me meet a lot of people and friends. I think that I am a very lucky person because I went to a very big university, USC, where they teach so many courses, also hosting 17 libraries where they teach so many languages. I learned how to memorize things by association. For example, if someone is named John, you remember the actor John travolta, or if someone's name is Thomas, you remember Thomas Edison. If there is a restaurant named Atlantic, you just remember the Atlantic Ocean. So, the memory course helped me in my education to improve my grades and helped me in learning languages. When I studied language in university, I started learning the basic things, such as hello and learn the basic easy words, such as car, pen, book, food, water, house, etc.… as well as basic questions and answers. Such as, "what is your name? how old are you? Where are you from?" I took a memory course when I was a freshman in the university of southern California. This helped me memorize the material in some of my difficult courses such as chemistry, physics, and geology. It also helped in easier courses such as languages. At the same time it helped me memorize people's names, their hobbies, and phone numbers. I also remember in my freshman year, when I took a French class in USC, I used to

practice my French words in my room.

17. My ex-roommate thought I was stupid or weird. I used to go early in the morning at 6:30 AM, to meet my tutor for French class, because this is the only time he has tutoring for me.
I was interested and keen to learn the French language and other European languages since I was fifteen years old and always thought of traveling to Europe and other parts of the world. My father used to give me some money as an allowance, and I used the money to buy books about foreign languages. Going to a big university like USC opened the door for me to learn languages. Later on, after I grew up, learning languages helped me meet more people and have contacts and connections. This led me to have businesses with different companies in different countries.
Learning a language requires practice. In a way practice is a language, and language is a practice. This means that in order to practice a language you must practice it with people so you will never forget it. Reading books is important. You have to be well educated in subjects people like to hear.
18. Every time when I travel to Germany, I practice the German language with taxi drivers or with people who work in hotels. Some of my friends think that the German language is not important, but I know that one day, I will gain something from learning the German language. I kept practicing the German language for a long time because I always like to travel to Germany. I like the countryside, also I like the fact that everything there is clean. The petrol stations are clean, the hotels, shops, roads are all clean.
I also have respect for the German people because they are nice people. Once you become a friend of theirs, they will become your friend for life. I am a patient person and knew that I will one day gain something from learning German. In Germany, there are a lot of good companies. Not just car and automobile companies like Mercedes, Porsche, and BMW.

One day I met a retired German manager who introduced me to meet a very good European company. European managers know each other. This good European company opened the door for me to meet other companies. I already mentioned earlier that in business, a door will open another door for you. It is like how one friend will introduce you to another friend. They call it networking. I remember when I traveled to Italy in the summertime, I always practiced the Italian language with the taxi driver. Some of my friends thought that I was wasting my time because they thought that the Italian language is not important, but I knew that someday I would learn something important. I always like to travel to Italy language because I like the Italian food, the Italian culture, countryside, and history. The Italian people are also nice and friendly. Later on, the Italian language helped me meet an Italian person on the beach, and after being very friendly, he introduced me to one of his friends who knew people and has many connections in the oil and gas industry.

19. I remember from my cinema class about acting, that I had to do a lot of research and read many plays and asked many students about the best scripts and plays for the theatre to choose. Finally, I found the best script and chose the best play – which was funny. I hired the right students to act in the play while I directed it. The result was good, my cinema professor was impressed and started laughing during the play. I then got an excellent grade, an A. This happened by doing a lot of research, reading a lot of scripts and plays and by asking a lot of people. Today I do the same thing in my business, I do research if there are projects in oil and gas. I start to read my old chemistry and physics books and ask my friends and engineers in my oil companies about the technicalities of the project in order to understand what the project is about. So, when there is a meeting, I will be ready

for it, so during the meeting, I talk and discuss the project with the engineers, and if there is any problem about the project, I talk with the engineers and work to solve or go around it.

20. I remember there as once a non-educated person who was impressed by how I made my money and was curious to know what I was doing. He asked me if he could work with me. He wished to attend a meeting with me but I told him that he is not an engineer and will not understand what I am doing. As I am not selling apples nor oranges.
I then brought him to one of my meetings and did not understand things. He thought it was a boring meeting.

21. When I travel to France or North Africa, they ask me why I like to practice French and not English, the reason why is because I like languages. I've been interested in languages since I was 15 years old.
At that time, I was full of energy, I wanted to travel and explore the world. I like adventures and seeing different cultures. When you speak French, you sound like a sophisticated person. French sounds more like poems and music. Also, I like the French history and French culture. France has a variety of things, when I go to France, I never get bored. Later on, the French language opened the door for me for success in business. Language helped me to meet people around the world and made my business easier in oil and gas. When I deal with people and companies related to oil and gas.

22. Usually, when I start talking to a person in his own language, he becomes friendly with me, and I get to know him quickly. This is because most people around the world are friendly by nature. And they like to make friends. Especially with the people that speak their

language. No-one likes to be alone or lonely.

23. Education helped me to learn communication, body language, and eye contact. It made it easier to understand people. If they like me or they do not like me. From their eye contact, I can also understand what subjects people like to talk about. I always start talking to people about different subjects. I then notice from their eye contact, what subjects they like the most. The same thing about body language, from their body reaction, I can study the personality of the person. I met a lot of people and made a lot of friends because I know what subject they like to talk about, and what they like to hear. All of this is because of my communication courses I took in university. Then I started to tell people what they like to hear, or the subject they like to hear.
History for example, politics, religion, sports, travelling, etc. This method helped me to make a lot of friends and make a lot of contacts and connections. It helped a lot in my business because I can tell if someone is lying or telling me the truth – which is very important in business, because there are a lot of times that you meet a lot of liars in the world of trade and business, and they are everywhere. My communication skills helped me to discover the liars easily.
You always need communication skills to deal with people to deal with your clients, your partners, your employees, friends, and all kinds of people.

24. When I go to a big party or a wedding, where there is a big gathering of people, I can tell from the eye contact of people and from how they are standing or sitting in relation to each other how well they know each other. So, if there is a key person that I want to know, I talk to his best friend, and that person will introduce me to the key person. I was once in the gym and there were two people talking to each other. One of which was a key person, so later on, the next day, I went to

familiarize myself with his friend. After a few days, that person introduced me to the key person who is important to my business, and I established a connection with him. Many times, when I travel to Asian countries or any other countries that I do not speak their language, I rely on my communication skills. Like body language and eye contact. I remember I once travelled to India, I arrived there three in the morning. When I rented a taxi, I saw the taxi driver discussing a few things with the other taxi driver. I did not feel comfortable from their eye contact. Half-way, the Indian taxi driver stopped in the middle of the road, I jumped out of the car. I knew they were planning on stealing my money. My communication skills saved my life. I once traveled to Turkey. I missed the boat, so I had to take the bus to reach the city of Istanbul I was staying at. When I arrived there two in the morning, there were no taxis in the station. I had to go with someone in their own car who would take me to my hotel for money. There was a nice person at the bus station. I told him that I needed someone to drop me off to my hotel, which is far away from the bus station. This person tried to find a private car for me, since at 2 AM there were no taxis. I noticed that this person tried to explain to the driver by looking at their faces and facial expressions, they don't speak English and I don't speak the Turkish language. I saw that they were friendly people and weren't going to try and hurt me. That person gave me a ride to the hotel, and I arrived safely to my hotel. I also learned in my speech communication classes in university which helped me give speeches. At the same time it helped me to analyze people when they give speeches on TV.

25. One of the good things I learned in my cinema classes is how to show a person's reaction on his face when he is sad, happy, or surprised.
Because, in filming, showing the emotions of the actors and

actresses is important. When I go to meet people for my business, I can easily tell if a person is happy or sad. I can see part of his emotions, even if he is trying to hide it. My speech communication classes helped me a lot to give speeches anywhere, and not to panic when I give a speech. I remember I once asked one of my employees about his best day and moments in recent years. So, he answered, the day I gave a speech to all the employees in our company, because he was impressed by the way I spoke and felt that we were together like one family.

26. In my communications class, we used to analyze people who gave speeches on TV. Whether someone had a lot of self confidence or not, we could tell the personality of a person, as well as the intentions behind the speech.

27. The point here is that living at university housing for 14 years made me have the talent of knowing people and understanding people. That made me street smart and made me able to use some tricks to get to know people and to make contacts and connections. Because the same tools and methods I used when I was a student, I can still use them as a businessman because people are people, they are all the same. Today unfortunately I found that there are a lot of people in the world who did not have the experience I did, they do not have the talent or even the basics of how to know people and how to make contacts and connections. They want to make contacts and connections, but they don't know how.

Self-Reliance:

Being in university, far from my family and I must solve my problems by myself, made me prepared and able to rely on myself. In the future, this made me able to start my career from zero without the help of my father or anyone else. This is due to how difficult education is, especially when you attend a big university, such as the University of Southern California where there are students from all over the world. This made me patient and strong and able to put up with bad times and bad circumstances, and later made me successful in business.

28.Education is not easy:

1. You have to have a strong will to always be in your room and study for exams and have to go to the library and spend a lot of time there, studying and writing papers and resist yourself from certain activities such as going to the cinema with your friends instead of studying. Your friends may want to play football or soccer, but you have to say no to study. Sometimes, your friends wanted to go to the beach on weekends, but you have to sit in your room and study. Education is not easy and this is why not everyone in the world can study and resist themselves.

2. Every week, every month, you will have some other problems. For example, sometimes you will have a shortage of money. You will not have enough money for your daily or weekly expenses. I remember in a semester, I had some financial problems. I was not able to make the payment for my housing. I did not have a car and did not have enough money to pay my tutor. I did not have money to eat out. That was a very bad year for me. I remember studying for one of my classes for a long time and still getting a bad grade – a D. I was frustrated and was thinking about myself, why I am not a lucky person.
3. Sometimes, you get sick during winter and have the cold and the flu. There is no one that is going to take care of you.
4. Sometimes, you are unlucky and get the wrong roommate,

who is not nice and has no manners.

5. Sometimes you may get a resident advisor or RA on your floor who does not like you, who will always be mean to you – he may be envious of you etc.
6. You may get unlucky with the people on your floor, some people may not like you, say bad things about you, knock on your door and wake you up at night just to bother you or scratch your car with keys because they are jealous of you.
7. You must rely on yourself to look for new friends and find good friends to hang out with which is not always easy. You must impress people with your personality, friends are not going to be coming to you, you must look and work for them.
8. You have to cook your own food, do your own laundry, clean your own room, and do everything by yourself because you are far away from your parents and family.
9. I never had a perfect month or a perfect year because every month or year I will have a certain problem. I will either have bad roommates or a bad resident advisor on my floor. I will also sometimes have a shortage of money and I have to live without money for a while.
   Sometimes, I will be very busy with exams and writing papers. Or, I will be sick with the cold and the flu. So, there is no such thing as a perfect month or a perfect year. Life is not easy. Going to university is not easy. However, in order to have a proper education, you must go through some suffering. No pain no gain. I was lucky that I attended a university like USC. There, I learned a lot and had a wider horizon on life. They do not have a lot of classes nor majors in small universities. They do not have student housing or dormitories either. They do not have sports events such as swimming, volleyball, soccer, football etc. They do not have marching bands, cheerleaders, and other amusements during large games. They actually do not have a lot of things. No matter how hard school is the exams or spending time

writing papers it is still a lot of fun. This is especially the case once you look back at it after 20 years or 30 years, you will remember the good old days.

The Good Old Days:

1. I still remember in my freshman year, how I was eager and anxious to learn new things and accepting challenges. How I was excited about life and about my future who I wanted to be. I had so many dreams. I was solely focused on learning and always told myself that I wished I had 1/4th of the knowledge my geology teacher had, or 1/4th of the knowledge my petroleum engineering professor had. At that time, all I had in my mind was attaining a 4.0 and graduating quickly. I was serious about university and life.

2. Every time I went to class, I always stopped to see the design of the earths different zones in the geology building. I knew that I would one day work there on the oil fields.

3. I used to go to my chemistry and laboratory classes late at night, for more than three hours. After I finished my classes, I would always go and buy coffee and a sandwich. This was a relief to me. It was the break I needed after hours of work in the laboratory. I was not alone, I saw many of my classmates doing the same thing. I sometimes went to the cafeteria to eat fried chicken which I liked because of its taste and texture. I also bought salad with beans which I used to like a lot.

4. I sometimes remember having tutoring classes early in the winter mornings, wearing my hat and overcoat, where my tutor would tell me that I used to look like Kojak; a popular T.V character at the time. I still remember my early morning math classes, where the classes were so early that

some students were still sleeping in the classroom. I still remember that students were moving so quick to different classes between different buildings, where I would constantly hear the doors banging and how everyone was in a hurry. When I hear that now, doors closing and banging feels like music.

5. When I went outside, I saw hundreds or thousands of students walking outside where everyone is in a hurry going to their different classes. At that time, I was walking with a lot of dreams in my mind about the future.

6. When I went to the library to study or write a paper, I would see students talking to their friends at their table and other students getting tired and sleep on the table – I would sometimes sleep as well.

   I accepted the challenge of staying in the library for that long because of the dreams I had and thinking of my future. After a while, I would go to the coffee machine, get coffee, and head back to the library. I thought that life was a game a game I had to win. One of my friends in university always used to say that. He used to say that life was a game and that he had to win that game.

7. When I was in university, I thought after graduating, many people would ask me so many questions about my classes and what I learned in university in order to share my knowledge with them like a school teacher, especially my father, my uncles, and my friends.
   Unfortunately, after I graduated, I was disappointed that no one asked me such questions.

8. I still remember that on a rainy day, many students would carry an umbrella going and coming back from classes. I

enjoyed the rain in California and the sound of the raindrops, they sounded like music. When I went back to the dorms, sitting in the lobby, I would see students closing and opening their umbrellas as they came in and out of the dorms, it felt like music. I would look at the different types of clothes people would wear for the rain.

9. Going back to my room on a cold rainy day and covering myself with a blanket was always so cozy.

10. Something I will always remember is sitting in the cafeteria during dinner, spending hours talking to friends, moving from one table to another and socializing like a butterfly. Hearing boys at a table talking about other girls. At the same time, I would hear the girls talk about other guys sitting on other tables. Hearing some students complain about the junk they used to eat in the cafeteria something I used to regularly hear. Waiting in line for some food or drinks was something we used to do every day.

11. Going to sporting events such as football games and soccer games was something I always remember about college life, when everyone was so excited. I would see thousands of people going there, especially in football games. All the students used to get so excited, especially for our rival university, UCLA. The night before the game I would see all the students making a rally before the UCLA game, seeing marching bands and the cheerleaders dancing. It was so exciting, it was a night that no one would forget.

12. The most important thing about university is meeting young people, having good friends, talking to them, laughing with them and making good jokes. Most of the time, they talk about funny things or simple things. Going with them to the movie theatre, to concerts, or to football games was always

fun. At the same time, every season is different. Every season has different kind of fun. We enjoyed the fall because of the football games, we enjoyed winter because of boom hockey, hockey games, snow skiing and the cinema. We enjoyed the spring to go to dinner, to the beach, when everyone was so excited about going to the beach after a long winter. In summer, we always thought of going to the beach and attending different summer schools in order to have different classes and meet different people.

13. Something I will always remember is the first week of school in the fall, when all the students are moving in to the dorms. Seeing the students come in with their parents in university, I was trying to help them with their luggage and meeting new friends. Students try to unpack. It happens to all students in different universities, something common.

14. No matter what, university life is a lot of fun. All students love university life. For one, they are far away from their parents so are free to do whatever they want. At university, you meet a lot of friends, and have fun with them, going to movies, parties, and football games. There is always someone who is willing to have fun with you. A lot of people in university talk about small and insignificant things. They are primarily funny; unlike the conversations people have as they grow older. Later on, when people grow older, they always think of the good old days when they were young and healthy in university. Even when we used to complain, we complained about little things in university.

15. I want to mention, that college life is a lot of fun during all four seasons of the year. In the fall, you get excited to meet new students and have new friends, going with them to football games. Walking to classes in the fall is so beautiful to see the leaves of the tree as they fall in different colors.

The wind comes and pushes the leaves away.
In winter, you would go snow skiing with your friends in college and see the white snow covering the houses and the trees. Smelling the smoke of the wood while walking with your friends at the ski resort is fun. Drinking hot chocolate or hot tea or coffee in a restaurant in winter when it's cold or rainy outside. In the springtime, we start playing tennis, and go to palm springs California. Everyone is excited about the weather.

16. On my way to classes, people are playing tennis, as I can hear the sounds of rackets hitting the balls. In the summer, everyone goes to the beach. Very crowded and playing volleyball at the beach. In the beach you hear loud music everywhere. Even taking summer courses is easier than in the school year. After taking summer classes, I would go with my friends to the beach.

17. I still remember going on geology fieldtrips in the springtime, on the mountains of California, sitting there between the mountains listening to the beautiful breeze of the wind - drawing maps for my geology class.

18. Summer is always fun, where you can ride bicycles by the beach, and stopping to eat juicy hamburgers by the beach and seeing people on roller-skates. Seeing people having fun and happy makes you more excited.

19. In the summertime, sometimes I go to summer school. I remember at one time I went to summer school in California state at Long Beach playing ping pong in the afternoon and it was a lot of fun meeting people in the cafeteria talking about girls also playing table tennis and going jogging on the track before sunset and enjoying the breeze in the evening. Going to movie theaters at night. There at Long Beach State I met a

lot of interesting people I will never forget.

20. I remember at one time I went to summer school at the University of California – Irvine and it was a lot of fun where I used to talk to my friend in the cafeteria and going with them to the swimming pool and going jogging on the track. Going to movies at the nighttime and playing tennis in the daytime. Also, there I met some funny students in the dorms that make me laugh.

21. Also, I remember visiting my friends at San Diego State going with them to movie theaters at night on the weekends and after that we go late at night to eat hamburgers in fast food restaurants and spending the night talking and laughing with my friends and eating good delicious hamburgers and walking along the San Diego beach in the day time.

22. I like San Diego a lot because it is a beautiful city and I had good memories even in the wintertime when I used to walk and feel the rain and hear the thunder.

23. I remember in the springtime going with my friend's horseback riding in the outskirts of San Diego. Where the weather is nice, and the sun is shining.

24. I remember in the summertime going out with my friends on weekends to eat Hamburgers in fast food restaurants talking and laughing all night.

25. I had a lot of goals in my life but didn't know the steps needed to be taken to reach my goals. I used to think of myself as the smartest person in the world, now, looking back at it, I simply laugh. Now, I am living in that future. I have come to realize that life is not easy. When I look back at those days, I tend to miss them. Sometimes, we would go to

movie theaters and restaurants with my friends, and sometimes the students in the dorms were very funny.

26. Also, I remember visiting my friends at University of California Los Angeles - UCLA. Eating with them at the dorms cafeteria and sometimes I go with them to nice restaurants in Westwood.

27. There was always entertainment around me and always had friends to do things with. Life was simple then. Even when a bad student borrowed 20 dollars from me and didn't pay me back. I remember that I once took girls shopping, and they borrowed 160 dollars from me to buy shoes. They wrote me bounced cheques. I trusted them, mostly due to the fact that one of their dad's was a professor and seemed like a professional wearing a suit. Today, life after college is hard. You have to work a lot. Also, when someone would steal money from you, they would no longer be taking 20 dollars, rather, thousands or millions.

28. Even visiting some students in Boston was fun in the winter when the snow is falling, the students and friends I was around were from Boston University and Harvard University, they were always talking about fun things. The same thing with students at the American University in Washington DC when all the streets are covered with snow during the winter time the students are all nice and friendly.

29. When I was at college, I used to only study during exams. After exams, I would have fun and go out with my friends. There are a lot of friends and good people to socialize with. It's the people and friends at college I miss the most.
I noticed that in the business world, things are not as easy as I once thought or dreamt of. I have to work every day, even on weekends. Sometimes, very late at night and on public

holidays. I have to mention that in business, there are good parts about it. These include, always having money in your pocket, traveling, purchasing automotive vehicles such as cars or boats, and the feeling of success and accomplishment.

30. During the four seasons, we were enjoying it fully. I used to have so much fun when we used to go to the places mentioned above. I enjoyed the times with all my heart. Today, as a businessman, I always have things on my mind wherever I go. I cannot enjoy things fully. The feeling is exactly like when I go to the movies or the beach during exams. I am not able to enjoy myself nor my time. When I was at college also, I used to do a lot of adventurers.
I remember that when I once finished my exams, I wanted to do something crazy. I decided to go to Aspen, Colorado on the weekend for snow skiing. I asked my roommate, floor mates and friends, but they all refused. I then asked a certain person in the building and he agreed, I had to pay, however. My roommate then told me that if I asked this man to go with me to Africa, he would go. We then went Skiing in Aspen Colorado.

31. Another time, I decided to go to Hawaii a weekend before thanksgiving with my friend John. This was a sudden and unplanned trip. John didn't tell his parents that he is going to Hawaii. Then, when we went to Hawaii, Jon lost his driving license there. Someone found the driving license and mailed it to his parents in Washington State. When he called his father, his father knew that he wasn't in California but in Hawaii. John didn't know that someone sent the license.
I was laughing all day because of this. The main point here is that no matter how hard your classes, and how hard university is, it is much easier and much better than working as a businessman. In university, you are controlling your time. In the world of business, the circumstances and

the problems are controlling you. For example, during the coronavirus pandemic, a lot of people who owns shops, restaurants are losing money. They cannot control the situation. It is something out of their control. The people who own shops, restaurants, and other businesses, their lives became a disaster. For students, the case is quite different. There are students who are suffering; however, they are not suffering as much as businessmen that lost their money, and everything, that have so many worries. For example, in Indonesia, some students leave their village riding motorcycles trying to get as close as they can be to their school to work on their computer. This is primarily due to them not having strong connections. These struggles are still not as much as what businessmen go through. The consequences of this would be you losing a lot of money. I once had a tutor who tutored me for some classes. Whenever I went to see him, I talk and socialize with my friends by the pool while my tutor is waiting. When I arrive however, I would pay him full time. In business, this cannot happen. You have to be on time, otherwise you partner will tell others that you are not punctual and are terrible.

32. I met one of my old roommates after 35 years. We were talking about college life. He was telling me about how we used to have fun in university even without having money. The tears started to come out of my eyes. To think that there was a time that I could have fun when not having money. However, when you are a businessman, you may have money but are still not having fun. You are always under pressure to work hard.

33. I once remember that in university, I thought that I was very smart and that making money was going to be very easy for me. It will be much easier than studying, because going to a hard university like USC, studying hard, reading books,

writing papers, there is a lot of competition from a lot of smart students from all over the world. It is very tough. I thought that business will be very easy because I am smart and have many connections. This was not the case.
When I entered the world of business, I found that it is very hard, and that it's not like college not having anytime at all, not even in weekends where I have to read a lot and do a lot of paperwork and sending a lot of emails as well.

34. When I was at university, we used to go to summer school in University California Irvine, and Long beach Estate University.
We used to have fun, talking to my friends, socializing with them.
Suddenly, we would go the beach and see thousands of people enjoying themselves, roller-skating, playing volleyball. We would decide to go the movies at night. When you are at college, it is important to stop and smell the roses, this is something you cannot do in business. You are always in a hurry and always have appointments. Time is money. I heard that a producer in Hollywood believes that wasting time during meetings is like wasting money itself. He says that him spending 5 minutes in the bathroom, is like him losing 5 thousand dollars.

35. I remember that when I was a student in University, I once flew from New York to Miami Florida with my father. I was very happy and excited during my flight even though my father was traveling first class, and I was travelling in economy class. But I was happy and excited during my flight to Miami, because soon in Florida I would see Disney world, and the orange farms, and the beautiful beaches of Florida. When I was at Disney World in Florida, I was happy walking with my father, taking a lot of pictures, buying souvenirs from Disney world. Even though my father gave me money to buy souvenirs much less than I expected, but I

was happy. The main point here is that student life is fun. Of course, you will face problems, but these problems are insignificant and small in hindsight.

36. I wanted to speak about USC in relation to my major, geology and petroleum engineering, and also because I like the weather in California, and USC is the only university that has my major, petroleum engineering in California. They teach petroleum engineering in Alaska university, but I did not want to study in a cold place, because I would not enjoy it.

37.I started to know how to deal with people in my freshman year of college when I was at the University of Southern California USC because is used to live in USC housing and used to meet thousands of people every year. The reasons why I chose to live in USC housing:

1. To save time instead of driving an hour or two away from the university since it was very difficult for me to live in the same
   neighborhood where there was a high crime rate. I just wanted to save time and be closer to the library, study with other students (group studies).

2. I was to be living in a university environment and the events, I also knew that university life is once in a lifetime, so this is why I wanted to enjoy going to football games, volleyball games, basketball games etc. Also, going to a university party after the football games or basketball games. I just wanted to have some good memories after I graduate,
   I remember the good old days of college life.

3. I noticed that students and young people are living a simple life and they always make me laugh because they do funny

and stupid things.

4. Also I noticed when you live in dorms, you get to know people from all around the world, you get to know their culture, you get to make new friends and you get to know about their majors. So, when you socialize or live with someone studying cinema, you will indirectly know about cinema and when you socialize or live with someone studying psychology you will indirectly learn about psychology. Also, the same when you socialize or live with someone studying economics, you will indirectly learn something about economics. 5. The reason to live in university housing is that you will never get bored, there is always somebody to do something with you. For example, if you want to play tennis, out 100 people, someone will play tennis with you. If you want to go jogging at night, out of 100 students, someone will go jogging with you. Same thing if you want to go to the movie theatre or to dinner, you will always find somebody to go with you. Also on the weekends, if you decide to go snow skiing or the beach, you will always find somebody to go with you. So, at university housing, you will never feel lonely.

5. When I graduated from USC, I felt a lot of relief. A huge burden was taken off my back. I felt like I did what had to be done, I worked hard and graduated. I thought that after university, life was going to be easy. University life always revolved around examinations and grades.
   Going in and out of the library, and using other tools was something I did daily. When I was in university, I was a big dreamer and very ambitious. I thought that I would be a billionaire within five or ten years. I thought that making money was going to be easy, because of the challenges I had already overcame. I had countless problems and conflicts when I was younger, more than the average student. I thought that overcoming the obstacles I faced made me

superhuman. I was always thinking about the future, even during my walks between the university buildings and on campus grounds. I always thought about my future, five or ten years from then. I thought that because of my education, making money would be unbelievably easy for me. I didn't know nor realize the importance of experience. I didn't know the importance of the other factors of success – mentioned in this book.

I didn't know that there are thieves and criminals everywhere in the world, who can affect your life. I thought that bad people were solely in films and movies. I remember when I was in the university housing - dorms, late at night, we used to have a lot of arguments with other students in the dorms, about how life would be after college. I was influenced by the many conversations I had with students who told me that life was going to be easy after university. An argument I repeatedly heard was that students study all day to achieve optimal grades, while life after college was simple.

People would work from 9-5, and have fun for the rest of the evening, and have fun on the weekends. At that time, I believed them because education is not easy it requires the will and you have to resist yourself in order to study and get the education. I spent 14 years at USC, working very hard, taking many classes, studying by myself, adding pressure, no matter the circumstance. In university, I always had exams and had to go the library to study or borrowed books from the library to write a paper. A lot of times, you would have to add pressure to yourself, and study between four walls in your room or study with a group of students to practice speech, in speech communication class, or going to a chemistry laboratory or physics laboratory late at night with a lot of concentration. You must force yourself to go to language laboratory's and force yourself to listen to tapes in foreign languages. The worst thing is going to an editing class for cinema, where you would have to sit by yourself

and work on it day and night, and drink coffee all night.
I spent 14 years at USC, working very hard, taking many classes, studying by myself, adding pressure, no matter the circumstance and graduated with a single degree in cinema. Whether I was sick, depressed, or tired, I had to keep studying and working hard. Education is not easy; it requires the will and you have to resist yourself. While your friends go out to a movie, party, or football game, you have to resist it and keep studying.
Sometimes, I had financial problems not having enough money for basic things, and sometimes I'd get sick with the flu (a cold, sore throat), or social and family problems. Sometimes I would get a bad roommate or bad guys on my floor. You have to concentrate and put it at the back of your mind. Education requires the will, hard work, and resisting yourself. That is why education is not easy, and why many people in the world are not educated. Even when taking easy classes such as horseback riding, not all of it is fun, sometimes you spend half the class cleaning the horses. We used to ride far away, between the hills of California, a far away from where the university is located.
Somethings I remember about horseback riding is that it makes you tired, forcing you to come back and sleep to wake up the next day. I once took a physical educational class, where we have to run for 5 miles, and do 200 push-ups and 200 sit-ups. I thought that it would be a fun and easy class. This was not the case. I ran for three miles, then got tired. When I took this class, I was not fit like the other students from the Marine corps. (There were a lot of students from the military in top universities because their education was paid for by the US army or US navy). I saw my classmates - who are primarily from the US marine-corps –finish the exercise and told the instructor goodbye. I followed them and told the instructor "Thank you, goodbye". He told me that I still had to finish the two miles. I was tired and exhausted by 6:30. I

asked my instructor if he had to eat dinner or go to his room. He said that he would not go until I finished running. I kept running, and after I finished the five miles, I thought that I was done. I then told him "Thank you, goodbye". He told me that I still had to do the 200 push-ups and the 200 sit-ups. I told him that I'd finish them another day. He said that I had to finish them tonight. I then slowly did them, then by nine o'clock, I was done and went to my room. The minute I entered my room, I fell asleep without having dinner, sleeping for nine hours and woke up the next morning.

Networking

1. The most important thing I learned at USC was networking. Networking at USC taught me how to contact and build connections later on for my business. Having the skill of meeting new people also made me able to know the key people everywhere.

2. One of the good things that happened to me in my life is that I started to learn how to meet people and make contacts and connections at an early age. This may be related to my family business and upbringing.
   However, going to a big university like USC and living in university housing helped in me getting smarter and meeting people and networking. I remember the historical day I had in university when I first started to learn about networking. It was during the month of August, the first week of school before classes began during the fall semester, where students moved their belongings into school. I was moving in just as the other students and decided to walk around in campus, closer to our dorms. Then I saw, some students, boys, and girls, playing volleyball. At that time, I was a nice and naïve young man. I did not know anyone. So, I was walking around, then I saw some students playing

volleyball. I started to watch them because I like volleyball. I asked them if I could join them and play volleyball with them. They agreed, and I started to play with them. This was in the afternoon. After that, I went back to take a shower. At dinner, I was standing next to my room, talking to one of the guys across the hall from me. Two girls were walking in the hallway and greeted me on their way to the cafeteria they are the same girls who played volleyball (they had to go through my hallway). We had some conversation about volleyball and then started talking about the room I was staying at. I invited them into my room and showed them around. There were many pictures framed in my room of me. They were impressed by the pictures of me playing volleyball, riding horses, playing tennis, snow skiing, and swimming. They complimented the number of hobbies I took part in. I replied by saying that I love sports and enjoy travelling. The two girls thanked me for showing them the pictures and continued to the cafeteria. I went alone to the cafeteria as my roommate was yet to move in with me. When I went to the cafeteria, I saw the same two girls sitting on a table with some boys and girls from their floor. They asked me if I wanted to sit with them. I agreed and joined them. They then introduced me to the boys and girls in the table that were from their floor. I started to talk to them. I found out that they lived on the third floor. At dinner, I met so many people, and started to talk to them.

3. That night, across the hall from me, there was a sophomore boy who was surrounded by the freshmen boys on my floor talking about life in the university. I joined them and was listening to him like the others and introduced myself to them. The next day, the two girls came by to my room on their way to the cafeteria, and they were talking to me, and they came to my room and were talking to me for a few minutes. They asked me if I wanted to go to dinner with

them. At dinner, by sitting with the two girls, I met more people from the same floor as them. The same night, I went upstairs to the same floor to visit those two girls and I ended up meeting and talking to more girls on that floor. I noticed that once you meet someone from a certain floor, you will then end up meeting everyone on that floor. This is called networking. That day, I learned something which helped me for the rest of my life, that when I visit a certain person on a certain floor, I end up knowing everyone on that floor. So, whenever I go to any company, all I have to do to get to know the people on that floor, I just need to know one person, and that person will help me to know everyone in that floor, in any company or organization. This follows in any oil company or place that I have business, because the people who work together know each other and will introduce you to others. So, by meeting them, you will end up knowing everyone on that floor.

4. There was a student who lived across the hall from me on the same floor named Mark. He was handsome and sociable, and many girls were attracted to him. He was a fraternity boy. He always spoke about surfing and having fun. He knew how to talk to and flirt with girls. The girls who came to talk to him are sorority girls. Usually, you will find more than a hundred boys in a fraternity house and over one hundred girls in a sorority house. They know each other very well. I started going with boys in the fraternities and the girls in the sororities to the movies since they needed a ride in my car. We had fun. I noticed that since they had a lot of things in common, they quickly got to know each other, and the clique started to form. The next day, Mark and I went to visit some of the sorority girls living on the second floor, where they introduced me to their neighbors. As time went on, the sorority girls I started to visit on the second floor started to have visitors from different buildings from the same sorority

house. I realized that once you know a person in a clique, from a certain sorority house, you will then know everyone from that sorority house. When I started to go to lunch, the girls on the second floor introduced me to more girls on different buildings. Mark also introduced me to more boys in his fraternity house. I remember that a boy from the fraternity house told me that when he used to meet his sister in her sorority house, he met so many girls from the same sorority. A few weeks later, I noticed that people started to meet each other from classes. The same kind of people who had something in common formed cliques because everyone likes to meet people who have something in common with him or with her. Everyone likes to meet people or is interested in meeting people who share the same interests as themselves. They say, 'birds of a feather flock together'. I also noticed that gossip and rumors spread quickly, for example, when a guy buys a new car, everyone in his fraternity house knows about his new car. Also, if a girl's parents get divorced, the word gets spread and all the sorority girls will know about it.

5. I also noticed that that the boys in the fraternity houses knew other boys in other fraternity houses, and the girls in the sorority houses knew other girls in other sororities, so, all the gossip and rumors will spread out quickly. Something I realized about fraternities is that people with common interests with the same cliques and same profession know each other even though they live far away from each other. This is applicable to what I see today, with how people in the same industry know each other. For example, lawyers know each other, even though they are from different cities, actors, producers and actresses know each other. Business men know each other even though some business men live in different cities and even in different countries. So, if something happens, like if a business man divorces his wife,

the other business men will know that. Also if a lawyer went on vacation, then the other lawyers would know this as well. In this case, the best way to know anyone, you have to know someone in his clique or in his profession, or the same group of people. Then, you will end up knowing everyone in his profession or in his level. So, the gossip rumors spread around. Basketball players sat at the same table as other basketball players, the same with football players tennis players swimmers on the swimming team (for both boys and girls) Then I learned networking, once you want to meet a certain person, you only have to know one person from that same group or clique. So, from this basic concept of networking, I started to meet people in oil companies, banks, and all other industries. Today, networking made me have a lot of contacts and connections, always asking me the same questions. How do I have so many contacts and connections, how I know everyone. If I wanted to meet someone in the film industry, like actors, actresses, producers, directors, he will just introduce me to one person and they will introduce me to the others. One of my professors who was in my script writing cinema class, knew a lot of script writers in Hollywood, and always invited them to our class. Also, he will sometimes invite big directors and producers to our classes because people in the same industry know each other. This is the also the case with taxi drivers and farmers. If you one day lose your luggage in a taxi, ask your current taxi driver how to reach the other taxi the one with your bag. Because, most of the time, taxi drivers socialize with taxi drivers, farmers socialize with farmers. Taxi drivers argue like taxi drivers and farmers argue like farmers Something I liked about college, was that I was socializing with students and all the students are educated people, so I learned things from them directly or indirectly. When farmers socialize with farmers, they learn more things about farming, and taxi drivers with taxis. A lot of times when I travel to some Asian countries I noticed all the taxi drivers have the same mentality and the same way of thinking. When you socialize with students for many years, you will learn a lot of educational things. Even when you argue with students, you will learn how educated people argue.

6. I always feel like I am a lucky person because I was in a big university like USC and not everyone was lucky like me. Our petroleum engineering professor always invited people from the oil industries and the big oil companies to our classes like Exxon-Mobile and chevron. Over the years, I developed my skill in meeting people and networking, this is why I have contacts and connections, in the beginning when I was a student living in the dorms in USC people who did not live in the dorms and went to small universities where they did not have dorms, do not know much about the skill of networking. The main point here is that going to university and living in university housing helped me a lot in having contacts and connections which is very important in the world of business. I want to mention something very important here. A person must be interested in meeting people and in networking. For example, all of my ex-roommates are not interested and keen to meet other people they are too lazy to put the effort to meet people. The important thing here, is that you have to be interested when meeting with people, if you are not interested, then you will never meet people. They are only interested in wasting their time on talking to their friends on their floor, or arguing with them all night, or watching football games with them on TV. At the same time, I was visiting other people on different floors and meeting new people every day and making new friends every day. Sometimes, when I sit in the cafeteria with my ex-roommate, many people come and talk with me, and I introduce them to my roommate. But, my roommate does not take advantage of the situation, and does not try to visit them

because he does not like to visit people. He would rather play with his friends on our floor. I always visit people because I think friendship is growing when you keep visiting people and talking to them. It is exactly like a tree, you must keep giving water to the tree every day, in order to make the tree grow. I had more than 14 different roommates in university housing when I was a student for 14 years in USC. Most of my ex-roommates are the same. When they graduate, they only have a few friends, and know a few people only.

7. The main point is that education will give the basics for a lot of things.
   Education is power, knowledge is power, information is power. So try to invest in yourself and spend money on education because that is the best investment. So try to educate yourself and try to read more books and try to learn more about everything. For example, to learn more about history, economics,psychology, science, languages, social skills and communication. So all what you learn today will help you tomorrow. It will help you sooner or later.

Chapter 19
Wisdom

A Chinese proverb says: the strong person is the one who can pass and walk through the problems and the wise person who can minimize the distance. So, wisdom can help you a lot to minimize the distance and to avoid the problems.

1. The world of trade and business needs and requires wisdom. A merchant or a businessman must be wise in order to grow and in order avoid financial problems. Being a hard worker is not enough to be a merchant or a businessman you must also be a wise person. If a person were not wise enough, they may lose everything.

2. Wise people in the world are very rare.

3. I know so many people who had the opportunity to make money. They lost it because they do not have the wisdom. They inherited the money and lost it because they did not have the wisdom.

4. Life is full of opportunities everywhere. There are many chances for a person to make money but most of the people in the world do not have the wisdom. It is like a blind person who is walking on the road or in the forest and there is gold under his feet, but he cannot see it. Some people cannot see the opportunity because they are dealing or socializing with the wrong people or with losers.

5. Some people are very greedy. They want to make a lot of money from the first day or the first deal. It is not wise to be greedy from the first day or the first deal. Greed is not good they say he who wants everything will get nothing. There is

a story of a greedy rich man in Russia who always likes to buy land and real estate. He once went to a village where the mayor of the village was a wise person. He told him in front of the others in the village, if you want pieces of land, we will give you pieces of land for free. He told him to go and place a flag in the pieces of land he wanted, but he had to come back before sunset. The further he went, the greedier he got. He kept delaying his return, trying to get as many pieces of land as possible. The time was getting closer to sunset. He suddenly noticed that it was right before sunset and he needed to go back. He didn't know what to do, he needed to run really fast to get back to the village in time. He put a lot of pressure on himself and his horse to run very fast. By the time he arrived, he was so exhausted that he had a heart attack that he fell down and died. The mayor of the village said that the man wanted everything yet he got nothing. All he ended up getting was a 2x1m grave.

6. Many people who inherit money lose their money quickly because they do not have the wisdom nor the experience.

7. There are a lot of poor people when they had an opportunity in business, they suddenly start to be overcome by greed and lose everything. Many times, I had to make deals with poor greedy people and it did not work because they are very greedy.

8. It is not wise to tell people of your business ideas. Some people, may end up stealing your idea because they have more contacts and connections and money than you do.

9. There are so many people who are not wise and cannot wait and do not like to listen. I already met a lot of these people. I tried to help them but they do not like to listen and cannot wait because they are not patient.

10. Sometimes, a person will go to see someone without knowing any basic things about that someone. Or they will start dealing with a person that they do not know that well. It is exactly like a man trying to marry a girl that he does not know well. Or a woman marrying a man without knowing any of the basic things about that man.

11. Even if you give people this book to read, they will not read it because they are not wise.

12. You will sometimes find a person that is not wise and try to help him and introduce him to the right people but he will end up being pushy and bother that person or he might be rude and make that person mad at him.

13. Sometimes, people don't understand that they have to be flexible with the money they want to charge for properties and houses. They lose the opportunity to rent out their houses or properties because of the high prices they put on them because they are greedy. They end up waiting many years to rent out their properties and houses while losing possible money they might gain and the opportunities present.

14. Sometimes, it is not smart to borrow a lot of money from banks to do business. Bank will constantly charge people high interest rates.

15. Sometimes, family problems and disputes between members of the family, it is not good for the company. Some members of the family are not wise or not flexible. This will lead to more financial problems in the company or even bankruptcy.

16. A lot of times, you will see people who only have a small idea on a business. He will start working on that business without the proper experience. For example, he never worked in a restaurant and yet he wants to open a restaurant. Or, he never worked in a hospital and wants to open a hospital where he will fail. That is not wise. There was a young man who worked at a hotel by the beach in California. I used to see him when I went to the beach on weekends. I used to talk to him late at night he used to work at the reception. He once told me that he has dreams of being rich. So, he told me that he wanted to quit working in the hotel and start his own business. He opened a shop to sell clothes.
Unfortunately however, he opened his shop in a very bad neighborhood because he did not want to spend a lot of money on rent. Some thieves ended up attacking his store and stole everything – all the cash he had all the goods he was selling while being held at gun point. They even used the man as a helper and accomplice, telling him to carry the goods to their car.They stole all his clothes and money at gunpoint. This young man claimed bankruptcy.

17. Sometimes, I draft an agreement with a company or a client letter of understanding before the formal agreement. Some people think I am stupid and keep telling me that this agreement has to be reviewed by a lawyer and that it will take a long time. However, I am trying to reserve the company or the client. The lawyer will take about 6 months to finish the paperwork. It is exactly like getting a fiancé before marriage, because marriage is more formal.
Sometimes, when I go to the beach, I leave my towel on a bench by the pool or beach and go eat breakfast – just to reserve the place during the weekends when it is crowded. When I see a line at a popular café, restaurant, or airport, I wait in line for a minute, talk to the person who is Infront of

me or who is behind me in line, and ask them to reserve my place. I step away to buy water or something else and come back. By doing this, I save time.

18. I know a person who always likes to push so hard for tough agreements from the beginning - arguing and fighting with the client or with the person he wants to deal with. He pushes very hard and is not flexible. He is still poor. He just wanted to get the maximum.

19. It is good for a merchant or businessman to stay in his own shop or business instead of trying to enlarge it. It is always good to stay in your own restaurant rather than trying to enlarge it. A lot of people who start to enlarge it lose their clients and their customers, not getting the same number of clients in the new location. Trying to do something that makes customers move away from your business and no longer use your services or product. This is evident in old shops, clinics, or restaurants. The owners think it is a good idea to expand and modernize however the effect is sometimes much worse and they up losing money and clients. Renovating for many months and wasting a lot of time will make his clients go somewhere else to seek services and products.

20. Making money is not easy, the only easy money you can get is inheriting money.

21. There was once a smart merchant who only made 5% profit. His neighbor who sold the same types of products was not making money he did not have many clients. The second merchant who does not have many clients does not know the reason why he does not have as many clients as him. One day, after a few years, during a wedding party the two met each other. The second merchant asked the first merchant why he has more clients. He told him his secret, that he was

selling the products cheaper than him. However, because of that, he is selling his products in big quantities.
Most people like paying less. By selling more quantity, I would have more clients. After telling his neighbor his secret of selling the products at a lower price, his neighbor followed in his footsteps and started selling his own products in high quantities for even less profit, where the two began competing for the best prices. Telling your competitors about your business secrets is not wise.

22. There was once an old man who sent his son to university to study business. When the son graduated from university and came back, his father gave him full authority to run his business which was a restaurant with a nightclub. It was a popular place a lot of people gathered by to have fun. There was a disease spreading amongst cows that made their meat more expensive. So, the son started to have smaller pieces of meat in his sandwiches and burgers just to maintain the price. The people who visited the nightclub criticized how there were smaller pieces of beef in their sandwiches. After a while, the climate changed: wind, hurricanes etc.. and the places where they were selling wheat and corn started to increase their prices. The son started to shrink the size of the burgers, just to maintain the price of the burgers.
Everyone in that nightclub started to criticized how much smaller the meat and burgers were than a long time ago. As a result, many people started to leave the nightclub and go to a different place to eat. When some people saw that their friends started to leave and go someplace else, they decided to join them and left as well, as the most important thing to them is their friends and their ability to hang out with them. Then, when other people saw that the nightclub and restaurant was empty, they started to leave the place. The son ended up claiming ankruptcy. This all happened because the son was not wise. What the son should have done instead, was keep the burgers as they were, but compensate by selling other things such as T-Shirts, caps, CD's, desserts or other things as well.

23. There is also a story of an old man and his son. The old man and his son started to buy shares. After a certain point, the shares started to make more money, so, the father decided to sell his shares. The shares reached a certain point where they were very high, so he sold his shares. He told his son to sell his shares and get out of his position. The son refused, thinking that the shares would go even higher because of what he was reading in the newspapers. The father sold a lot of his shares and made a lot of money, getting out of the stock market. The son's shares went down, and when he did eventually sell his shares, he lost money. Here, we can see that the father is wise, because he has a lot of experience in life, this is why he made money.

24. A person who respects his clients, and gives them compliments is a wise person because he increases the number of his friends and clients every day. He is nice, well mannered, and gives them compliments. While a person who is rude and has no manners lose their clients and lose their friends. That is not wise. There are also some people who have low self-confidence and feel very bad when you tell them anything because of their low self-esteem and their low self confidence. So be wise and be careful when you talk to those types of people.

25. People who lie and cheat lose in the long run.

26. It is always wise to deal with a good bank, you deal with bankers and not banks. This means that you deal with banks because the people in the banks are nice to you and because of how good their loans are, not because of the furniture and looks of the bank. When your business grows, it is always good to have more than one bank to deal with, because every bank is good in something, every bank has its own unique qualities.

27. Sometimes, you see some partners discussing some plans for the future which has not happened yet. For example, they are expecting money but did not receive money, so they keep discussing the plans for the future and what they should do with the money, and how to invest it. They start to waste their time by arguing and shouting at each other. It is like buying a fish and it is still in the sea. This is not wise. Let the money come, and then they should talk about it.

28. It is always good to maintain a good relationship with people and customers. It is good to give compliments to people. However, sometimes if a person has very low self-confidence, even if you were to give him a compliment, he may think that you are insulting him. For example, when you say "I like the way you talk or your accent". So be careful, as some would think that you are insulting them or insulting your race. Sometimes, the management in a company makes a mistake when they replace a smart manager with experience and connections knowing how to make money for the company. They replace him with someone else who isn't as capable as him, just to save money. Later on, in a few years, if you become successful in your business or your shop, or your company, do not try to expand suddenly and drastically and have the burden of spending more money on salaries and rent for your new employees and paying more money for expanding and the extensions. You have to be wise and stay where you are making good money every day, or every month. Save your money in the bank, after a few years, you can expand. I have seen many people fail when they become greedy and start to expand suddenly. Sometimes it is wise to stay with your old shop, old restaurant, and old office when everyone goes there, rather than moving to a bigger office and suddenly you do not get people there. And you lose your customers and clients in the process. In some cultures, they say, the older places have more blessings.

29. Most rich people think about prestige, fame, and what people are saying about them. Try to remember that whenever you approach rich people, you must consider fame and prestige. For example, they want people to know they are driving the best car, wearing an expensive watch, and in this case, they do not care about the prices. In this case, their priority is the prestige and not the prices.

30. Everyone must start a small business with a very small budget, otherwise, you will lose money and gain experience. Many entrepreneurs end up losing money on their first business venture because of their lack of experience. It is always good to start with a small business in order to gain experience. Even if you lose, you will lose little money, however, if you start with a big business, there will be a higher risk of losing larger sums of money.

31. It is sometimes wise to not talk about your plans, so do not talk about them, because some people will steal your ideas. Try to be low key because some people are jealous. No matter how nice you are to them, they will still be jealous of you, because, they do not have what you have. Sometimes, if a salesman sells something and makes 50 thousand profit, and this happens to you for the first time or once a year, some of your friends will wonder that if you made 50 thousand a week, how much would you make in a month. They will think that you are making 2.4 million a year. They may think to themselves "Wow, he is very rich" Some may start to be your enemy and will begin to hate you. Other people will come to borrow money from you. So, if you do not lend them, you will start losing your friends, even if the story started because you were bragging about making 50 thousand dollars on a single deal – and it was the only deal you made. When I was studying at USC, some students on my floor were very jealous of me. I had a nice and expensive

car, a Porsche. They used to scratch my car, and shake my car – whereby the alarm would go off. And sometimes, they would knock on my door, late at night, just to wake me up. They would knock on the door and run away.

32. It is a must to have good management and organize verything in your company. Also, be nice to your employees, and at the same time, be firm with them. Always remember that your employees will be talking about you.
33. There are a lot of companies around the world that make large projects, however, every time they take large projects, they lose money because they take a risk and put a low price just to become famous and well known to simply get more projects. Sometimes, this is not wise, as in the long run, they lose money, their debts increase, their losses increase, and finally file for bankruptcy.

34. Sometimes, when some people see a successful friend in business, they think that they can do the same thing and try to imitate him without knowing the factors of success he has.

35. Sometimes a successful businessman becomes greedy which makes him do mistakes where he will put all his money or his income in shares or in a new project. He does not know very well which led to lose everything and go through financial problems which is not wise. He is supposed to put only 10% or maximum 15% only.

36. Sometimes you see a successful businessman is doing good in his business, but instead of relaxing and enjoying his income and his success for few years. He becomes greedy and start to put most of his money and his income then he starts to suffer and have bad times and financial problems to expand his business quickly. Then he starts to suffer and have bad times and financial problems. That is not wise because he is supposed to relax for a while or only use 10% or 15%

of his income.

37. Sometimes a person would see that his best friend in high school become a successful businessman and would try to imitate his and do exactly the same business and would not consider the fact that his best friend's father is a businessman or comes from a family business where he learnt about business ever since his childhood for example the father was saying the reasons why the others are not successful in business. So, it would not be wise to imitate someone else because his circumstances are different than yours even though he would be your best friend.

38. It is wise not to borrow a lot of money from banks. In order to create and launch a business, it is better to use your own money. This is because banks sometimes charge you high interest rates and the business or investment did not make as much money as you had expected.

39. Wisdom is also important for the employees. There was once a big manufacturer which started to help a lot of poor people in the community by offering them jobs. Within a few years, the lives of the employees in the community changed. The standard of living in these communities got better, where the residents started to have nice cars and a good life. Unfortunately however, some employees started to steal money and started to get corrupt because some people are very greedy. Then, the manufacturer of the company went bankrupt, and everyone in the community lost their job.

40. Greed is not good. Some people who have no experience in business are very greedy. They always try to get more money than they should, and they do not want to start making money slowly. So, they lose everything, from the point they started.

41. They say the others, is you. Which means that a person is always optimistic and thinks that bad things will happen to others and not to him. This can come in the form of car accidents, where it can happen to other people but not to him. Or, other people will have diseases like diabetes, cancer, COVID-19, etc… but not him. The same thing can be reflected in business. When a person opens a shop or restaurant or any other business. He thinks he will make good money and will never go through financial problems and bankruptcy. It is wise in the beginning to think and consider that will happen if things go wrong.

42. A lot of rich people think about prestige. If you look at the order of needs in the form of a pyramid, you will see that the first and most essential thing a human will think of is having food, second is shelter, third is maintaining good health, fourth is to live in a secure and safe place, after that comes ambition and prestige. A lot of rich people or people with prestige think of buying big houses, big boats, expensive cars, souvenirs, or many different types of expensive items.
Sometimes, part of this is an investment, and sometimes, it is not a good investment. They invest in things outside of their line of business. It is not purely for investment, but for prestigious reasons as well.
At the same time, there is a good opportunity to invest their money in different things, with clearer profit.

43. Sometimes if a rich person goes on a vacation in London, Paris, or anywhere else in the world, he might invest some of his money in houses and farms driven by emotions and not investment.

44. When a person gets older, their mind gets stronger where they become more wise, however their body gets weak. A young man's body is strong like a horse, but his mind is small like a bird. If you are a young man who just started your business, it is good to take advice from older people who have more experience than you do.

45. A lot of times, some people like imitating their friends or others they know, without knowing the potential of the other. They think that if someone else made money, they can make money the same way just like the other person. He will say that the other person is not as smart as him, and he ends up failing because he underestimates the others. Maybe his friend in high school who he used to play with became a doctor and opened a hospital which became successful. He then tried to open a hospital and he is not a doctor and ends up failing because he is not a doctor.

46. When I was a student at the University of Southern California, there were a lot of athletes living with me in the dorms or in the other buildings. I would see them everywhere. USC, established in 1881, is very famous for sports and athletes. Football, volleyball, basketball, swimming, and tennis are all examples of sports the university endorsed. During the Olympics of 1976, if they had considered USC as a country, it would have been number four in the world, after the United States, the Soviet Union, and Germany. I know a freshman girl who lived in our building who was on the track team and had a baby face. She always used to come visit my neighbors the boys on my floor. I had always underestimated her. I once saw her on my way to class and asked her to race. Within a few minutes, I was shocked and surprised with how fast she was, much faster than me. I looked at her like a normal freshman who is

younger than me. However, I had forgotten the potential she has since she was on the track team training for the Olympics. The mistake I made thinking that she was at the same level as me while being on the Olympic track team is an example of what it means to mistakenly think that everyone has the same potential. Just like how a businessman cannot compete with a specialist in a certain field, I could not compete with the Olympic level track runner. When a businessman sees one of his friends or someone successful in a certain business, he thinks that he has the same potential and circumstances as him.

47. It is always wise to make a feasibility study before pursuing a project. This company will estimate how realistic the project or business you are intending to startup is estimating everything from the costs to the benefits and profits you will make in a year. Those are consulting companies as well as auditors at the same time. They are well known in the world of business and finance.

48. A lot of times, when I want to start a business with some people, I draft an agreement. Some people think that I am stupid because it is not a formal agreement, however, I do this just to reserve the company or partner to work with me in the near future. In most cases, they will have the moral obligation to work with me. It is just like putting a towel in a certain area on the beach, you do not own or ensure that others will not take your place, but it is morally unaccepting if people do. You will save that spot for you while you go off doing something else for an hour or two. The same thing happens when I make an informal agreement to reserve a client or partner. It is not attested or signed by a lawyer or foreign body, but the other person or party will have the moral obligation to work with me instead of going after someone else. I remember when I once traveled to England,

there was no limit on my credit card, I wanted to reserve a room in the hotel before anyone else did. I was able to even though the card would normally not work in such situations, but I did and we ended up getting the room.

49. Sometimes when I am on my way to lunch or going to the gym, if there is a business deal or someone needs to give me money, I prioritize the deal or money since this opportunity is not going to happen again. So if this happens to you, take the money now and go to the gym or lunch later and do not say you will do it tomorrow, because the person who offers you the money or deal might be sick tomorrow or may be a rainy day or something will suddenly come up and he has to go somewhere else tomorrow. So never say that you are busy and pre occupied with something else and save it for another day. These chances and opportunities are not always there, so do not lose them.

50. You will notice many people start their business by working very hard and saving money but later on in their life start spending a large amount of money on charity and helping people. Also there will be more blessing in the business and good for his reputation so if you become rich later on ty to help people also try to focus to help your relatives, people in your community, your childhood friends and old friends who were nice to you and supported you when you started your business because helping people once is not enough, life is rough. For example, if you help an old friend who had debts and solved his problems temporarily a year later, he might have some problems and would need your help because life is always full of problems and people always need help.

51. Change your mindset. For example, a rich person buys assets like gold to sell it at the right time. A poor person would buy gold to wear it and show off. A rich person will buy a house

to sell it and a poor person will buy a house to stay in it and show off.

52. It is wise to read all chapters in this book because every chapter is important. It is not wise to leave or skip one chapter.

53. Don't take a loan to open a business because success is not certain but the loan and paying the money back is certain. For example, if somebody borrows 11 million dollars from the bank in order to buy real estate for 11 million dollars hoping it will go up to 13 million dollars. But the price of real estate only reaches 12 million dollars after a few years while the loan of the bank with interest will reach 14 million dollars. Similarly, if somebody borrows 9 million dollars from the bank hoping the small hospital will make money of around 12 million dollars but after a few years all the profit of the hospital reaches 10 million dollars while the interest with the loan reaches 13 million dollars.

54. Chasing the right timing for starting the business is important or at least considering the timing.

55. Bank loans make some people lose money after a while because those people are taking the risk, they think about today and they don't think about the future. It is similar to a story that is well known in the Middle East. There is a person his name is Juha who was a funny character. The story About a king who wanted to find a teacher to teach his donkey to read and write within 20 years. The king said that whoever can teach his donkey how to read and write will be awarded with 50,000 pieces of gold coins. which is worth millions of dollars in our currency today. He has to sign a contract with the King to show the King's donkey how to read and write within 20 years or else the King will have him killed.

Most of the people in the kingdom were scared of signing the agreement with the king because they know they would not be able to teach the donkey, except for Juha who went to the King to sign the agreement, received the gold and the King's donkey. When he left the palace, the people asked Juha is he was crazy or stupid and told him that he will be killed after 20 years. He replied: "within 20 years something will happen, either the King will die or I will die or the donkey will die. Now let me enjoy life with all the gold and money I got." This story shows you that there are a lot of people like that, where they only think of the present and not the future, by borrowing money and spending money.

56. There are people whose debts will increase as time goes on. For example, a person who would borrow money from one of his friends. First borrowing from his first friend (Friend A), then his second friend, (Friend B), and finally Friend C. He will go back and pay Friend A with the money he borrowed from Friend C. As time goes on, because this person pays interest to his friends on his standing debts, the interest will increase and the debts will increase. Within a few years, the person would have financial problems.

57. There was an Italian person who had a trick in the early 1900's he used to borrow money from people and then return the money with high interest telling the people he was investing the money for them then more people started to give him their money as time goes on more people gave him their money then he had a lot of money in his hand. finally, people knew his trick then he was arrested.

58. If a person were to take a credit card from a bank (Bank A), and take another one from Bank B, and a third card from Bank C where he pays for the debt on Bank A. Then, he will

open a credit card in Bank D to pay the debts of Bank B. That person will reach a point after a few years where he will not be able to pay the interest or the fees. This is not wise. Many people try to borrow money from Bank A then Bank B then Bank C and pay their debts by using the other banks all the while the banks are charging interest. After a few years this company or this person will start to have financial problems. Because the interest rates will increase, the debts will increase. There is a term in the world of banking called turnover. This is how much money you are depositing in your account every month and every year. From that, they can tell the financial size of the company. It will be completely different than an average person who has a salary of 7,000$ a month, where he keeps the money in the bank constantly withdrawing almost finishing his money on daily expenses before his next salary. For example, if the company were to deposit 20,000$ every day, within one month, it will be around 600,000$ and within a year it will be around 7,000,000. The owner of the company can go to the bank at the end of the year and borrow large amounts of money, 3 million for example.

Unfortunately, there are some people who like to cheat the banks. By constantly depositing and withdrawing every other day or every three days the same amount of money just to make the turnover of their companies very high. By doing that, when the turnover becomes very high, they can borrow very large amounts of money from the bank as a loan. Because, the computer in the bank can count how much you are depositing every year. It shows that the company has a big turnover, which means that there are a lot of daily transactions and daily business in the company. The bank computer does not process that this is a trick. Finally, the owner of the company will start borrowing large amounts of money from the bank. For example, 5 million dollars a year for the first time, and then 20 million dollars for the second year, and 100 million for the third year and so on. All he is doing is simply depositing and withdrawing money from the bank, and it is not actually a real business – it is simply a trick or a show off. The owner of the company may do the same with other banks by playing the same game. After a few years, they will reach a point where they cannot pay their debts. This is not wise. It is not only about turnover. At the same time, some owners of companies know how to borrow money from banks, or they have the skill to borrow money from banks by having good credit with the banks, and paying the bank their installments on time. When this happens, the bank begins to increase their credit limit also having the skill to know the right people in the banks and how to deal with them and how to ask for more loans. They have the skill to manipulate the bankers and bank manager and tell them that their company is making a lot of money and has a good future, telling them that it is getting bigger and bigger every day. They even exaggerate the income by having a large monthly turnover; which may be due to the deposit and withdrawal actions taken daily. The monthly bank statement shows that the company has a good business and a solid income. They deceive the banker just like how a playboy would want to meet with a beautiful girl. He would try to tell his girlfriend or fiancé that he has many cars in his house, even though he just used a bus or a taxi because he was in a hurry, and is very rich. Or he will tell the beautiful girl that he is in good health and plays all kinds of sports and is the smartest person in the world and that his father is very rich – having a big boat and a big yacht – possibly even saying that his father is a big producer in Hollywood, so he could hire the girl to be an actress in one of his films. After a while, his girlfriend or fiancé will discover that the boy was lying to her. This applies to the companies as well, where the bankers will realize that the companies are going through bankruptcy. This is why some owners of the company know how to borrow money, but not how to make money. In the long run you will find that that person will have a lot of credit cards and pay a lot of money on his credit cards. His debts will be increasing, and that is not wise. When you take money from card C and pay the full amount of card A and B, they will consider you a good client and constantly increase your credit limit. I remember in university during summer, I went to London and the hotels were full and I wanted to reserve a room in one of the hotels I liked so much. I gave them my visa card with a 300 dollar limit to reserve the room in the hotel. I later received the money to pay for the hotel. The most important thing is that this example shows how to reserve a room or something similar. In real business, it is very important to reserve a company or a client.

59. 80% of rich people are born poor. Save money to invest not to buy a nice car or a nice house. Invest your money in something you know to increase your income.

60. You must be wise to take every factor of success in this book seriously because every factor of success in this book is important. Not taking some factors of success seriously is a disaster and not wise.
61. Sometimes it is hard to maintain the wealth. Sometimes you see somebody who became rich because he has some of the factors of success which are mentioned in this book but then he loses everything suddenly because he does not have the other factors of success and he think that the other factors of success are not important. For example, I know some students at USC who took the entrepreneurship program at USC business school. When they started they were successful and made money and the media was talking about them. They had some factors of success:

1. The money to start
2. The experience and they know what they are doing
3. They loved their job
4. They made the contacts and the connections.

Then things went wrong because they were not wise. They were greedy and they wanted to expand quickly and lost everything. Then I noticed that they did not have the other factors of success. For example, besides the wisdom they lacked, they were:
Not optimistic, they gave up quickly.

5. They were lazy, they did not have to work hard to recover.
6. They did not want to sacrifice and life with low budget even though they lost their money they were still living in luxury apartments, luxury cars etc.
7. They were not strong to resist and start again.

Also, there is a story about a man who became very rich, and the media was talking about him and his big parties on big boats. This person when he started had the factors of success like:

1. An education
2. Contacts and Connections
3. Luck, he came at the right time and met the right people at the right place.

So, this man did not have the factors of success to maintain his wealth. For example:

1. He did not have the experience in business or in investment, so he invested hundreds of millions in the wrong projects.
2. He was not wise because he did not focus on his business but instead, he kept focusing on his parties and meeting people. He is an entertainer not a businessman.
3. He did not work hard and was not persistent. He was lazy.

64. It is always wise to start your business when you are young, healthy and are able to take risks before the age of 35 years old and before you get married.

65. You must focus on one thing, or one business so don't jump from one business to another business every month. It is wise to start a business you know very well. Because sometimes you see a person making little money from his business which he knows and has experience in it then he hears that there is another business he does not know which makes a lot of money then he jumps to that business and he starts to lose money. This is not wise; you have to stay with the business you know very well. I know a person for the last 40 years who has dreams to be rich and he works hard from early morning to late at night but his
problem is that he is not wise, he keeps jumping from every business from every month to every year. This person is very poor until today, he has no car and no money and no nice clothes to wear.

66. Don't put all your eggs in one basket, have multiple sources of income. Examples include real estate, gold, stock, or any kind of business.
Because one day you might need those things. Also, a good investment is when you have good friends. Good friends will help you in case you go through financial problems. Don't rely on one business or one source of income. Don't put all your eggs in one basket because the time will change after a few years you will find certain business go up and others go down.

67. Greed is not good. For example, if somebody bought shares or real
estate the price of it went up but he did not sell it because he

is a greedy person and he waited hoping it will go up again and did not go up because of unexpected bad years in the economy then he will lose a lot of money. Especially if he had borrowed money from the banks which will charge him high interest rate.

68. Greed is not good. He who wants everything will get nothing.

69. Every job has some secrets other people don't know. Only people who have long experience in that job know about it so the same thing goes for a business. Every business has some secrets other people don't know, only people who had the experience for a long time in that business know about the secrets of that business. So, try to know those secrets of that kind of business.

70. You must start with a small project in order to gain experience. Those who inherit money lose their money quickly. The same thing with those who win money from lotteries. They lose their money quickly because they don't have the experience and because they don't know how to start with small projects. By starting with big projects in millions, they suddenly lose everything. The wise person would start a project with small amount of money and grow his business over the years.

71. If your father is a businessman, it is more likely that your mindset will be like a businessman.

72. Sometimes you see an old shop or an old restaurant has many clients and making money. It is wise to leave it as it is and not to expand it. Sometimes there are people who make mistakes the minute they see their business from an old shop or old restaurant is generating money they start changing the

shop or the restaurant or the gym and spending a lot of money on doing the changes then they lose a lot of money and a lot of clients.

73. They say don't put the eggs in one basket. It is always good to have another source of income like real estate or a building. If you have real estate or a building try not to sell it because once you have cash in your hand it is very easy to spend it and one day you might need this source of income. For example, if somebody has $1 million in his hand, he will buy a nice car for himself or will go on a vacation with his wife or he will spend on things not important. Also, good friends are good assets in cases of bankruptcy.

74. It is always wise to keep some properties or building in your own name and not to sell it because once you sell your properties and get a lot of cash it will be very easy for you to spend it. For example, you might spend the money on buying new cars, new furniture, or you might go on a vacation with your wife, etc. Then a year later you will find that you have no money left and of course, no property.

75. There are millions of ideas and millions of opportunities in the world to make you rich. Think, read, and look around you. You will find that every day, somebody had new ideas or new opportunities and became rich. So if you had a chance, or an idea to start a new business and you have a doubt, it will not make enough money to cover your expenses. Just wait for a few months or a year and you will find a better idea or a better opportunity because in the world, there are always opportunities for new business.

76. Sometimes, a person might change his line of business from having restaurants to rent a car business and maybe he will

find his second line of business suits him better and will be happy with it and then he will, in the long run, be happy that he went through bankruptcy and then changed his line of business.

77. When your company starts to grow, try to start a different business, don't put all your eggs in one basket. Businesses are always like this, some businesses will be booming in certain years, and some businesses will go down in certain years. So, it is wise to have different kinds of business.

78. It is wise to repeat things to your clients just to remind them and again it is wise to repeat things to your employees because in spite of repeating things to people, they still take time to understand. In business you want to make money and not to lose money.

Many times I was disappointed because though I explained to some of my friends and some peoples I know about the stock market in a simple way, and they understood me. Then few days later those very friends and the other peoples who listened to someone else talk about the same subject, in a very complicated way, followed them and then they lost a lot of money but at the end they regretted it and came to me and said we wished we had listened to you but now it's too late.

79. Also in business regarding making money I explained things in a simple way and repeat things many times just to help people, but i noticed some people don't appreciate me and they said you repeat things many times and use very simple words and terms and I tell them I'm like a school teacher in a high school and University Professor who try to help students so they repeat things to the students before the examinations but some students still gets bad grades. So this is why you might notice I repeat some important things in this book many times.

80.Most of the people like it when I explain things in a simple way, even my school teachers when I was in 6th grade and also later on my university Professors at USC used to like it even though I repeat certain things many times but I make people understand my point more than some people who talk and write in complicated way and using difficult words and difficult terms and ideas.

81.Many times I noticed when I explain things and repeat things people tell me that they learned something they are not aware of, for example when I explained things in Geology to a person who was working in an Oil company for the last 25 years, he told me he learned things about the subject more than the people he met before.

Also the same thing in history when I explained things to some people who are interested in history they tell me they like the way I explain to them and things became more clear to them even though they heard about the same subject before but it was not explained to them the way I did it and they tell me that now, they understood the subject much better.

82. Sometimes I talk about psychology to people about a person they know that he is a bad person even though I repeat many times and I explained to them in psychology why he is a bad person but they don't believe me. Few years later they discover that I was right and that person was indeed a bad person.

83.There are some people even if I explain to them and repeat to them hundred times they don't understand.

84.Most of the people don't know how to start a business, usually when a person wants to start anything he starts asking his friends or the people he knows, sometimes he will end up asking a stupid person who thinks he knows everything, but finally he will end up misleading him.Same times it is good to start asking your friends and the people you know to lead you to another group of people more professional and have more experience.

85. I remember that I met many students who went to the wrong universities and they choose the wrong major after that they regretted because they started to ask some unintelligent people for an advice, I even noticed some students choose the wrong apartments to live in and they start to complain because they started asking the wrong people for an advice.
The problem is when the man marries the wrong wife and the woman marries the wrong husband because of the wrong advice. I know a person who married a woman who beat him up every week because his friend told him to marry that lady.

86. The same thing when a person start any kind of business like a restaurant or shop, he starts asking his friends or the people he knows which is step 1 because he was focusing on step 3 and step 4 he didn't know step 1 is the most important step. He fails because he asked some inexperienced person. There are a lot of people who don't know how to start because they start asking the wrong people for advice.
87. When a person wants to build a house the first step is to ask a good consultant so if the design is good the house will be good. The same thing if a person wants to build a manufacturing unit the first step is to bring good company to do the feasibility study and good design so the manufacturing unit will be successful.

88.There are people who don't know the first step to approach people and start conversation to make friends.

Chapter 20
Vision

1. When a person has a vision, he has good planning. Usually, education and experience makes a person have a good vision.

2. If a person with a vision sees a small village growing due to the village's location being next to a gold mine, oil field, or next to the mountains (which became a tourist attraction), there will then be new roads because of the location.
   The person who has a vision can see in the near future that there will be more people and more visitors who will be coming there to start and buy real estate. The person with a vision will start buying real estate when it is cheap, knowing that in the future the prices of the real estate will increase and become more expensive. He will then start building houses and apartments for rent. He may also open a hospital or a supermarket knowing for certain that the business will grow in the near future, where he will tell his wife to suffer and sacrifice with him by not going on vacations for the next few years, until he becomes rich from investing money and real-estate.

3. In business, one door will open another door for you. Just be optimistic and wait, and things will work out for you. This means that a particular business could lead you to another.

4. The important thing is to start now, and things will work for you. For example, if a college student living on campus in university housing started selling candy and chocolate to students, but after a few months, he noticed that he's not making good money. He is wasting both his time and money. Then, some other students will give him advice to sell a special type of soap and shampoo to other students

especially to other girls on campus. Then, things will work for him and he will start to make money. However, he might regret that at the beginning, where he was selling chocolate and candy, might have been a waste of money. However, I see it as a good start for him, where selling the candy and chocolates allowed him to gain the experience.

5. There was a poor student in our buillding who was tall and big this student was walking with me late at night to the library.

Then i paid him 5 five dollars because i was a fraid to walk alone at night.

However i noticed that this poor student had a dream to be rich and famous.

He started to sell soap and shampoos, to the students on the campus.

Some students in the building were making fun of him because they think he is stupid and wasting his time.

But at the same time i was encouraging him to continue his little business on the campus.

Later on he gained the folloing things:

A. He started to know how to approach people to sell them things.soap – and shampoo.

B. He started to know when to approach people and find the right time.

C. He started to gain self confidence in explaining his products to people.

D. He started to go to different places on campus and different buildings on different locations.

E. He started to know that there are nice and respectful clients, as well as rude clients.

F. He started to meet more people and make more friends.

G. He started to know what people and clients like and the type of products they like.

H. He will then start to know about the best days and events to sell his products, for example during football games or on the weekend.

I. He will then start to think as a merchant or businessman about how much money he is making and how much money he is losing by doing simple calculations every night.

6. The city of Los Angles has high crime rate, So this is why im afraid to walk alone at night.So sometimes I used to ask a big tall guy to walk me to the library or to my car in the parking lot, then i used to pay him 5 Dollars. Also when the library closing at 12 midnight i called the same person to come to pick me up from the library even if he is sleeping i wake him up.

Sometimes If the big guy is not available i ask two short guys to walk me to the library or to my car. Then i used to pay them 5 Dollars each. If they are too nice people they refused the money the next day i buy them a pizza. Sometimes i even ask 2 girls or 3 girls to walk me to the library or the parking lot, then the next day i buy Them Pizza.

My ex roommate he used to make fun of me and call me

a chicken.
I remember at one time i asked a tall volleyball player to walk me to my car.But i told her i need 2 girls to walk me, she said she is strong enough to beat up all the guys on my floor.Then my ex roommate started laughing.

Also i remember one nice tall guy from mississippi who was too nice he always walk me to my car and he always refues to take the money or to buy pizza for him.

7. Let us go back about how one door opens another door.This man i assume he started by selling chocolates and candy, another door will open for him and he will ended up selling soaps and shampoo. Maybe, someone will start selling bicycles and another door will open for him where he will start selling cars. for example if we assume there is a man who started by selling choclate and candy and soon another door will open for him and he will end up selling soaps and shampoo, I assume in the future over a long period of time. He will start having more clients and making good money, then, he will start thinking like a real merchant or businessman, then he will start to get more ideas about business

I assume he will start having more clients and making good money, then he will start to get more ideas about business, then someone may give him an idea or some advice to open a pharmacy, in order to sell more of his products and some other cosmetics and things. Then, he will sell more of his shampoo and cosmetics and medicine. By doing that he will end up meeting many different pharmacists and doctors. Those people, the pharmacists and doctors, will advise him to open a clinic to treat patients or a small hospital. Then after a few years, he will realize that he will need x-ray machines for his patients.

He will also come to realize that the same companies selling him x-ray machines for his patients are also selling x-ray machines for airports. Then, after a few years, some of your friends will give you some advice to sell x-ray machines to airports. By visiting the airports and dealing with the people in the airports, you will start to know about firefighting. Then, the door will open for you to sell things related to firefighting, which will be like a new business for you. After a few years, you will end up selling firefighting extinguishers to power stations generating electricity for the houses. This will lead you to be in the power and energy industry which will allow you to have much more money and increase your income. Oil companies always need power, this may lead you to an even bigger business, oil and gas.

8. The main point here is that a lot of businesses are connected to each other. This is what I meant when I said that any kind of business will lead you to another business or how one door will lead you to another door after a certain amount of time. Also, the oil and gas business might lead you to the roads and construction business, because you might see that in the refineries you will have to build small roads and small civil construction projects. All this will lead you to have a civil construction company.

9. When you have a good vision for the future of your business try to divide in many steps. Step 1, step 2, and step 3. Just do it with good planning and things will work for you. The same way things will work for others and other companies, it will work for you. It also worked for me. So, when you break your plan or problem into sections, it will be so easy for you to accomplish your dream.

10. In order to achieve your goals and dreams, you must have a vision and divide your steps. So no matter how hard or big

your goal, it will be possible over a long period of time to divide it into steps. So, you must always consider the time factor. For example, in order to do step one, you need three years, in order to do step two, you need one year, and to do step three you need two years etc. So, you must be realistic and think in the long run. So, if you do that you must have a good vision about the future of your business.

11. A business man must be patient when he starts his business. And, he will go through some kind of sufferings also. For example, he will save his money and not go on vacation when he starts his business, and not live a luxurious life. And not live the same life as his friends, who works as employees. You will find that the employee will spend all his money on vacations, buying nice cars and luxuries, and will always listen to his wife. He must save his money and go through some suffering to establish his business, it will take him seven years or even ten years, and he must tell his wife that now is the time to suffer, but later on, he will live life like a king and she will live a life like a queen.

12. You must have weekly goals, monthly goals and yearly goals.

13. You must know where you are going in order to achieve your goals and dreams. You mist divide it into steps: step one, step two and step three etc.

And do it slowly but surely.

14. Choosing the right timing for starting the business is important or at least considering the timing.
15. A smart person who has vision can see what people need or what kind of products they want now or in the future. Do

people need in this town fast food for cheap hamburgers or diet and healthy food like the Japanese sushi. Do they need a restaurant or a hospital or weekly flights to the moon or cars that work on electricity or solar energy.

16. Usually businessmen and merchants cannot grow their business without the help of banks. Because, bank are always good partners. They will be supporting you. You must have banks as partners to expand your business. You must maintain good credit with the banks. Banks will help you once they start trusting you. They will keep giving you loans to expand your business, so, try to invite bank managers to your office or your house. The person who has a vision will maintain a good relationship with the bank, so the bank will giving him higher credit and more loans to grow and expand his business.

Chapter 21
Careful-Thieves

1. Be careful and do not be too nice or naïve and don't trust people.
   Because, there are a lot of thieves and bad people everywhere. Those people always have different tricks and methods to steal money.
   Sometimes, the thieves will be your best friends or best partners, or even your brother or sons. A lot of employees steal money from their own companies, restaurants, and shops. Thieves are the biggest problem in business, always has been, always will. A lot of times unfortunately, the thieves are the people you trust.

2. A lot of employees steal money from the company they work at. They start having ways to steal because of how they know the system of the company. Because they have been working at the same company or same shop for many years. They will always try to steal whenever they have the chance to.

3. A lot of companies collapsed, disappeared or went bankrupt throughout history because of theft or because of bad people who stole money. Before you start having any business, no matter how small, you have to think and consider that there are a lot of thieves and bad people everywhere. And one day you might be a victim of those thieves and bad people. As I have mentioned earlier, those thieves might be your best friends or your brother, or even one of your sons. Thieves are everywhere in the world and in every country. Thieves have no nationality.

4. I Remember when I was a freshman in the dormitory at USC. I met a freshman student on my floor. Everybody was

talking about him in the building, because when he received the money for tuition from his parents to pay the university. He decided to use the money to travel to Europe. When I asked him why he is doing this, he replied that he wanted to travel to Europe and see the world and to have fun.

I was shocked to hear that because his parents trusted him and they wanted him to have the education in a good university but the son was not used to having a lot of money in his hand. So he decided suddenly after the first week of school to travel and to have fun. He did not think about his future or his education he was thinking just about travelling and having fun.

5. Bad people and thieves can fool you and start business with you and can approach you in a nice way and tell you about making quick and easy money while investing your money in their companies. Bad people in your client's company can also hurt your business because they do not personally like you, or are jealous of you, so they will help your competitors against you. When the bad people or thieves meet you for the first time, they try to impress you by telling you they have a lot of money or they want to be your friend or will start talking to you about a subject you like to talk about. They may talk about your hobbies or sport of interest as well. In the long run however, they will convince you to work with them or be your partner. A lot of rich people are used by those faked friends. If you are not rich then do not worry, no one will approach you.

6. When I was a student at USC, one of my best friends used to tell me that his father used to own seven restaurants in Los Angeles, then the employees started to steal money from the restaurant since they kept receiving money or cash from the customers, where they would end up putting the money in

their pockets. Then, his father lost a lot of money and sold all of his restaurants, because he was losing money and his employees did not appreciate that he was giving them jobs they were too busy stealing his money.

7. When I was in Hawaii, a taxi driver told me that he was once very rich, but he made a mistake by trusting his partner who was his best friend, and he stole the money and ran away. He now lost everything and this is why he became a taxi driver.

8. In one of my trips to Morocco, I met the owner of a grocery store, who told me that he was once rich and when he asked some people to do paint job for his shop, he noticed that one of the employees was a young man who used to come in the very early morning before the others. He noticed that this young man was very clever and very ambitious, so, he trusted him and hired him to work for him. So, that young man started to cheat his boss in quiet a unique way. This young man found a way to use the public telephone without a charge. The store used to charge their clients 5 dollars for using the telephone line, however, since this young man could use it for free, he charged the clients 3 dollars and kept the money all to himself without his boss knowing. After one year of using this method, the telephone company came to realize that someone was exploiting their services. The telephone company sued the owner who had no idea of what his employee was doing and lost all his money made from the store, the employee on the other hand ran away with all the money he had been collecting for the past year.

9. The owner of the grocery store also told me that there was a person who had a worse case than him. He works most of the time and never socializes with people, always busy working in his department store or super market. He once went to a wedding where some people asked him why he was working

24 hours a day. He replied saying that he was not working 24 hours a day. They said that they saw the backdoor of his store open at 3am and that there was a truck, where some people were moving things from the store to the truck. He said, that it was impossible, since no one has the keys to the backdoor except his manager who has been his manager for the past 20 years while also being his childhood friend. He finally realized why he was not making good money after 20 years – it was because his manager was stealing products from his store.

10. In Saudi Arabia, an owner of a pharmacy told me a story of one of his employees who he trusted the most. He used to sell products and medicine in the pharmacy to clients while putting all the money he would receive straight into his pocket. This was possible because of the fact that every time he would sell a product to a client, he would replace the product put on stand by the same product in the store. The owner had not realized this.

11. In Egypt, a rich person thought a person was very smart for opening a good restaurant, since there were a lot of people visiting Egypt to visit the pyramids and other tourist attractions. He thought he would make good money since tourists always had money to go out for dinner. After a few months, he noticed that he was losing money because the employees are stealing money from the restaurant, as well as salt shakers, pepper, sugar, forks, knives, meat, fish basically anything they could get their hands on.

12. On my trip to Morocco, in my hotel I met an accountant who used to work in Sudan as an accountant for a company selling peanuts. He told me a story of two brothers from the middle east who are in the business in buying and selling peanuts. One of the brothers is located in Sudan, who

is buying the peanuts and exporting them to France, where his brother is distributing the peanuts. He was surprised when the brother in Sudan told him to forge the invoices. Suppose that the peanuts costed 700,000$, he would tell his brother that they cost 900,000$, so he would put 200,000$ in his pocket. So, this accountant confronted the man and asked why he had been cheating his brother and not honest with his brother. He answered by saying he is working very hard in the hot weather in Africa, while my brother is enjoying life in Paris, France.

13. There are some reasons why people steal money.

1. Because they have no morals and this is the way they were brought up. When children do not learn morals and that stealing is wrong or their parents do not teach them that stealing is wrong, kids grow up not thinking that stealing is a really bad thing.

2. When there is no control in the company and no prevention, stealing will increase in the company.

3. They steal because they wanted to make money in an easy way, so they do not want to work hard for it. Especially if they were born poor in a bad neighborhood and suddenly noticed that it is so easy to put money into their pockets. Say for example, they saw the struggles of their parents while growing up, and how hard it was for them to make money, only for them to reach an age where making and stealing money comes very easy.

4. Some people steal money because of greed. They think they deserve the money because they work harder than their boss and maybe work harder than the owner of their company. They think that their boss is just a lucky person and worked

harder than him, so they believe that they deserve a larger piece of the company.

5. Some people steal because they think that it is fun to steal and stealing is a habit for them.

6. On a larger scale, there are many people in the world who steal millions from their companies, because they know the system and have the experience in the company, so, they find it very easy to steal Some people steal because they see other people stealing from their companies so they take inspiration.

7. If an employee is working hard and is not appreciated by the boss and believes that he is working harder than their boss, he starts to think that his boss is not nice to him and starts stealing money from him.

8. Stealing is everywhere, it is a part of human nature, I have noticed that since I was young and a student. You do not have to be a businessman to be cautious or careful of thieves who are everywhere. Even when I was young and in university I was careful of such people.

9. There was someone who used to come to our refrigerator in the dorms and drink our milk when we were not there.

10. My ex-roommate always used to try and steal mugs, knives, and spoons every time we went out to a restaurant.

11. I also remember when living in the dorms at USC, every time I tried to do my laundry for my clothes, I have a problem. Because, when I put my clothes in the washing machine and go to bring the coins and detergent, someone will steal some of my clothes or throw some of my clothes and start using the washing machine. When I put the coins in the washing machine just so I reserve it until I come back

and go to bring my clothes and detergent, they would be gone by the time I am back, either stealing the detergent or coins I left as a reserve. I finally learned to wash my clothes at midnight or early in the morning when no one is there.

12. I remember when I went to Japan, I stayed in a 5 star hotel, where they stole my Rolex watch.

13. Also, in California, I rented a car and when I asked the employee at the desk of the rent a car company whether he wanted cash or a credit card, he gave me a receipt not mentioning I paid, stealing the money and putting the money in his pocket. That same popular rent a car company repeatedly kept sending me invoices telling me to pay even though I had already paid. When I told them that I already paid in cash, they told me that it wasn't their problem and that a lot of their employees had been stealing money so I wasn't supposed to pay in cash.

14. Sometimes the manager will ask why his employee is stealing from him even though he is nice to him. Why do some people become bad people and thieves. As I mentioned earlier in the book about psychology and marginalities; that some people have a lot of marginalities and problems in their childhood.

1. Someone who has no father nor mother an orphan.

2. Someone that was born half blind or crippled and the kids at their school are making fun of them.

3. If someone is very short and everyone is taller than them in the neighborhood, that is marginality.

4. If someone's parents are very poor, while other people at school have rich parents.

16. Usually, it is the nice and naïve people who are the victims of thieves. So, when it comes to money, don't trust people and say that a certain individual is your best friend or brother. So, if the boss is a nice person and had a good childhood, he should not expect that everyone in the world is like him.

17. There are also thieves who are:

1. Ready to steal your business ideas that would make your projects or businesses their own by taking the idea of your business and copying it.

2. There are many people around the world that steal Hollywood movies; the big hit movies, that will only change few things in the script according to their culture so that their target audience can relate and understand.
3. They steal a book from an author and print and distribute it without paying or dealing with the author piracy.

4. There are some other types of thieves that claim to be investment firms that call people in order to get them to invest with them or into their company but end up running away with their money.

5. There are a lot of thieves everywhere that come up with different ideas and different tricks to steal other people's money, so be careful.

6. The most important thing is to be aware of your employees be careful of your employees. A lot of times, one's employees are the boss's own enemies. They will keep

stealing their company's money until it goes bankrupt.

7. Thieves are not the same, some are smart, some are stupid. However, all of them will damage your company or run away with your money, so be careful.

8. There are a lot of people who will try to approach you once they hear that you have a lot of money. They will try to convince you to have business with them by mentioning big money, big names, big things, and brag a lot about different things, and they lie a lot if you are smart enough you can tell that they are lying to you.

18. There was a rich Indian lady who likes to purchase gold. After a while she noticed that the amount of gold is decreasing then she became suspicious of the servants in her house. At the same time her daughter became sick in the hospital, and they discovered that there was a lot of gold in her stomach.

19. Also, thieves are not the same. Some of them are smart thieves and some of them are stupid thieves, some of them are very greedy and some of them are less greedy. Every thief is thinking differently than the others and that he has the right to steal because:

1. They think they worked hard for it and deserve the money.
2. They had a miserable life and a bad childhood; they are not nice people.
3. Some of them were born poor and they become very surprised when they see a large amount of money Infront of them which encourages them to steal money.

4. When there is no control in the company and there is no good management, it will be so easy for thieves to steal money and

thieves are not afraid of stealing because there is no punishment.

If it happened that at one time you met somebody and you hired him as one of your employees. After he steals money from you, you will say that if was the worst day of your life when you met this person because you will have a regret and it will be too late for you to get your money back.

20. If you are rich, thieves and bad people will always approach you and everybody will try to be nice to you and everybody will try to be your friend. The thieves will be exactly like the flies who fly around the honey so be careful.

21. There is a young person from one of the Asian countries who had a dream to have his own business. The only thing he knows about is cars so he opened a show room and started with one car is his show room. But he chose the wrong person to work for him in the show room. That person was born in a very poor country so one day a client came into the show room to buy that car. The client asked the man in the show room whether he prefers a cheque or cash. The client said that he would prefer cash and when the person in the show room say a lot of cash in the client's hand, he became very greedy because he has never seen such large amount of money in his life. He took the money and gave the client the car but never gave the business owner the money. He ran away to his country and never came back.

22. I know a person who bought a travel agency in California thinking he will make a lot of money. He traveled a lot and always bought tickets from a certain travel agency in California. He noticed that travel agencies have a lot of clients and they make good money. Then, he decided to buy this travel agency thinking it will be easy money for him.

Then, he decided to approach the owner of the travel agency in California and started negotiating with him the deal to buy this certain travel agency. Unfortunately, the owner was a bad guy. He accepted the offer to sell his travel agency office but at the same time, he started to tell his clients that he's moving to a new location because he opened a new office for a travel agency and kept telling his clients to go to the new office. When the Californian bought the agency, the next day, he found that there were no clients there. The clients disappeared and he was shocked, there were no clients coming this travel agency. Not making any money, he knew what happened. But it was too late for him.

23. Finally, even you are not a businessman you always have to be careful because thieves are everywhere. It happened to me back in 1987 when I travelled to London. Some thieves followed my taxi from the airport until I reached my hotel in London. One of the thieves was standing next to me at the counter and replaced his black brief case with my briefcase. I ended up sleeping in a youth hostel.

24. I remember at one time when I went to India, I always had in my mind all Indian people are too nice and very friendly. Also, since I am a cinema major and I like the film industry, I like Indian films because they have good stories. Even though some criminals and violence were in the movies, I never believed it because it is just a film, specially that in India they make more movies than anywhere else in the world. But when I arrived there at 3am in the morning with a briefcase in my hand, I noticed the taxi driver discussing a plan with his collogue another taxi driver, so I became suspicious. What happened halfway between the airport and the city of Mumbai was that the taxi suddenly stopped, and the taxi driver said that there is no petrol. A few minutes later, the other taxi came and stopped 100 feet away

so I knew for sure that they had a plan to rob me, so I jumped out of the car with my briefcase.

25. Evil of money. The point here is don't trust people. Even a brother might steal from his brother. A son will steal from his father. A father will steal from his son.

26. There was a man who was travelling a lot in Africa, an average young man who has no experience in business. He noticed that in one of the big countries in Africa with a high population, a lot of people there drink tea. He has no experience in business. But, he did simple calculations with his calculator, and thought that he would be able to sell the tea to the millions of people there, and he would make millions easily. He convinced a boy who just inherited a lot of money to finance the business importing tea from India to Africa and sell the tea in big quantities. He rented a very large storage unit for the tea. He hired security for the storage as well. When the competitors of that country heard that new tea was getting imported, and that there would be more competition, they bribed the security guards and put bad things in the tea bags. This was to spoil the tea. So, when they started to distribute their product, the people didn't like the tea and the tea's reputation was terrible, its sales were disastrous. No one wanted to buy the tea or try it they didn't like it. Both the man and the boy were naïve in not thinking about the competitors and didn't think that in this world, there are a lot of thieves and bad people. People who have no experience in business think that everyone in the world is nice and honest.

27. Some people have the skill to take loans from banks by fooling the banks. They deposit a lot of money and withdraw at the same time so the bank will calculate the turnover because the computer is not a human being. All it does is

calculate the turnover because computers do the calculation only. The turnover shows that the company and that businessman has a lot of business and they end up borrowing a lot of money and not paying the bank back.

28. Unfortunately however, there are people who do not have a good vision and only like to cheat the banks. Sometimes, they get more loans than they deserve. They just try to fool the banks for different reasons. Sometimes – when people try to get more loans from the banks they lie and exaggerate their income and turnover just to fool the banks. It is exactly like when a man sees a beautiful girl in a nightclub and tells her that he has many cars and lives in a big house in Beverly hills, or when a person tells his fiancé the best things about his personality and never tells her about the negative things. After their marriage, she discovered that he is not a perfect person and he has a lot of bad points. The same thing is true with banks, the person tries to show that they are making good money daily or monthly, and that the turnover is very positive, where they are actually playing with numbers and exaggerating. Such as depositing the money and withdrawing, also knowing the key people and managers in the banks who can help them a lot.
29. There was once a rich man who married a young beautiful girl. He arranged the wedding party in his farm and a year later he divorced the young beautiful girl. The girl became sad and started to cry and then she went to the Judge and told him that she was divorced and her husband did not pay her any money, then the Judge asked her if she had marriage certificate and witnesses she said there is no marriage certificate and 2 witnesses were present during the wedding and they were the friends of her husband, then the Judge asked her husband and the 2 witnesses to come to the court but the husband denied and said he does know this lady and that he has not seen her before also the 2 witnesses the

friends of the rich man said the same things, they don't know the lady and they have not seen her before, then the girl started to cry even more and the Judge asked her if there are some people living in the farm, she replied there are only dogs and horses in the farm so the judge decided to go the farm with the lady and there in the farm , the dogs and horses seemed familiar to this lady and they knew her. Then the Judge said he trust the dogs and horses because dogs and horses are more honest and they don't lie like human beings. Finally, the Judge helped her to get her money from her previous husband by filling for a case.

Chapter 22

Work With Good People

1. The world is full of good people, but you have to look for them because there is a balance in the world. Without the good and nice people, life will be miserable, and there will be no life. Every good person is like a piece of gold every nice person is like a piece of gold. So, good and nice people are treasures. Look out for them, work with them, and deal with them they will not cheat you, they will pay you your money on time. Also, when you need help they will help you. Good people are everywhere, some of them are doctors, engineers, taxi drivers, farmers, ordinary people in the street,businessmen, actors, actresses, or even presidents, kings, and queens. The point here is to look for the good people, deal with them, work with them and stay with them, while at the same time stay away from the bad and evil people as much as you can. It is possible that some of those good people are not your type, or do not have the same mentality as you, or not educated like you, or do not like the same type of sports or hobbies like you, but they are good people, and you must appreciate the good people – knowing those good people is good for you maybe, the good person is not perfect but he is still a good person. A good person is a person who is nice and has a big heart, or a heart of gold. The important thing to get from this is that you must always have the intellect and knowledge to know the difference between the good people and the bad people. Always try to deal with good people and good clients. You must know how to select good clients it is like selecting your friends because some clients will lie a lot and not pay you. So, what is the use of working hard and selling products to clients that will not pay you or delay their payment to you. There are a lot of people who lie to you or cheat you, so, companies are like people.

There are a lot of good companies and bad companies. It depends on their people. Because, companies are run by people not angels.

2. Working with good people is good for the following reasons:

a. When good people buy things from you – they pay you.
b. Good people will pay you on time.
c. Good people will help you if you need help or go through bankruptcy.
d. Good people will help you and give you advice from their heart.
e. Good people will let you learn things from their experiences in order for you to learn about the world of business. They will tell you the truth about their experience.
f. Good people will introduce you to businessmen, CEO's, and managers of big companies.
g. They will give you good ideas about business from their heart.
h. They will try to help you to start your business when you needed the money, or, when you lose your businesses or go through bankruptcy, they will try to help you.
i. They will introduce you to the key people in the business or industry.
j. They will explain things to you from their heart and with passion, about businesses, and will show you the way to be successful.
k. They are not going to be jealous of you.

3. Always try to meet and socialize with people and successful people, because they will always be helpful to you and never regret. If you are a student in university, always try to meet and socialize with

educated people, people who have the ability and ambition for success and to succeed. At the same time, these must be nice people who have the ability to succeed, if they are bad people then they will ignore you or might also be arrogant and pretend that they do not know you not be nice to you. I know a person who had a dream to always become a businessman and to make money, but he always socialized with losers, and I knew that he will never make it because he does not have the ability nor potential to be successful in business and is always socializing with people who are losers and do not have the ability or potential to be successful in business or anything else. After 20 years, I met that person, and asked him, if he started his own business, he replied and said that no he hadn't.

4. There was once a king who had three sons, and he had to choose one of his sons to be the future king.The king asked his advisors to give him an advice about the best way to choose one of his sons to be the future king. The advisers suggested that the king must give each of his son's a big amount of money to travel alone for one year and when they come back they have to give an account of how they used the money.Based on that the king will decide who is the wisest son.

The king gave his three sons the money and asked each son to travel alone for one year.

A year later the king's sons came back. Then the king asked the first son about what he did with the money.

The first son replied that he bought a lot of goldThen the king asked his second son about what he did with the money.

The second son replied that he bought the best hundred horses Then finally the king asked his third son about what he did with the money.

The third son replied that he used the money to make good friends and to meet good people, so he had more than hundred friends, then the advisors told the king to wait for one more year to see the results.

So within one year many things happened.
The thieves followed the first son and knew where he was hiding the gold and then they stole the gold.
Also within a year an epidemic disease came and all the horses died, then also the neighboring country wanted to invade the kingdom so the third son who had many friends went to seek help from his good friends and the good people he knew, and they came to help him and defeated the enemy. Then the king decided that his third son is the wisest son and chose him to be the future king.

5. Nice friendly employees who smile to their clients can bring more business to you. No matter what your business is: hotels, restaurants, car sales, shops, shoes, clothes, airlines, and even hospitals.

6. Try to avoid bad and evil people, because, bad people are always with bad people – they say that birds of a feather flock together. They will never help you, they might hurt you, and they might also feel jealous of you.

7. They will be honest with you when you deal with them in business. Even those good people are your employees, they will be loyal to you, and honest with their work.
8. Dealing with bad people will make you lose everything in the long run. Or, they will teach you about cheating, bribing, making you lose your reputation, and no one will trust you.

9. A rich merchant had two sons and he wanted to test them as to which son is the best in business so he gave each one of them plenty of money to travel and to buy goods so they will learn the skill of making money.

The first son was naive he just wanted to travel Quickly on his first trip in order to come back quickly and also to impress his father. The first son chooses the first caravan to his city

destination without checking if they were good people also he did not ask about the reputation of the leader of the caravan, but unfortunately they were bad people.
The second son was smart he kept asking and investigating about the people in the caravan and also asked about the leader of the caravan if he had a good reputation and finally he choose a good caravan with a good people and a good leader with reputation.
His father noticed that his second son did not travel quickly and was late but then he realized his son was asking and investigating about the people in the caravan and the leader of the caravan then he knew that his second son is a wise person.
So the first son who traveled with bad people they kept asking him how much money he has, as they were curious about how much money he had because they planned to steal his money so when he reach the destination, his money was stolen and they replaced the money in his bag with sand and stones so he end up working in that city as a servant just to make money to go back to his father. He became a failure and this this happened because he choose the bad people to travel with him.
The second son who choses good people to travel with, and the good people noticed that he has no experience so they kept teaching him about bargaining and negotiations. Dealing with people and how to choose good product with low prices and also told him about the best merchants and honest merchants in the city.
So when he reached his destination city he was ready to make good deals and bought good quality of goods with low prices. So when he returned to his father. He retunes as a successful person then he sold all the goods and made good money.
This happened because he traveled with good people and he was dealing with good people.

10. Bad people will sometimes not pay you your money, so you will end up going to court – wasting your time with lawyers.

The best course of action is to avoid dealing with bad people all together.

11. Also if you are an employee don't work in a place with a bad manager who is rude and mean to you and does not appreciate you, also don't work in a bad company where they don't give you salary.

Always try to work with good people where they pay you and appreciate you, but if there is no alternative wait until you find another job in another place with good people.

12. I remember when I was 14 years old, my father told me to follow up on a construction company which owed him money because my father and he had done a lot of services for them. The amount that the construction company must pay my father was a big amount of money at that time and my father promised me to pay me 10 ten percent of the amount if I helped him to collect the money and I was so excited so I started calling that company and visiting them. I thought it will take few days or few weeks but it took 3 years but nothing happened and finally I learned that it is so easy to lend people money or do services for them but it is very hard to get your money back .

13. Sometimes owners of shops and stores sell things on credits to their friends who don't pay them back. Their friends at the beginning they say they will pay them after 3 days. But it takes 3 weeks or 3 months or sometimes they takes 3 years and they don't pay back also some people borrow money from friends but they don't pay them back or even don't appreciate it .

14. I remember when i was 9 years old, a school teacher borrowed a golden necklace from my aunt for school party only for one day. But the matter took many weeks , then my aunt kept sending people to ask her to return her

golden necklace. Finally the school teacher returned the golden necklace to my aunt with a letter saying bad things to my aunt and did not appreciate what my aunt did to her.

15. When I was 16 years old many students borrowed my comics books - Superman, Batman and Mickey Mouse also they borrowed my small tape recorder.

At the beginning they say they needed it only for one day but it takes them few weeks and few months to return it back and they don't appreciate what I did for them, they just shout at me. When I asked them to return my things back to me they shout at me and they don't appreciate what I did for them.

The point here is to be careful because some clients and some business associates are not honest and they will not pay you because they are not good people.

Chapter 23
Management

1. When you see a good company, it means there is strong management. Also, when you see a bad company, it means the management is weak.
   Management is an art, not everyone is smart in management, there are a lot of employees who do not like each other. You have to be able to make them work together.

2. If you are good with management, you will make money, if you are not good with management, you will not make money. For example, if you are only one person who paints or are offering services to houses, you will make a little money, however, if you hire a hundred or five hundred people to paint and service houses, you will make a lot more money and you will be very rich, but the question is do you have the right management to run the business or company?

3. If the CEO or an executive of a company is unable to run the business or company in the right way, the company will suffer a lot and it will start to have a lot of problems.

4. Sometimes you see a shop or a company has a lot of clients but they don't make money because of bad management for example they pay high salaries and high rent etc…

5. At the beginning, when you want to establish your company, you should start it with the right people, whom you trust, intelligent and hard workers. Even if you start with as little as 3 or 5 people.

6. There was a Swedish person named Daniel EK who was a genius in computers. He started to form a company with

Martin Lorentzon, who had capital. In April of 2006, they founded an audio streaming service called Spotify Technology S.A with 574 million monthly active listeners. It became one of the world's largest music streaming services.

7. Organize everything from the beginning, your papers, documents, because one day, you will need them.
8. Be careful when you choose your employees when starting your business – they must be qualified with good ethics and morals. Always put the right person in the right place.

9. Sometimes I avoid dealing with certain companies after they change their management.

10. Good managers know how to motivate employees to do better work and make them more loyal to the company. There was an owner for a company who always visited his 3000 employees and memorized all their names and the names of their children.

11. Later on, when your company starts to grow, you need a financial consultancy firm to do a financial chart for your company, and will give you more advice and ideas of management and how to run your company this of course comes at a fee.

12. When you start your business, whether you are one person working alone or even if you have three thousand employees, you have to have filing paper work and good records, no matter what, you might need such files after a few years, so, it is always good to keep things organized and in record, so never lose your records, even if it is a small company and there is only person in your company. Slowly, when your business is growing, you can see what type of

people you would need to work with you.

13. Do not be too nice to your employees, it is always good to be fair. At the same time, it is good to have positive incentives for them to work harder.

14. No matter how nice are your employees, if they see no control in your company and no management, they will not do their job right, or they might come later, or they might steal money from your company. Without good management, nothing will work. Because, this is human nature.

15. Every employee must be specialized to do something that they are good at and have good teamwork. However, you first have to choose the right people.

16. The good management make their employees work as one team.

There is a story I learned in my childhood. In the story, a donkey, a dog, a cat, and a rooster, were mistreated by the masters and they heard that soon they will be killed by their masters because they were getting old. So they decided to run away and to go Bremen- Germany.

So the donkey, the dog, the cat, and the rooster met each other on their way to Bremen and decided to cooperate and work together as one team. On their way they saw a lighted cottage. The dog stood on the back of the donkey the cat stood on the back of the dog the rooster stood on the back of the cat and when they looked inside through the window they saw three robbers eating their good meal so they decided to scare the robbers away by making noises, and then the robbers ran away. Then the animals took possession of the house ate good meals and settled in for the evening. Later that night the robbers returned and sent one of their members in to investigate. Then things happened in quick succession. The cat scratched his face with her claws, the dog bite him on the leg, the donkey kicks him with his hooves and the rooster crows and chases him out of the door. The terrified robber tells his companions that he encountered or faced a horrible witch who had scratched him with her long fingernail (the cat), a dwarf who had a knife (the dog), a black monster who had hit him with a club (the donkey), and a judge calling out for them on roof top (the rooster). The robber abandon the cottage to the animals, and the animals lived happily for the rest of their days.

17. At one time I asked the person who was an entrepreneur about his dream to be rich and he always talked about business and making money, as to why he failed after trying for more than 37 years and that he still was poor, he replied because 37 years ago when he met his partner who was an entrepreneur like him and both of us have a lot of things in common and the partner always talked about business and making money. But recently he realized his biggest mistake that he was very bad in management and he thought that he knew everything about every kind of business and that he was the smartest person in the world. He thought that he could do 5 employees, or 7 employees work all by himself and that he wanted do everything by himself. He did not want to hire specialized employees who are perfect in doing their job because he thought he could minimize the cost and save money.
    He thought that he could work as a finance manager and at the same time he could work as a technical person and also he could work as a delivery man. He just did not know anything about management because he never worked as a manager and also his father was a poor farmer who did not work as a manager.

He said he and his partner tried many kinds of different businesses for more than 37 years and they were not able to have good quality of services and deliver on time and their work does not run smoothly, this made their clients to always complain and they remained unhappy always and then they used to end up losing money and though they tried to enter different kind of usinesses ,the same thing happened over and again, all because his partner was a bad manager .

18. I once asked the CEO of a successful company what he thought would be the reason behind the success of his company and how did his company grow over the years from few employees to about 500 employees, he replied I don't know everything so I hire employees who are specialized and perfect in doing their job and over the years every employee will be perfect in doing his job because he is doing it every day over and over again.

19. You must have the discipline in your work and at your company, for example, attending meetings on time, doing the paperwork the proper way, and in everything. Do not worry, things will work out for you over time. Because, you will start to gain experience over the years, and will know how to choose your employees, and know how to organize your business and your company.

20. Your employees will always be looking at what the other employees are doing. Make sure there are no bad employees at your companies, some people might imitate them. Employees also look at their employer and bosses. They view their boss as an ideal person.

21. A good manager should consider the consequences before making a decision, and should consider the following:
    1. Finances
    2. Environment
    3. Politics
    4. Legalities
    5. Operations

6. Technicalities
7. Sociality/Ethics

22. To have the right people in the right job is very important, to have the right secretary, the right accountant, I noticed that in some companies they do not have the right secretary, accountant, or lawyer, and this is probably due to weak management.

23. Try to listen to others, they may have good ideas. Sometimes, the other employees have better ideas than the people on the board or in the management.

24. Eastman Kodak company, An American manufacturer of film and photographic supplies and provider of digital imaging services and products,is one of the historic brands in photographic history.
Headquarters are in Rochester, New York. Kodak used to make money from negative filming. In 1975 an employee in Kodak suggested to the management to use digital but the management refused the new idea. Then this employee Steve went to another company Sony. Sony accepted the new idea about digital and started to make money. Kodak filed for bankruptcy in January 2012.

25. Try to compliment your employees, however, they have to be true compliments from your heart, so they will appreciate both the compliments and you.

26. There are financial companies specialized to do the management and organization chart in your company. They are specialized to do auditing and accounting for you. And they will help you and tell you what to do to organize your company, but of course, you have to pay them.

27. There are also companies specialized in doing feasibilitystudies for you, before you do any project or business. They will tell you if the project looks successful and will detail the costs of the project or business.

28. Always make sure to make agreements with those financial companies to give you the required letters and documents.
29. It is a must for a big company to switch the employees from one place to another for the following reasons:

1. The employee will learn something.

2. If the employee stays in the same job, he will get bored, if the employee stays in the same position for a long time, he might steal money or accept bribes. Once the employee knows more about the people working with him, he will have more confidence and begin hiding things or exploiting things for personal gain. Do not give such people a peace of mind, always shift and move them around your company.

30. When someone asks you for something or a proposal, do not make a decision immediately, tell them to wait until the next day. I never make an important decision on the same day, I must wait 24 hours. For example, if someone wants to sell you his car, do not accept immediately, give yourself some time to think about it. Do not take or make quick decisions.

31. When there is a problem do not panic. Relax, go for a walk, or a swim, think slowly until you find a solution for the problem, because, when you are relaxed, you can think better.

32. Management must motivate the employees to be loyal to the company, to work hard, and to maintain the good reputation of the company. Always study the business case and create

plans to organize
(plan A, B, C).

33. It is always good to start with a partner or partners to help you at the beginning. Because, it is possible that one of them may have the money, while the second would have the contacts and connections, and the third partner would have the knowledge or technical background, but most of the time in the long run, partners do not get along with each other, because, everyone is different with different ways of thinking and planning etc.. In the end, people think that having partners is a big headache, or, they might fight with each other. It is like putting two lions in one cage, so, they will kill each other off.
Sometimes even brothers do not get along with each other.

34. Choosing the right people, making them work as a team, and together. This is a very good and strong skill if management can do that. Then, things will be done and the employees will save their time and focus on things more useful, to produce more and to make more money. This will also make the work very smooth.

35. Good management is the management which is making the employees happy and not complain a lot. Because, sometimes, there are companies that make the life of their employees miserable and unhappy.

36. Sometimes, the employees know how to solve a problem better than the management. Because, they have lived through the problem and can see it better. So, it is always good to ask their employees about their opinion.

37. You must make an interview with your employees to see their ability because people are not the same. Some people

have more energy than others. People who have the ambition of love to win and accomplishing things.

38. Good management can find the right people, the smart people, and the qualified people and of course the honest people. They must let them work as a team work because they cannot work alone.

39. You should choose your employees who are honest not selfish and who love their job and have a talent and skills.

40. Finding the right people for certain jobs is difficult, it is not easy to find the good people and the right people for any job. Also, for certain jobs, it is very difficult and very hard to find the right people. For example, it is not easy to find a good accountant, a good CFO or a good secretary or a head of projects etc. Of course, it is not easy to find a good CEO to run the company.

41. Negotiation is a skill and not everybody knows how to negotiate.
    Sometimes you have to be firm with the other party or client so they could give you a better deal or better prices.

42. Don't take a quick decision and wait for at least 24 hours just to think it over.

43. Legal issues are very important and must be always considered.

Chapter 24

Strength and Vigor

1. The person must be strong and ready for the challenges and financial problems. You must be strong and able to resist challenges. There are a lot of challenges in the world of trade and business. Making money is not easy. Many time things can go wrong. For example, wars like World War I, World War II and earthquakes. The world of trade and business is always affected by bad events and circumstances like wars, world financial crisis, diseases like Covid-19,natural disasters like earthquakes, floods, hurricanes, tornadoes. Sometimes, bad management or bad planning or theft could cause bankruptcy.

2. Business is a risk and 90% of the people who try their hand in business fail, only 10% succeed in it. In order to be successful in the world of trade and business, you have to be ready for shocks and sufferings. Once you start to have financial problems and bankruptcies, you start to have infinite problems and all kinds of problems. So, your life will be miserable, however, you will learn a lot because people learn things when they have problems. For this reason, you have to be very strong and patient, to overcome the problems. Because people learn many things when they have problems, so, for this reason, you have to be very strong and patient to overcome these problems for a few years. If a person overcomes and passes the financial difficulties and challenges of such problems, the person will come out of it with different experiences, skills, and knowledge. They will know better and more detailed things of the world of business and have very good chances to be successful in business.

3. Be strong and don't feel bad during the good times if your clients don't appreciate you or some of your employees don't appreciate you, no matter how good you are and how hard you work.

4. Most of the time, things go wrong suddenly and unexpectedly. For this reason, a businessman or merchant has to be very strong and patient to go through the pain and suffering of financial problems for a few years. Once the financial problem started, the businessman or merchant will be like a paralyzed or a crippled person.

5. Unfortunately, 90 percent of people who start their business lose their money. If you lose your money, you have to be ready for the bad consequences. Suddenly, you will have many problems from all directions, and life will be miserable for you.

6. There are many reasons behind bankruptcy. Most of them are unexpected. Sometimes some new banking rules and environment rules and regulations can make a company lose its money and go through bankruptcy. Also, family dispute between partners can make the company go through bankruptcy.

7. There is a Persian proverb saying "if you eat a lot of watermelon, you have to put up with the consequences". Meaning, if you eat a lot of watermelon, you will have diarrhea or a stomach ache. Meaning, you have to be ready for the consequences. Same thing if you have to enter the world of trade and business, you have to be ready for the financial problems. For this reason, you have to be very a strong person. No matter what you do to shrink your budget and save money, you will still have a lot of problems and you must be strong. Sometimes, shrinking your budget by as

much as 50% or 70% and start to lay off 50 – 70% of your employees, sometimes even that is not enough.
It depends on your situation and your problem, you will still have many other problems and you must be strong. You might go through bad times and struggle for a few years or 7 years. It is up to you and your circumstances, to continue in the same line in business, or change the line of business.

8. Life is full of good days and bad days, good years and bad years, the same thing can be said with business, sometimes there are good years when you will make money, but also bad years when you start losing money suddenly.
Because, in life, there are a lot of unexpected surprises and events, and circumstances beyond your control. For example,

1. The world financial crisis in 1929 and also in 2008.
2. The corona virus/ Covid-19 pandemic in the year 2020.
3. Wars like WW1 and WW2 and many wars continuously happening around the world.
4. Natural disasters like earthquakes, volcanoes, tornadoes, tsunamis.
5. Human errors, for example, large fires, nuclear plant meltdowns, etc.
6. Bad management
7. Employees who steal money from the company

9. Without loses or going through bad times you will not learn much, so bad times will be good for you to learn more about business.

10. Money is very important, you need money in your daily life, traveling, and to run your business. However, once you start to have financial difficulties, you will not be able to run your business smoothly. You will be like a paralyzed or crippled person, or like a ship sailing without water, far from the

shorelines not being able to move. Your life will be difficult and miserable.

11. Maybe things went wrong so you now have to recover, it is not the end of the world, now you gain the experience and contacts and connections which is very important for the business. Just imagine you were in a sinking ship and started swimming towards an island. Once you reach the island, you will try to adapt yourself to your new life on the island. You must live in a small hut and eat fish and fruits every day, waiting for a big ship to come and save you. So, do not worry, life does not stay the same, it is always changing.

12. When you start to have financial problems, you will have a lot of worries and no peace of mind, and sometimes, a lack of sleep. And you will eat a lot of junk food and will always be in a hurry and you may end up with diseases or sicknesses such as diabetes and high blood pressure.

13. My friend's father told him staying away from business is a good business, because business is a big headache and not easy.

14. A lot of merchant and businessmen in big companies have financial problems but a lot of ordinary people on the street do not know that businessmen, merchants, and companies are struggling.

15. Making money is not easy. You always have to be strong. Even during the good years, when you are making good money, you will have problems. It is not easy to make your clients happy. They will always be complaining about something. It is irritating. You will face problems, stress, and unexpected bad news like losses, theft, people not paying

you, etc... Because, sometimes, things go wrong, things do not go as smoothly as you expect it.
Unexpected things happen.
Sometimes, some bad people may take you to court and try to take advantage of you by taking your money just because you are rich.

16. Sometimes, your employees will make mistakes, for example, if you send one of your employees to buy green apples, he will buy red apples.

17. In the world of trade and business there are a lot of challenges and daily problems so you have to be strong because things do not go smoothly and the way you want it. Sometimes, your clients will make you tense, sometimes your employees or partners will make you tense, sometimes your income is not enough to cover your expenses, or there will be a delay in payment from your clients. So, you will have worries and will not know what to do. When you start to have unexpected financial problems or face bankruptcy due to some events in the world, things will get worse for you. Unexpected things happen in the world like wars, financial crisis in 2008 or 1921 or the COVID pandemic in 2020 or natural disasters like earthquakes, floods, typhoons, hurricanes, tsunamis, and many other events. So, you have to be ready for problems like that. You have to be strong and ready for problems like that. A smart person is a one who can survive during the crisis and act immediately by lowering the company's budget and cutting cost, firing most of his employees laying them off. He must start living like a poor person and put up with difficulties and challenges.
18. A lot of strong people go through financial problems and learn a lot, becoming better businessmen. They then think that what happened is good for them. They may suffer for several years but most of them will get over it and overcome

such problems. There is a Japanese proverb that says "the wind of tomorrow will blow tomorrow" which means that tomorrow is another day, and things may change so you must be optimistic. For this reason, a person must be very strong and ready for shocking and unexpected events. To me, a person who wants to enter the world of trade and business has to be strong, and be ready for it exactly like a soldier who joins the military who has to go through grueling weeks of training, running for many miles, doing hundreds of pushups and sit-ups. Being in shape could also be said for someone who wishes to scale mount Everest, where one has to be strong and prepare himself. This is why that one will not succeed in business if they are not strong or repared. This is because businessmen must be well trained psychologically if there were any problems such as, pain, grief, and misery - exactly like a young soldier who can take the stairs on the 75th floor to escape a burning building while the weak old man

cannot, thus not being able to survive.

19. It is very hard to make all of your employees at your company happy. Some people in your company may not like each other. Your goal is to have them work together for them to achieve things.

20. I remember that as a kid I would always see my father spacing out and did not understand why until much later, where I know see myself thinking and spacing out just like him. Nowadays, I am always spacing out even while I drive – this is why I have a driver who takes me to places. It is not like when I was a student in university when I used to drive as fast as I wanted to in my sports car without any worries or spacing out.

21. When things go wrong, or during bad years, business

requires patience and sacrifice. So, a merchant or businessman must wait a few years until the situation gets better or the circumstances get better. For that reason, the businessman or merchant must be patient and strong.

22. If you go through financial problems and bankruptcy you have to live on a small budget like a poor person for few years and then pay your debts then be patient and wait until the economy picks up then start making money again.

23. You will be worried about thieves and stealing things from your company.

24. Most of the people learn when things go wrong or during difficult times, so you will learn a lot of things about business and then you can start all over again. Without losses or without going through bad times you will not learn much. So bad times will be good for you. So, it is always better for you to start your business at the age of twenty five to thirty years old single not married. So, you will recover at age of thirty-five to thirty seven. But it will be very difficult for a fifty years old man to start a business, with a big family, incase he goes through financial problems then his wife and kids will be suffering too.

25. You will always be thinking about the problems mentioned here, improvements to your company, and the cliental. So, you will always be dosing off and may take the wrong road or speed or not concentrate doing everyday tasks such as driving.

26. When you have financial problems or a disaster, you must cut down your expenses by 80 – 90% and act fast. However, many people and companies are very slow to act and when they do, they only cut by about 30%. This is because most

company owners and managers are optimistic and are not used to big shocking problems. They believe that the problem can be solved and the situation can recover within a few months rather than years. This may also be because they do not expect big problems or a disaster like that in their lives.

27. When you have financial problems, every day you will hear bad news, possibly even every hour. This will make you tense and sad. And you will have so many problems. You will be struggling a lot just to survive or for your business to survive. Your life will be miserable for many years. For this reason, you must be strong until this problem goes away.
28. Once you have financial problems, you will be paralyzed and will not be able to move, because of all the problems you have. For instance, if you have a friend from another city offered you some money, around 5 dollars, to get yourself out of such a situation, you are being paralyzed financially won't even be able to take a bus or cab to reach that friend that is offering you his help.

29. When you do not have money, you will suddenly face a lot of problems from all directions. You will have problems you didn't expect. You will be wasting your time on worthless things. For example, you will be traveling from Los Angeles to San Francisco or anywhere for hundreds of miles just to borrow 500 dollars from your friend. You have to go there in person just to convince him, because it is easier to convince a person in person than on the telephone or some other reasons. Your good employees won't be happy to work for you when you do not pay them their salaries. You will have difficulty to concentrate and focus on your job. Every day and every hour will be full of suffering. It is a nightmare. You will receive bad news every hour and you will have problems every hour. But do not worry, they say that what

does not kill you only makes you stronger. Every week you will face unexpected bad news such as losses, theft, people not paying you, etc... Sometimes things go wrong and do not go as smoothly as you expect it. When you are just beginning, you will have problems since you do not have the starting capital you will always be tense and will have to be patient and put up with people and things.

30. In case you go through bankruptcy, you must know how to adapt yourself to know how to live like a poor person for a while or possibly for one or two years. You must be strong enough to live that life without a car. Also, some people will be very mean and rude to you. Some other people will take legal action against you and take you to court. You may be spending a lot of your time with your lawyers because of this.

31. 90% of people lose their money when they start a business. A lot of times I see people when they start their business, in their first year they are very happy and optimistic. But after a few years when I meet them again, they start complaining and tell me that they lost money and things went wrong.

32. When you lose money, your employees will shout at you and threaten to take you to court because they want their salaries. Your friends will shout at you and threaten you because they want their money back. You will also receive a lot of phone calls asking you to pay them money. This can take the form of specific bills you are yet to pay or late for specific payments. So, your life will be miserable. You will be spending a lot of time going to court or talking to your lawyers. It is not fun.

33. Survival is very important during the crisis. A great person is one that can survive during a financial problem. And it is

the great people who can survive and adapt themselves when things go wrong. In the middle east, there is a story about a famous scientist named Ibn Sina.

34. Having financial problems is not always a bad thing. This is because:

1. They say that whatever doesn't kill you makes you stronger. This will make you a stronger person.
2. You will learn a lot of things you did not know before. You will learn about the weak point of your company or business and will learn about your mistakes.
3. You will learn who your good employees are and who the bad one are.
4. You will learn about saving your money.
5. You will learn about your friends, who are the good friends and who are the bad ones. You will also learn more about people.
6. You will learn about how to improve your business and how to avoid making the same mistakes in the future – after a few years or after the crisis passes.
7. You may end up choosing a different line of business.
8. You will learn a lot of things you did not previously know. Everyone hasdifferent businesses and different lives. So, one will learn many things in their own way and choose the business that is most suitable for them. The person will be very happy since they now know that the business they end up in is the business is for them. They end up being grateful for their failure since they now find themselves in a business that suits them better and works with them better.

35. When you do not have money, some people will give you dirty looks and not respect you. Even your friends will shout at you and not respect you and will even insult you. Especially when you borrow their money and do not pay

their money back.

36. You will notice some stupid people do not know or understand what your financial problems are. Even if you told them that you did not have enough money, someone like your lawyer and land-lord would ask for something of a compromise like 20%. The bank or some of your employees would also not understand and ask you to pay. One of the reasons why I am writing this book is because I heard many stories of the people who went through bankruptcy so I always feel sorry and have sympathy for them and their families because of the amount of pain and suffering they go through, even for some of their health problems. It has happened also to some of my close friends, and at those times I wished that I could have helped them but I was not able to. This is one of the reasons I had the incentive to write this book.

37. When I read and heard many of these stories, it gave me the incentive to write a book explaining that making money is not easy and that it is always a chance or risk that you will fail.

College Students:

1. When I was at the university of southern California, I noticed that there are a lot of students who have dreams to be rich and famous but are very spoiled and complain about all the little things and get annoyed and bothered for the smallest of reasons and get frustrated by small problems and cannot tolerate stupid or rude people. They get annoyed and cannot absorb little problems and complain about little things. Those people have no chance to survive in the world of trade and business in case things go wrong or in case they go through bankruptcy and financial problems. I do not believe that some of those types of students are ready for the world of

trade and business and the trouble they will surely have to encounter and face. Here are several stories of such instances:

2. There was once a boy at the university housing who wanted to hang himself because he was not able to get a girlfriend. He used to see hundreds of girls around the campus and could not get a single one so he wanted to kill himself.

3. There was a girl who was visiting a handsome guy in our building that she liked but when he told her he only liked her as a friend, she had a tantrum a psychological mental breakdown hitting things with her hands and legs.

4. A student who lived on the same floor came to our room and urinated by our door thinking that we were asleep, however, my roommate had heard him and was very mad. He asked me to go and seek revenge on the student by urinating by his door.

5. My roommate and I had made an agreement in the beginning of the year that we were to write down the messages or calls we would receive on the telephone if the person they wished to talk to was busy so I had always written down the name of the person and their message to my roommate while he did the same for me. I had another roommate who did not like girls that complain and whine. So, whenever girls would send me voice messages on our shared telephone, my roommate was complaining about the girls who called and constantly whined because he does not like girls who whine and act as if any small inconvenience is the end of the world. I played a joke on him by paying a girl 35$ to constantly call him and whine on the phone while talking to him for over half an hour. He gets annoyed when they call for one or two minutes, so when she was whining

for over thirty he was furious.

6. In 1989, I always wanted to listen to a song called for U-2, with or without you. I had always played this song before I went to sleep. The music cassettes and tapes had belonged to my roommate not me, so I always asked him to play them 2 or 3 times a day. He started getting bothered by it so I began paying him a dollar every time I asked him to play it. At the time, two dollars was a decent amount of money. He was annoyed by the repeated song even though I paid him.

7. I once had a difficult financial year. I had no money at all. I was not able to pay for my housing, telephone bills, or tutors and had no car. I got bad grades even though I had studied hard for the exams. So that specific day was really bad, it had felt like the end of the world. So I went to eat junk food at a cafeteria and didn't have enough money to go somewhere else to afford a good meal. I was so frustrated and disappointed and felt like an unlucky person. After that I went to sit outside by the lounge and saw a very beautiful girl walk by while talking on the phone. She was speaking to her friend complaining that she had no plans for the day and didn't know what to do. It cheered me up seeing someone struggle in such a different way, where in comparison to me, she had no need to worry about tutors because she is majoring at something extremely simple at university, meaning that she had no reason to worry about exams or tutors and since her father was very wealthy, she had a car and a place to stay with a sufficient salary to not worry about any other expenses. She was able to smell the fresh air of the beach and relax there or can go to her sorority house and start laughing with them.

8. At the beginning of the school year, I have always tried to help the freshman girls move into their rooms on the second floor and third floor of the dormitory. I once asked my roommate to help me carry the luggage for the girls.

After we finished, my former roommate was complaining and acting like it was a big deal. He said that he is not going to do it again.
Because, to him, it is a big hassle. On the other hand, to me, it was a very easy and simple thing. I would like to mention that those types of students that complained a lot are almost never strong enough and not ready for the problems they will face in the world of trade and business. They are weak people who complain and are bothered by little things and they will not be able to face the problems and challenges in the world of trade and business like when there are disasters or financial problems such as bankruptcy. And the most important thing is to survive and make your company survive when you are in business and ready for the shocking events and unpredicted and complicated problems. I usually travel for seven or nine hours in my car paying for gas only to meet potential business partners and people. I sometimes end up sleeping in my car never complaining about these things while my former roommate was continuously complaining about helping these girls for twenty or thirty minutes.

9. I had a childhood friend who I used to call during my time in university, and he had continuously heard the background noises from my roommates such as them pulling the fire alarm, playing golf down the hall, and playing loud music. He asked why it was so loud and I had told him that I was in the dorms. He said that he was not able to live in dorms since he believes the people there are not real people and the rooms are not actual rooms. I noticed that he was not able to cope with pressure. When he grew up, he was not able to handle his father's business and would always take vacations.
10. One of my ex-roommates was very rude and very mean. As soon as he used to open his mouth he was very mean to

me. This is because he grew up in a very bad neighborhood and most of his high school mates were trouble makers and gangsters. I finally told him that I did not want to talk to him and that if he wanted to communicate, he would have to write on a piece of paper and I would write back. I put up with people like that and things like that because I do not want to stay far away from the campus and I do not want to drive my car every day for two hours – to commute to my classrooms for two hours far from the library, university, and classes. There were no other choices so I had to put up with the pain and mean people.

11. I was once traveling on one of my international flights, it was a long trip for many hours. I was sitting next to a rich family, a mother with her sixteen year old daughter, I was talking during my trip to a mother and noticed a girl who was crying the whole time. I thought that her father or one of her brothers died I thought there was something miserable going on in her family. By the end of the flight I asked the mother why her daughter was crying and she told me that they were supposed to fly first class because they always fly first class and her daughter is used to first class only, but since all the flights were booked, they had no chance to fly first class so they had to fly economy so for this reason her daughter is very depressed.

12. The world of business is full of problems and shocking events where a lot of things can go wrong. It is much more difficult than going to school or university. Because in university, you can control your time and a lot of events, and things are more simple in university. However, in the real world, things are much harder. If someone is complaining about little things in university and is very spoiled, when he grows up and tries to get into the world of trade and business, it will be very hard for him to survive since life

is much harder in the real world in the world of trade and business. Even if someone in university wanted to cheat you in university, they would ask to borrow 10 or 15 dollars and not pay me back. It happened to me many times. There was once two girls who asked me for a ride to a shoe store. They bought shoes for 160 dollars. I paid for them and they wrote a cheque to pay me back but it bounced back. This was the most money I had lost in university. In the real world people fool you for much more, reaching amounts worth thousands and millions. You will end up wasting your time and money needing to see your lawyer every day and going to court. This is why most people, when looking back at college life, think it is a good memory and simple life and fun in comparison to life in the real world.

13. Of course, there are a lot of students in college who are strong and put up with pain and misery. For example,

A. I once saw a very poor girl who doesn't even have bedsheets on her bed and doesn't even have clothes. Except the jeans t-shirt and jacket she was wearing.

B. One of my ex-roommates was very poor, he used to cut coupons from the mail for discounts he would use for meals. He told me when he was young in Colorado, he was always walking with his shorts in the snow. Because he grew up faster and could not buy new shorts and new pants for himself to fit. I asked that poor boy why he came to USC even though he was very poor. He said that to find a good job he had to come to a prestigious and good university such as USC. He was willing to sacrifice any form of luxury toestablish his future.

C. Another story, there was another boy who used to live in our apartment and would sleep on the sofa even though his father was rich, he was not paying for him, because he has a very negative relationship with his father. I noticed at one time, his father came to give a speech at university and the boy was running after his father's car, however, his father did not stop for him.

D. I once had a roommate who was overweight. I asked him why he was overweight. He told me that when he came to university, he was very skinny and very poor. He was not on a full scholarship so he had no money to pay for food in the first semester. He used to eat an apple a day just to keep him going. At the second semester, he got a full scholarship and started to eat in excess as if to compensate for his lost means.

14. I noticed that a lot of students could not go anywhere during Christmas, thanksgiving, or spring break. This is because they are from the East coast far away from California and they don't have the money to travel.

15. I always respect people who are suffering because it is those people who are going to make it in the real world those who cannot find a bed sleep on the floor or those that do not have clothes or money are the ones that are going to be great people. In the world of business, if you read the stories about the successful people in business and the billionaires, you will find that those people suffered a lot and had a weird life and were lonely. So, if you see some of them like that, do not underestimate them and think of them as weird, it is very possible that it is those people who are going to change the world and be successful. Usually those people were born poor, are hard workers and sacrificed more. Sometimes in business, you have to sacrifice, there is no time so sleep, no time to go on vacation, no time to even eat lunch or dinner when you are supposed to eat because you are always in a hurry. You have to sacrifice and put up with a lot of pain and even some people sacrifice their health – not taking their

medicine on time, and this is why we see many rich people with a lot of health problems such as diabetes, high cholesterol, and heart problems. Sometimes, they may even have stomach ulcer.

16. I always recommend sports and maintaining a fit lifestyle to people in order to see very positive outcomes in the long run. This is because sports release the tension and is good for the health. When you do sports, you can think in the right way and you can slowly solve your problems and will find solutions to your problems when you are relaxed, and sports is what makes your mind relaxed. I always come up with new ideas for writing or business during my time walking and swimming. I always go for swimming in the swimming pool during the day and walking at night. I always make time for that no matter what. However, before, when I was a student in university, I used to do all kinds of sports. Such as jogging, playing tennis, playing squash, racket bowl, playing soccer, cycling, scuba-diving, snorkeling, horseback riding, water skiing, snow skiing, I may not have been excellent in any of them but I could still play those sports, because of sports I never get bored and sports always releases any tension I may have and makes me think better and think well. Now however, I am only swimming and walking. So, I recommend anyone with stress and facing difficulty to do the things I mentioned above. Also, I recommend people to always eat good and healthy food and avoid bad or junk food in order to maintain their health, because many people who start to have stress because of their business or financial problems do not care about food or their habits of eating. And they start to eat bad food or junk food. This is not good for them in the long run. Also, I recommend people to maintain a good relationship with their friends, to visit them and talk with them and laugh with them. I always try to make time to see my friends whenever I have time to do so. I am

also lucky to have a sense of humor that many find to be friendly and joyful. You should also try to get enough sleep, because sleeping is good for your body and your health, and after getting enough sleep you can work better and think better. You also have to think positively about life. Whenever things go wrong for me, I always say that I am lucky because something good or rewarding will happen to me after the difficulty. So, I wish that everyone had this mindset and thought positively when they face any challenges such as bankruptcy.

The difference between working as an employee and working as a businessman

1. If someone is not strong enough, I recommend them to work as an employee for a salary and not even think of having their own business and entering the world of trade and business. Because he will feel more secure and less at risk while working as an employee. I just wanted to mention the difference between being an entrepreneur and an employee. These are the good and bad parts of running your own business and being an employee:

a. The good thing about having a business is making a lot of money.
b. You have no boss to tell you what to do.
c. The son of a merchant or businessman starts from where his father ends. Suppose that his father died with several properties or left his money his child will start from there and will work to increase his family's wealth. However, an employee would start the same way his father started from the beginning.
d. When you are a businessman or a merchant. Sometimes you can live like a king and have a big birthday party or a big wedding party. You can accomplish one of your dreams even if you don't have the money you can borrow.

e. The businessman always has the freedom to organize his schedule sleep whenever he wants, gets up whenever he wants, go on vacation whenever he wants. While the employee has to ask his employer or line manager about the simplest of things they are the ones in control of his life.
f. Even if the businessman does not have money on him, he might have good credit where he can borrow a lot of money from banks.
g. He can accomplish some of his dreams, for example, if he wanted to throw a large party he can borrow the money to use it however he wished to buy his dream house by the beach, or have his dream boat or car.
h. The bad point about business however is that business is not easy.
You sometimes have to work harder than most, 7 days a week, 20 hours a day, you cannot enjoy life when you are very busy and might get sick with diabetes, blood pressure, heart problems.
i. i. A lot of times, businessmen don't have a lot of time to enjoy
themselves. They are not able to see their friends, go out on the
weekends, go to the beach, or generally just have a good time.
j. Business is a risk. 90% of people who enter the world of trade and business lose money. So, if you lose money, life will be miserable and you will go through a lot of pain.
k. The good part about being an employee is that an employee has a
secured income, where they regularly have a salary coming in. He knows his budget; he knows how much he should spend monthly or weekly.

2. Most of the time, he is living a normal life, he goes on vacation once or twice a year. He can enjoy his weekends like going to the beach or play tennis or go horseback riding

etc.

m. He can visit his friends and go to wedding and parties.
   The bad thing about the employee is that he has a boss that tells him what to do.
n. He has to come to work a certain time and leave at a certain time.
   Sometimes, his work is boring, he will do the same work all the time, see the same people every day, and discuss the same subject every meeting. There are a lot of employees who do not like or enjoy their job.
o. His son will start his career exactly like his father, as a small employee with no head-start. The employee does not have plenty of money, only enough for him to live a normal life. He will be working in the same place, same building, seeing the same type of people. A businessman makes a decision, but an employee does not make a decision.
   Employees still need their boss or the board to make decisions for him.
p. The businessman takes risk, while the employee does not take a risk. The mentality of the businessman is different than the mentality of the employee.

Chapter 25

Luck and Fate

1. I believe in luck, and I also believe in fate. Luck is true, I have seen it happen to me and the people around me. It happened to my family and the people in my neighborhood, also to my friends and the people I know. I have seen it happening all over my life. For example, my father, is more educated than my uncles – the brothers of my mother, however, they have more money than him. Even though he used to work harder than them and is more educated than them. When he first started his business in 1941, he was even richer than them during the 1940's and 1950's. My father is a businessman. My three uncles, the brothers of my mother, are also businessmen and merchants. Each one of them have different kinds of businesses.
   The only thing they share common is that they respect the profession of business and want their kids to be businessmen or merchants, but not employees.
   Speaking of myself, I grew up in a business family.
   My father was a businessman who was very well educated. He traveled a lot and has seen a lot of things, experiencing many different businesses when he started in the 1940's. He is a humble person even though people respect him because of his famous father and always likes to talk about business and the future of business and has a vision for the future. He always believed that experience is very important in business, he also believes that patience is very important and that things will slowly but progressively grow. I recall him always complaining about his employees who constantly stole his money and how he could not control them. He most notably believes in the importance of education. He also used to proudly talk about his powerful father and powerful grandfather. Even though my father lost his father – my

grandfather - in 1919, at the age of 3. The thieves stole all the gold my grandfather had, so my father has to start from scratch and suffered a lot during his childhood and started to work at the age of 12 – where he used to go to school simultaneously. My father started his many businesses in 1941 then he became successful only in 1946. My father started with the food business then selling shoes then clothes then finally settled with pharmacies and medicals because he noticed there is more money in pharmacies and medical business. My father, self-made man started his business at an early age from scratch in 1941. My father's personality is completely different and the opposite than his father my grandfather. This is because my wealthy and powerful grandfather was in control of things. He was bossy, he liked to give orders, and he told people what to do. He is wise, a good speaker, and generous. People respect him and listen to him. When he died in 1919, he left a lot of gold, unfortunately however, my father was only three years old and did not inherit the gold, because the thieves stole all the gold and took everything. This sad event made my father concentrate more on his education. His education helped him later to become successful in business.

2. My mother who married my father in 1948 was too nice, had good manners, humble and respected people. I was a blessed child to my mother because she had two sons before me who died in childbirth due to complications in her delivery. She learned to be nice to people from her father.
   My grandfather who had a lot of morals and was generous was always helping poor people and giving charity, always giving people extra time to pay him back for what they purchased. He lends people money whenever they needed it. My grandfather started his business at an early age in 1893 with a small shop for selling food then moved up and entered the business of shipping. My grandfather believed

that in business, a person must be honest and trustworthy. He always wished to give back to his community until he died during the same week as my grandmother due to a flu/fever in 1942. My grandfather's reputation for being a successful businessman and having a lot of morals and generosity, made him marry a good wife my grandmother who married my grandfather in 1905 who was from a good and well known and famous family, that had a lot of contacts and connections and was well respected in the community also her father and her mother and her aunt all have strong contacts and connections for many decades before 1905.

3. My aunt my mother's sister was the one who raised me and took care of me after my mother's death in 1968 when I was 12 years old. She was a good speaker, and generous; always trying to help poor and less fortunate people, always kind to me and to my younger brother. My aunt was different than my mother. She was sociable and knew a lot of people and learned how to establish contacts and connections from her generous mother, who knew a lot of important people in the community because of her father and mother and aunt of her mother the sister of her mother. My aunt always used to visit people with her mother, such as her mother's friends, and maintained her contacts and connections even after her mother passed away. My aunt was bossy and had many leadership attributes. She was very well known in the community. She always had visitors in her house until her death in 1997, just a year after the death of her billionaire brother. There were all kinds of people, she had contacts and connections and whenever she spoke, everyone listens to her; men, women, kids, poor people, rich people, everyone. My aunt used to read a lot of books and knew a lot of things. She encouraged me to read books when I was little. She was also brave, patient, tough, and had a strong personality. She always gave orders and told people what to do. Even though

she was fighting with our aggressive neighbor whose farm was next to her farm that caused a shortage of water to her farm.
At one time she even shouted at my father because my mother at one time got tired of the housework cooking and cleaning. My aunt was brave and generous like her mother and her uncle her mother's brother.

4. I also want to mention that I was influenced by my three uncles the brothers of my mother who used to always visit my aunt in her house. This was the aunt that raised me after the death of my mother.
The circumstances I was put into since my early childhood made me learn a lot from my three uncles. My three uncles all have a different personality and mentality with different approaches to business. My three uncles respect businessmen and they always want their kids to be businessmen and not work as employees. I realized that my father was more educated, a hard worker, and has more experience in business than my three uncles. However, he did not have more money than them. This was because they were luckier than him. My first and eldest uncle who I liked the most, was a nice person and was nice to me. Also, he has good manners. He was dedicated to his work day and night but always had a problem with his employees who were not honest and always stole money from him. My second uncle, who was nice to my mother and to my aunt, always visited them. He did not care and always believes in the power of fate and destiny, and always said sit and wait until the opportunity comes to you. He does not believe in working hard or in all of the factors of success I mentioned here in this book. He's a lucky person, and things always work out for him in the last minute. My third uncle and the youngest one, who became a billionaire has strong connections and contacts. He has strong connections and contacts everywhere

and knows how to deal with people. He is very generous but he always likes to give orders and tells people what to do. He also gets angry quickly and shouts at people. My father was not lucky like my billionaire uncle who had strong contacts and connections. My father lost his father at the age of three years while my uncle, his father lived for a long time and he inherited his father's connections and contacts in business. Also, my billionaire uncle, his mother and her family had strong contacts and connections everywhere. While the mother of my father and her family does not have strong contacts and connections.

5. I once asked my cousin, his eldest son of my billionaire uncle who is running his father's business which is mainly in real estate, hotels, cars, oil and gas and many other things. I asked him about the reason behind their success in business. He said, honesty and credibility, because they established credibility with the banks a long time ago. They established this by paying their installments with the banks on time and never missed a payment by a day. They sometimes even sell some of their properties to maintain their reputation and credibility with their banks. So then, the banks began increasing the loans they would give. Then, they started to grow their business even more. Today, they never go to banks, but banks come to them. This is because banks see that they are honest and have credibility. My cousin also said, that when there is a problem related to contacts and connections and he could not solve it, his father would get involved and use his own contacts and connections to solve it.
   I consider my billionaire uncle as a lucky person luckier than my father because his mother also his uncle, the brother of his mother had contacts and connections, as well as the aunt of his mother who had contacts and connections. All the while, my father lost his father when he was three years old and his mother did not have contacts and connections. My uncle met some important people in his school and childhood

but my father did not.

6. I would also like to mention a cousin I have, whose mother is the sister of my mother, my aunt. He is in the real-estate, business and farming and has a lot of contacts and connections. He knows a lot of important people and always likes to talk about people and believes in luck, fate, and destiny. He has a lot of stories to share about luck fate and destiny. He also believes that people who cheat and lie will lose their money.
This cousin, whose stories I enjoy listening to, once told me that when he was a teenager, he asked my father to help him find a job. This was because he was desperate to find a job to make money. In 1948 when he was at the age of 15 years old, he traveled with my father. He thought that my father could help him find a job, because of my father's limited connections. My father deserted him alone in the airport without trying to help him find a job or giving him any money. My cousin was shocked by the behavior and actions of my father. Luckily, my cousin found another family who knows my aunt very well and from there, started to live with them for a while, where he then started a small business by selling perfumes in small quantities. He met many people who empathized for him as a young boy. Finally, he started to have the experience in business for selling perfumes and started having strong connections over many people over the years. 50 years later, he became much richer than my father, he is just a lucky person. Even though oday, my cousin does not like my father and says bad things about him, my father indirectly did him a favor when he deserted him at the airport. My cousin started his perfume business because of my father's actions in the airport. If he had gotten a job like he wanted to at the time, he would be an average employee but because after my father left him alone in the airport, he stated to rely on himself by selling perfumes and meeting

people and started using the contacts and connection of my aunt and my grandmother. My cousin is luckier than my father because my father does not have an aunt or grandmother who has contacts and connections.
This cousin had a brother, that's older than him, and died a long time ago in 1985 at the age of 58 years because he did not care about his health and diet since he was fat and overweight.
However, this cousin was a wise person, and had a big effect on me for writing this book. This is because when I once asked him about the world of trade and business, he told me that it is a big headache. At that time, I was a young man and a student at USC and was anxious to have my own business like a lot of other USC students. He told me to stay away from business because it is a big headache and making money is not easy. He told me that I should try to work as an engineer or employee, it would be better and easier for me. What he said to me made me think all the time, why business is not easy, why making money is not easy. He did not explain it to me in great length because he does not talk much and was a quiet person, he did not know how to explain things, even though he has a lot of experience in business and inherited money from his rich father, he believed that making money is not easy. This made me question why making money was not easy for the longest time. My old cousin had businesses in selling gold, clothes, and real estate. After a few years, I asked him about business again. He said, that making money is not easy and that business in general is not easy, and that it is a big headache. He finished by saying that there are a lot of problems in the world of trade and business. This cousin was not educated like my father and did not work as hard as my father, but he had more money than my father because he is a lucky person because he inherited money and real estate from his rich father but my father did not inherit anything

from his father. Finally, I would like to mention that my father was successful in his own business and owned properties, real estate and a hotel.Also he encouraged his kids to get educated and study. He was still not as lucky as my uncles and cousins even though he lived longer than the others and died in 2015. My father had a lot of employees working for him and many of them became businessmen and one of them became a billionaire. This proves that luck is a real thing, it exists. They became luckier than my father.

7. Sometimes a person does not have a lot of the factors I mentioned in this book. He, the lucky person, may only have 3 or 4 of them, but suddenly fate and luck will be on his side and the opportunity will present itself in the right place, the right time, and with the right people. You will see that this person has become rich and successful because he was brave enough to accept the opportunity coming to him. This person already has the potential and the basics and ability to be rich and of course, he has some factors of success such as courage and bravery. This opportunity came to him at the right time, in the right place, and with the right people. Some may call it luck; I call it fate.

8. There is a triangle theory. The right time, right place, and the right people; rich people, leaders, presidents, and all successful people throughout history became successful because of the circumstances that they were in, where they were at the right time, place, and met the right person. If you have all three, you will be a very successful person.
   For example, if two twin brothers go to two different universities, one of them attends a university in New York, and the other brother attends a university in Los Angeles, if the one in New York has a roommate whose father is an ordinary engineer, and the other brother in Los Angeles, his roommate in college, his father is the CEO of a big studio for

films in Hollywood, there are more chances that the one in Los Angeles will get a good job in Hollywood because of his roommate's connections. In the long run, this may mean that he will become rich and famous, due to the fact that this brother came to the right place Los Angeles, the right person whose father was the CEO of a big studio, and at the right time when the son of the CEO was a freshman like him.

9. In Morocco, North Africa, a simple poor man wanted to go to a toilet, then, he went to a public place at the corner of a big empty space or yard (much like a parking) and relieved himself. After he was done, he saw a group of people gathering at the parking. He was curious to see why these people were gathering there. The people were gathering there because there was an auction to sell steel. They then offered him money to leave. He was surprised. Because of how surprised he could not talk, he was in a state of shock and kept silent. They then offered him more money. He was even more surprised, and they offered him more money. They gave him a lot of money and he eventually left. He left with a surprised look on his face. Those people actually had a monopoly for selling steel. They thought that this person would participate in the auction. They had no idea that this was a simple a man who had no idea what was going on. Then, this person kept asking many people about what had occurred, until he found out what happened. Then again, the following weekend, he went to the same place and they offered him more money. He became interested and decided to join the group. He became very successful with them and learned about the steel business. This story shows you that this happened in the right place Morocco and that it would not occur in another country or continent like Europe because it is very unlikely for someone to go to a public area to relieve themselves.

10. A Scottish man who was working as a photographer for TV won the biggest lottery in Europe in 2011, worth 161 million sterling pounds. His wife was unlucky who was working as a nurse in the hospital. At that time, she was celebrating her divorce in a nightclub with her friends. Just a few months earlier before she received the divorce certificate from the court. This came after 38 years of marriage. She would at least get more than 80 million pounds sterling if she had waited a few months, however, she was an unlucky person.

11. Luck is a true thing and it is happening, and this is why we sometimes see a very stupid person whose rich or sometimes we see a non educated person who's rich because that person came at the right time, in the right place, and met the right people.

12. I know a rich person who told my friends and I, while we gathered at a friend's house, that he went to Moscow in Russia, and realized that Russia does not have a strong economy and that they have very limited drinking water. He saw that they were selling imported bottled water from foreign countries. He does not know that Russia is the largest country in the world and has a lot of rivers and have a lot of snow in Siberia and have plenty of water everywhere. Also, it has a lot of natural resources, oil & gas, coal, cobalt, and magnesium. This stupid person however became rich because he is a lucky person and he came at the right time, at the right place, and met the right people.

13. Sometimes, you see two restaurants located close to each other on the same street. They almost have the same food; however, one will have more customers than the others. I consider that one is luckier than the other. In other cultures, they may say that it has more blessings than the other. The same with pharmacies or shops for example. They may be located next to each other, one the same street, while one of

them will have more clients than the other and make more money than the other.

14. Sometimes, you will see a shop on the right side of the road selling shoes is making much more money than another shop selling shoes on the other side of the street. You may even see the other shop selling the exact same products but is not making money. The point here is that luck is present in all of these situations.

15. Timothy Dexter was born in 1747 in Massachusetts Bay in the United States and dropped out of school at the age of 8. He is not an educated person but he was a very lucky person He was an unintelligent person. His rivals wanted him to go bankrupt so they told him to sell coal to Newcastle in Britain. He did not know that Newcastle is exporting coal to the world. He started to export coal to Newcastle but by the time his ships with coal arrived in Newcastle there was a miners strike, so then he sold his coal and he made a lot of money. Then his rivals told him to sell gloves to the Sea Islands where people don't use gloves but when his ships arrived in south Sea Islands, at that time the Portuguese boats were on the way to China and bought all the gloves so he made a lot of money then his rivals told him to sell the Bibles to the Caribbean Island by the time his boats arrived there the missionaries came and they were in need of the Bibles so they bought all the Bibles and he made a lot of money. In conclusion, though he was asked to send the wrong stuffs to the wrong places, he still made money and became wealthy because he was lucky.

16. If you read books about billionaires, they will tell you that they became billionaires or they became rich because they are billionaires. They will never admit that they were lucky at a certain point. They will tell you that they used to work

hard all the time. They just want the public or people to sympathize with them and respect them. They just wanted to be seen as smart people or as heroes. However, the truth is, that at certain points, they were lucky. They will keep repeating that they simply worked hard. There are a lot of people who work much harder than them and did not make money. They did not even make 1/4th or 1/10th of the money billionaires are making. The reason is because luck was playing a big role for certain people at a certain time. Just think about it, what would happen if that billionaire on the same day that he is supposed to sign an agreement had a car accident or missed his flight or that person he is supposed to meet or sign an agreement with him got sick, or died, or something happened to him. A lot of hard working people don't find the right partner or don't meet the right person in their university as a roommate. Or they do not find someone as a classmate in high school or a friend in their neighborhood. All the while, the billionaire has everything working out for him meeting the right people at the right time at the right place.

17. I admit, that I was lucky at a certain time. I am a hard worker and sacrificed a lot, however there were certain points in my life where I got lucky. I met the right people at the right time at the right place. Even though, many times, I was an unlucky person and things went wrong for me, I did not give up.
18. A long time ago, a friend of mine told me that his father had told him that sometimes in life when you plant onions, you get tomatoes and when you plant apples, you get oranges. What he meant by this is that life is full of surprises. Unexpected things happen, sometimes good things and sometimes bad things. Things don't work out the way you plan or expect it. I believe that life will be boring if everything works out the way you plan or expect it to.

19. Throughout my life and the lives of others, I have seen unexpected things happening, even in social life. For example, you see a person engaged and have a fiancé or girlfriend for a longtime, while at the last minute, he ends up marrying someone else or the girl will end up marrying someone else.

20. One of my friends at USC told me a story about her mother. She said that her mother was engaged to a man and he was supposed to marry her. They went to a restaurant one day and while the man went to the bathroom, another man had seen her mother and approached her. He asked for her number and kept calling her, so, she ended up marrying this man who ended up becoming my friend's father.

21. Christopher Columbus was on his way to discover a new route to India, however, he discovered America in 1492. Unexpected things happen all the time.

22. The same unexpectedness comes about in business. Just imagine that someone has three shops and a restaurant. He was expecting to make more money from the restaurant. The first shop was selling clothes (A), the second was selling furniture (B), and the third shoes was selling shoes (C). He expected to make more money from the restaurant, and the least from selling shoes – the opposite however ended up happening. The shop selling shoes was making much more money for him than the other shops selling clothes and furniture. The same could be said when dealing with companies as a businessmen. Some companies could unexpectedly generate more money than others. The main point here, especially in businesses, is that you may unexpectedly receive more money than the others.
In addition, planning does not work all the time as expected.

23. Life is full of events and unexpected events and circumstances that may be good or bad for certain people. Throughout history, these unexpected circumstances made certain people rich and certain people poor. For example, wars, earthquakes, volcanoes, floods, hurricanes, tsunamis, World war 1, World war 2, the great depression of 1929, the crash of 1987,the financial crisis of 2008 tornadoes, pandemic diseases such as COVID-19 etc.. These events could make certain people very rich or very poor.

24. Nobody can control they future, whatever will be, will be. Sometimes unexpected things will happen. Life will be boring if things are always happening in the way you expected.

25. A long time ago, there was an aerospace engineer who was working in Airplane manufacturing. His name is James Smith McDonnell who was born in Denver, Colorado, on April 9, 1899. He graduated from Princeton University in 1921 with a bachelor's in physics. He then earned a Master of Science in Aeronautical Engineering from MIT in 1925. In 1928, McDonnell left Huff Daland and set up J.S McDonnell & Associates, and with the help of two other engineers, McDonnell set out to design his first aircraft with his company name. He was working for many years without getting promoted. He joined another aircraft company and did not get promoted there either. He then went to a third company for aircraft and didn't get promoted. He felt bad because he has a lot of experience and did not get promoted. Then, in 1938 he decided to open his own company related to aircraft production. He borrowed money from his wife and his friends. He needed even more money from banks; however, they refused to lend him money. In 1939 Adolf Hitler invaded Poland. He founded McDonnell Aircraft

Corporation. Then, World War 2 started. The United States started to produce weapons and supplies for the war. There was a lot of business related to the aircraft industry. James Smith McDonnell found one bank who was willing to lend him money. He then started his business. He started growing and making money. More banks started to lend him money. In 1967, McDonnell Aircraft merged with Douglas Aircraft Company to create McDonnell Douglas. He kept growing. Finally, he made a lot of fighter jets, such as the phantom and the f series (F-15, F-18), dc-9, dc-10. He became a billionaire. The point here, is that James Smith McDonnell started a business related to his job aerospace engineering. It was something he knows.Also he was lucky because of world war 2.

26. There are some financial companies that specialize in doing feasibility studies on the current market for you. For example, if you have four different restaurant in four different locations; A, B, C, and D. They may come up with different calculations or different results that will tell you location C will make more money than location A and B, and that location D will make the least money. However, it ends up that location B makes more money, while location C and D are doing decent, and location A is the one struggling and performing the worst. Restaurant B covers the losses of A this how business survives, they do not put all their eggs in one basket.

27. Even in the movie industry, in Hollywood, some of the biggest studios such as paramount, Columbia, and MGM, sometimes make seven or eight films, and believe that film A will make more money than C and D, while film A becomes a disaster where no one ends up seeing it, while film D will be a successful film and will make more which will cover the losses of movies A and B.

28. Sometimes, a person wants to become a manager at his work when he is still young. However, things don't end up working out for him and he becomes a manager at the age of 50. This however turned out to be a good thing as he had more experience. The same thing could happen with someone who wants to be rich at the age of 30 and yet things didn't work out for him so he became rich at the age of 50. The point here is that many other unexpected things are happening in life.

29. I believe in luck and I also believe in fate. Everything starts from early childhood for the person. If you read psychology books, or if you take psychology classes in university, like I did, you will understand why certain people act a certain way. Everyone or every person is the product of their family upbringing, as well as a product of their environment and circumstance. You will know why certain people have factors of success – it grows with them since their early childhood. The potential and basics for everything as well as the skills and ability for success will start at an early childhood for any certain profession. For example, if someone wants to be a doctor, he will find that he excelled in science when he was young, and his parents were encouraging him to learn science and bought him many science books since his early childhood, where this made him love science books from a very young age. He had a very good family life, where his parents are encouraging him and made his environment very healthy and inspiring to get good grades at school. Also, some other events might give him the motivation to study medicine. If he sees something on a film on TV, like a doctor helping patients across the world and is like a hero curing his patients, he may be inspired to become a doctor when he grows up. Also, if someone is encouraging him to study math, then later on, he will become an engineer, or if his father was an engineer, if he repeatedly saw big bridges or

sky-scrapers created by engineers in his childhood, especially if he sees movies about engineers. Fate will work and help the boy who always wanted to be a doctor. For example, when he wants to go to the mountains for snow-skiing, if there was a big storm in the mountains on the weekend and he had an exam on Monday, things might happen for his own good, like his professor being sick on Monday or something that stops the exam from taking place. Also, when he applied for the medical school, that year, something may have happened where his grades may not be high enough to be accepted, something may happen around the world that will have the demand of doctors increase, and he will be accepted into medical school. I call this fate, and not luck.

30. In Russia, there was a seven year old boy walking with his father when the father met Tolstoy, the writer of the novel War and Peace and many other famous/best-seller books. The father was talking with Tolstoy for a very long time and looked at his son after Tolstoy left, asking him if he knew who he was. He told his son that it was Tolstoy a very famous writer. The father kept complimenting Tolstoy and saying many good things about him, talking about his work and sharing many stories of him. The boy was impressed and later on became a big writer in Russia called Vladimir Nabokov who wrote Lolita, a story of an old man that loved a young girl and started to talk to her mother in order to get to know the girl. He later immigrated to America.

31. I remember seeing an 11 year old boy quietly reading a book when I was working as a counselor in summer for YMCA kids. I asked why he was reading his books quietly and alone. He answered by saying that his mother is paying him a few pennies for every page he reads, so that he reads more. I was impressed by his mother’s commitment to making her

son read books helping the kid grow a habit of reading and fall in love with books.

32.If you read the stories of many rich people and billionaires, as well as many leaders around the world, you will notice more than 90% of them were born poor and had miserable lives but gave them the motivation and ambition to work harder to achieve their goals to become very rich and big leaders. Motivation for success comes after somebody suffers because of poverty for example:

1. his parents are poor while others are rich so he will have the motivation to work hard and be rich like the others;
2. he is not healthy or a crippled person or people look at him because crippled, he will have the motivate to work harder; or
3. socially if people in his society or his relatives treat him badly because he is ugly or because of his family background or any other reasons, this person will have the motivation to improve himself and will work harder to prove to the others they are successful people.

32.Usually people who are born poor or crippled or socially excluded, these people work hard, take a risk and have more courage to prove themselves and they usually leave their comfort zone. Usually, people who are born in upper middle class family, they become lazy and they like things in the easy way and there is no easy way in business and usually a spoiled kid does not like work hard or sacrifice or to leave his comfort zone.

33.Sometimes a poor kid will see his father or his mother working all day for making little money or when the kid sees his mother or father insulted. This will motivate the kid to work hard and to decide to be rich so he will take a risk to be rich. There is a story that happened in Spain for Mr Orteiga who saw his mother insulted when he was at the age of 13 because she wanted a loan from her boss and her boss kept insulting her. So he decided to be rich one day and he decided to work in the clothing delivery business and then worked as an assistant for a tailor. In 1963, he made a manufacturing company for clothes. Finally, he got the idea of designing clothes. In 1975, he made the trademark Zara.

34. Charles Darwin's father considered him a useless boy and a failure because he was not good at school. When this boy, Charles Darwin, found out that there was a ship sailing around the world, he wanted to go with them. His father refused to let him go, saying that if he would sail with them, he would cry halfway and want to come back since he is useless and a loser in his eyes. Charles Darwin asked his uncle to help him convince his father to let him go. When his uncle tried to talk to his father, his father said that he was a loser.
The uncle responded by saying that if he is a loser then he does not need him and that he should give him a chance. However, Charles Darwin had the motivation and wanted to prove to his father that he could grow up to be somebody and be a useful person and not a loser, he started to write on his notebook, his observation and his comments, of what he saw and experienced on his journey around the world. Charles Darwin is the person who had the theory of evolution, where he said that the man is descended from apes. His theory created a lot of controversy around the world. Also, his theory of life of the fittest.

35. During one of my acting classes at USC, I felt sorry for a girl when our professor asked her to perform a romantic scene like something out of Romeo and Juliet. The girl was always

depressed because she had a bad childhood. She was an unhappy person and never smiled. The teacher asked her to do a love scene, and knows that this girl could not do even a part of it. She could not do any of the expressions, not her face, hands, or body. The professor asked her if anyone had ever loved her in her life and she said that they didn't, she had a terrible childhood and was adopted. Since she was never loved, she could not do well in that scene. The professor kicked her out of the class and forced her to change her class. I felt very sorry for this girl, who never had anyone to love her in her life.

36. If you study the psychology of criminals, you will see that they became criminals because of their miserable childhood. At one time, a visitor from the Los Angeles Police department came to our sociology class in university to give a speech. He gave a speech to the students in our sociology class and mentioned a story that he once gave a speech to some teenagers who were criminals. One of the teenage criminals raised their hand, and said to the speaker that his life was different than the speaker's. He had loving parents, he did not. "I was an adopted son and had very bad adopted parents beating me up and mistreating me. I had a horrible childhood and was an abused child, so do not expect us to be like you, you who had loving parents growing up." Then, the speaker from the Los Angeles Police Department said that he stopped talking and didn't know what to say.

37. Sometimes a spoiled kid who has a rich father and rich mother that gives him everything might be more involved in having fun and having different hobbies when he grows up, he might not pay attention to his father's business and will not be serious about his father's business.
After he inherits his money, he might end up losing all his fathers wealth and will become poor at the end of his life

while you might see a boy whose father or mother is very poor this story happened in Spain to this Spanish boy who ended up establishing the very famous clothing line, Zara and the boy sees that their boss is insulting his mother and when he grows up, he will insist on working very hard in order to get rich and powerful. This was possible because he had the motivation and incentives to be rich from his early childhood.

38. The same thing can be said about all the factors of success in the world of trade and business I have mentioned in this book has to do with the early childhood of a person. For example, if his parents teaches him manners when he is a child, he will grow up with good manners and this is one of the good factors of success.
39. Also, if his parents taught him that patience is a good virtue, and if he read good books about patience, then when this child grows up, he will become a patient person, and this is a good factor of success for the world of trade and business. The same thing is the case if his parents had taught him about honesty in order to be an honest person, then, when he grows up, he will start to become an honest person, which is a very good factor of success.

40. I remember when I was living in the dorms at USC, there was an aggressive boy. Whenever I hung my towels during my shower, he would take the towel and throw it away. When I wanted to use the water on the sink, he would close the tap. This happened at the beginning of the school year. I noticed this boy because he is so aggressive and did not have manners, the boys on my floor didn't like him. His behavior made me curious. I knew that he had problems during his childhood. At the end of the year I invited him to dinner.
I asked him to tell me something about his childhood. He

said that he had a weird and miserable childhood since his parents were homeless and were hippies during the 1960's, living in the streets of New York with his parents as a homeless person. He never felt secure or safe on the streets, especially with the high crime rate. So, someone who is aggressive and not friendly and does not socialize, he cannot have friends or establish contacts and connections. The factor of contacts and connections is very important in the world of trade and business.

41. If a child tries to talk to his father or his mother, they shouts at him or beats him, or smack him, the kid will be afraid to meet people and socialize with people when he grows up. When he becomes an adult, he will not be sociable, and it will be hard for him to have contacts and connections. And of course, contacts and connections are a very important factor of success in the world of trade and business.

42. Because I believe in fate, I believe that fate made me write this book, because all the circumstances and reasons worked for me to write this book.
I was a blessed child for my mother because my mother had two sons before me who died at childbirth during her delivery and I was the third child who survived. So maybe because of this, I was spoiled by my nice mother. Also, I remember at my first day at school, my rich father then bought me many pens, pencils, colored pens and other stationary more than I needed while other students in my classroom do not have things. They just come and borrow pens and pencils from me so I started to like to go to school and education since my early childhood.

43. Since my early childhood, I used to read a lot of books and stories for kids, as well as a lot of comic-books like Superman, Batman, and Mickey Mouse. I used to spend most

of the money I received from my parents just to buy comic books and kid-story books. I used to spend a lot of my spare-time just reading books. Reading books made me good with writing papers. It gave me the talent of writing. I noticed that when I was in 6th and 7th grade, many of my teachers started to say that I am very good at writing. When I was a teenager, I lived in England with an English family as an exchange-student and my English mother used to go with me to the library to read books all the time, because she enjoyed reading books. She had always told me that the pen is mightier than the sword. This was especially the case during some of my history exams, where my teachers would complement my writing.

Reading books opened my mind to travel and to have other hobbies like collecting stamps and collecting coins. Collecting stamps abled me to understand the cultures of other countries, the history of other countries, and the arts of other countries as well as a lot of general information about other countries. Of course, this made me interested in traveling. I had the chances to travel to Europe when I was a teenager. I travelled to Greece in 1969 and I travelled to England in 1971, to France in 1973, also I was in a boarding school in 1971, a boarding school in Switzerland in 1974.

Traveling made me interested in learning languages. Languages encouraged me to travel more, also leading me to have more contacts and connections for my businesses. I have traveled around the world twice and have traveled to Europe over one hundred times.

44. Since my childhood, I used to like nature and was a boy-scout. I liked all kinds of sports. Also, I was a boy scout and used to enjoy camping. All these things lead me to study geology because I noticed that if I study geology and petroleum engineering, I will be living in nature outside the

city. That became my dream in life, to live in nature and far from the cities.

45. Reading comic books and stories for children during my childhood helped me in writing. Since my childhood, I had the ability to write and helped me to progress the skill and talent of writing. I even remember that I started to impress some of my school teachers starting from 6th grade.

46. Later, in the University of Southern California, I took many communications classes and wrote many stories. My classmates told me many times that I had many stories, so why didn't I write all my stories in one book. My professors noticed that I was very good at writing spending 14 years at USC, writing papers for different classes. All these things made me gain the confidence to write a book because I realized that I am talented in writing books.

47. In my early childhood, I noticed that my parents had always been respecting businessmen and merchants. So, I had always thought of being someone respected like a businessman and making a lot of money. I also noticed that a lot of students and people I socialized with at USC had a lot of dreams to be rich and famous. When I socialized with a lot of students that attended the universities of Colorado, UCLA, San Diego State, University of California Irvine, Long-Beach State etc. they all had the same dream of making money but didn't know how since they lacked the factors of success mentioned in this book. Also, during the 80's they liked the tv show to do with the oil business called Dallas, as well as JR who had his own series about his oil business.Taking a course of US business history in USC explained how the big corporations started in the United States impressed me. Like Carnegie who started the steel industry, as well as Rockefeller who started the oil companies. All this gave me

the dream to be like one of them.

48. Making money is not easy. Some people do not have the potential nor the ability for it. I noticed some of the young people wanted to be rich businessmen or rich merchants. They do not know the basics of business and do not know the factors of success in business. They only think that making money is easy. They will tell you stories about successful people who became rich. And they do not know about a lot of people who tried to be rich but failed even though they are the majority of people. They only think that making money is easy but it is not as easy as they think.

49. Then, when they start any kind of business, they will realize that making money is not easy, especially when they lose their money and go through bankruptcy.

50. I wished that there was a book to guide me when I started my first business. A book that could make things easier on me by avoiding some mistakes. Unfortunately however, I learned things the hard way.

51. In my life, I have heard a lot of sad stories about people who went through a lot of pain and suffering and had a miserable life because they went through bankruptcy. For this reason,I decided to write this book, just to help people to help them avoid the bankruptcy.I have noticed that many people who started businesses around the world are suffering because of debts and failures within their business. I noticed that some of my friends and classmates attend the first year of university but are unable to continue to the second year because of financial difficulties and that their parents have financial problems. This made me think of helping others and reduce their pain because a lot of time, when a father loses money, it has a lot of negative implications on his wife and

kids who go through so much suffering, something very sad and regrettable. Traveling around the world made it possible for me to make this book into somewhat of an international book and for this reason, I put stories from different cultures and different countries to make everyone reading this book happy.

52. I remember in 1990, I was waiting in line in San Diego for a movie with some friends. I started to talk to an old man with grey hair behind me. I was surprised when he asked me how old he was. He said that he was only 35 years old but looked much older because he tried for many years to get rich and ultimately failed. He went through bankruptcy and a lot of suffering and had a miserable life because he failed in his business. This event made me think why people are struggling so much for money and made their lives miserable and had to go through a lot of pain with their families and their kids. Then i decided to write a book to help people, to explain things to them about business.

53. I noticed that even good businessmen do not know how to explain the factors of success in business and why making money is not easy. Before I started my business, I asked a successful cousin of mine about making money. He said that making money is not easy, however he never explained himself. I have realized that many successful businessmen are not able to explain business or making money, because these people are merchants and people of trade, not schoolteachers or educators. Also, one of the things that gave me the motivation to write this book, every time I ask a merchant or businessman to explain the other factors of success in business, they just tell me one or two factors, like working hard, or being patient. Then, when I bring something up like contacts or connections, they say it is very important. When I say management, they say yes very

important, dedication same thing, sacrifice, same thing. The problem with these merchants is that whenever you say something about the factors of success, they agree that it is very important. Because I noticed that these people are not writers and cannot write about the success in business. Since I have the talent of writing, I asked why I don't write a book to help the young people in the world and to help them avoid the mistakes of failure and going through bankruptcy.

54. When I was a student at USC, I noticed many students late at night in the dorms talking about their dreams to be rich and they think that making money is easy and they are not aware of the factors of success in business. But for me as a person who came from a family or a community and friends of my family in the world of trade of business, I knew it was not that easy as they think. But I was not able at that time to explain to them because I did not have the experience in business.
I was just a student just like the other students. But now after 30 years of experience, I am able to explain everything to them. Some young people think it is easy to make money if you are having only one factor of success like working hard. It is not true, you must have many factors of success, it is a combination of factors. This is why rich people are very few in the world. They talk about a few people who became rich and keep talking about their stories of success and they spread those stories around but don't talk about the millions of people who failed in business everywhere around the world. For this reason, I declined to write this book because most the people who failed in business don't have the factors of success mentioned in this book and even not aware of them. Also, some people don't have the basics and the potential for business exactly like not everybody can be a doctor or an engineer or a singer or a football player. Business is a talent and potential requires a lot of factors for

success.
I noticed that young people do not know that there a lot of factors and combination of factors, they think that there are just a few and that it is easy to be successful in business. For this reason, we see that the rich people and successful people are very few compared to the world population. It is good to have dreams about being rich but at the same time, it is good to be realistic and to know the real world of business.

55. Wherever I go people ask me about the factors of success and also at the same time I heard some sad stories about people suffering and they also go through some financial troubles and bankruptcy. This is another reason that made me write this book. Because I noticed a lot of people are struggling with debts and their life became miserable for themselves and their families.

56. Also, I was surprised that a lot of people and a lot of my friends do not have the basics of knowing the business and making money. They just think that making money is easy, they do not know that making money is very hard and not easy because they do not know about the factors of success.

57. During one of my trips to Spain, since I speak French fluently, I met a nice French family and be-friended them over a few days while we were staying at the same hotel. The father of that family asked me about the factors of success in business. Then, I kept asking myself, how is it that in the United States, many people do not know all the factors of success in business, in most Asian Countries too, and even in Europe they lack the knowledge of them.

58. Also, when I decided to write this book on the factors of success, I am not discouraging young people. I just want people to have the full picture or full idea about business and be ready for it before entering the world of trade and

business. It is exactly like if a person is going on a fishing trip or a picnic, he must be ready and take all the necessary clothes, tools and equipment with him for the fishing trip or the picnic.

59. My turning point to write this book was when one of my close friends in the oil company, who is very well-educated person who always likes to read books and who always likes to learn and seek knowledge and was an excellent student when he was in high school and had excellent grades in high school and who graduated from a university in Oregon. Fate and circumstances made me meet him by coincidence in the oil company. He was a nice person with good manners and has high morals. As time went on, I started talking to him about knowledge and books and at one time I told him that making money is not easy and a person must have the factors of success then I mentioned to him that I am thinking about writing a book. Then he said why don't you write a book. He encouraged me to write this book – to explain the factors of success in business since I have the experience of writing. I answered him saying that writing a book will take a lot of time and that I do not have time for it. He encouraged me by saying, "If you write a good book, you will help people" and kept encouraging me. My friend also told me "If you don't do it, who will do it? You must not be selfish, do something for the people." Every time he saw me after that, he kept asking on updates about the progress of the book. He was very interested in this book. About myself, I always like to help people because I was raised that way but my big problem was that I do not have time for it. I do not even have 20 minutes a day for things other than work but at the same time, I was thinking about people who enter the world of trade and business and go through a lot of suffering who in some cases end up in bankruptcy.

60. To me, writing a good book requires a lot of time and effort

and research. It is like writing a hundred research papers for your classes at University. If for example, it requires approximately three weeks to write one paper for your classes at the University, it means it will take you about three hundred weeks which equal to six years because writing a book is not easy, it is time consuming. It takes many years to write a good book and I don't have 20 minutes a day to do anything besides work related to my business. Also, there is a lot of frustration during writing a book because you always have to change things in the book and deleting things that you are not happy with or satisfied with. You will be feeling like you have to change a few things or feel like you are not explaining enough or you may be missing something and not have free time, especially since I am not retired yet so I am still working which is why I do not have enough time to write a book.

61. I first started writing this book slowly, not having that much time to work on it in December of 2017. Then, Covid-19/ the corona outbreak happened in 2020, it opened up the time for me to write this book every day and spending more hours on it. I looked at Covid-19 as a blessing, not a curse. Like I mentioned before, I believe in fate and destiny, I do not have regrets or feel bad about Covid-19. I am always optimistic as I have mentioned earlier. Whenever a bad thing happens, I always think of a good thing that will happen after it.

62. Luck is important but it is not everything, you can't rely on luck only because you must have the other factors of success in this book. Many people were lucky and inherited money or won a lottery and millions but they lost the money because they don't have the other factor of success for example experience, working hard.

63. I think that I believe a person must try to obtain the factors

of success or at least to be aware of them because those factors are the tools to success and will make you ready to make money at the right time and at the right place with the right people. So, the day will come to you when destiny, fate and luck will be on your side. This may be at the age of 30 years or at the age of 40 or even at the age of 50 so wait and be ready for the right time and the right place and the right people.

64. The Chinese billionaire and the founder of Ali Babba Jack Ma Yun who is the fourth wealthiest person in China and the 39th wealthiest person in the world. He was an unlucky person when he was young after he graduated from the university in 1988. He applied for thirty one different jobs and was rejected. He even applied to KFC and was the only applicant out of twenty four that was rejected. He and his cousin applied to be waiters. While his cousin was accepted, Jack Ma Yun was told he was too short and got rejected. Then, he began building websites for Chinese companies with the help of friends in the United States.

65. Finally, I want to say start working and luck will be on your side because most of the successful people in history become successful after they start working. They may fall a few times but finally they make it.

www.ingramcontent.com/pod-product-compliance
Lightning Source LLC
LaVergne TN
LVHW052030200926
848481LV00005B/1637
* 9 7 8 9 9 4 8 7 1 7 2 0 1 *